New Directions in Development Economics

New Directions in Development Economics

Edited by

Amitava Krishna Dutt
Department of Economics
University of Notre Dame

Kenneth P. Jameson
Department of Economics
University of Utah

Edward Elgar

Published by
Edward Elgar Publishing Limited
Gower House
Croft Road
Aldershot
Hants GU11 3HR
England

Edward Elgar Publishing Limited
Distributed in the United States by
Ashgate Publishing Company
Old Post Road
Brookfield
Vermont 05036
USA

CIP catalogue records for this book
are available from the British Library
and the US Library of Congress.

ISBN 1 85278 535 7

Printed and bound in Great Britain by
Billing and Sons Ltd, Worcester

Contents

List of Tables

Acknowledgements

The papers by Lance Taylor, Joseph Stiglitz and Keith Griffin are based on lectures they delivered at the University of Notre Dame in the American Telephone and Telegraph Company Visiting Scholars Lecture Series on the Future of Development Economics in the fall of 1989 and the spring of 1990. We thank Professors Taylor, Stiglitz and Griffin for coming to Notre Dame to participate in the AT&T Visiting Scholars series and for contributing their papers to this volume, and to AT&T and the Institute of Scholarship for the Liberal Arts at Notre Dame for making their visits possible. We also thank Ajit Singh for participating in the Lecture Series on the Future of Development Economics in his spring 1990 visit to Notre Dame in the Scholl Chair, and for contributing the paper based on his lecture to this volume. Finally, we thank Edward Elgar and his production staff, especially Julie Leppard, for efficiently and expeditiously seeing this book through to its conclusion.

Contributors

Amitava Krishna Dutt is Professor in the Department of Economics, University of Notre Dame, US

Keith Griffin is Professor and Chair in the Department of Economics, University of California, Riverside, US

Kenneth P. Jameson is Professor and Chair in the Department of Economics, University of Utah, US

Ajit Singh is Reader in the Faculty of Economics and Politics, Cambridge University, UK

Joseph E. Stiglitz is Professor in the Department of Economics, Stanford University, California, US

Lance Taylor is Professor in the Department of Economics, Massachusetts Institute of Technology, US

Introduction

During the 1980s a number of prominent development economists, in some cases 'pioneers of development' such as Albert Hirschman, looked back at the history of their subject and concluded that it was experiencing a decline. The fact of decline was largely acknowledged, although the question of whether it was warranted or not was hotly disputed. At the same time the momentum of development which had brought about dramatic changes in developing countries seemed to be lost; whole regions such as Africa and Latin America faltered and began to reverse the achievements of the previous 30 years.

The arrival of the 1990s calls for a reassessment of these realities and a reexamination of the decline of development economics and the pause occurring in economic development. The papers in this volume attempt to point out new directions which may hopefully be followed in coming decades.

The first three papers reexamine the state of development economics with the purpose of understanding its future course and its role in fostering economic development in less advanced economies.

Dutt argues that, contrary to claims made in the 1980s, there is no evidence that the subject is undergoing decline; significant developments are in fact occurring in several of its branches, representing alternative approaches to the subject. Dutt describes how such alternative approaches are distinguished according to methodology, vision, strategies and meaning of development. He argues that particular methodologies are not necessarily linked to particular economic visions and strategies and that, although there is disagreement on the meaning of development, this is not as sharp as is often thought. He observes a recent convergence of views between the proponents of alternative approaches which makes it possible to reduce dogmatism and increase communication; moreover, the coexistence of alternative methodological approaches and visions is beneficial for the continued healthy development of the subject and for the formulation of appropriate strategies for economic development.

The papers by Taylor and Stiglitz, respectively, discuss recent developments in what we may call 'new structuralist' and 'new neoclassical' development economics, two theoretical approaches to the subject which have experienced impressive growth in recent years.

Taylor, the leading force behind the recent growth in structuralist macroeconomics, concentrates on two areas in which structuralists have made major contributions – income distribution and growth, and money and finance. On the former issue he contrasts the Mill-Marshall neoclassical view with optimizing agents (which ignores important structural features) with the richer Marxian, Schumpeterian, stagnationist, two- and four-gap, fixprice-flexprice and Cambridge approaches. On the latter issue he develops a synoptic view of the history of monetary theory, distinguishing between alternative positions according to whether they focus on money or credit, whether they take these to be passive (endogenous) or active (exogenous), and whether they emphasize their price or quantity effects. Drawing on this discussion, Taylor argues in favour of a structuralist approach to development economics which takes an economy's institutions and own patterns of change as the basis of analysis, as opposed to one that focuses on optimizing agents.

Stiglitz, the leading contributor to new neoclassical development economics – or what he has called the information-theoretic approach – concentrates on the role of government in the light of recent moves towards greater reliance on markets in both capitalist and socialist economies. In his opinion government is not the cause of underdevelopment; in fact, there is much potential for government to improve the working of the economy, for instance, by providing legal infrastructure and helping to reduce the difficulties caused by informational problems (in the presence of which the economy is essentially always constrained Pareto inefficient). On the other hand, he argues that state planning and government intervention give rise to rent-seeking behaviour, and to information and incentive problems. Thus, though governments do have an important role to play, there need not be a choice of political freedom and economic liberty on the one hand, and economic progress on the other. He also argues that microeconomic issues relating to efficiency are more significant than macroeconomic material balance relations and capital formation rates; more important than the choice between sectors is an emphasis on dynamic comparative advantage, taking organizational complexity into account.

These three papers focus primarily on recent theoretical issues in development economics and are unanimous in their conclusions that significant advances in development theory are currently occurring. Thus the announcement of the demise of development economics was premature.

The next three papers take up the same refrain from the perspective of the experience of developing countries and the prospects for development in coming decades. They all agree that the 1980s represented a clear break in development processes, but that the 1990s and beyond hold the possibility of a viable redirection of development.

Singh highlights the differential economic performance across geographic regions during the 1980s, ranging from improved performance in East Asia to virtual economic collapse in Africa and Latin America. He disagrees with the conventional explanation that misguided policy was responsible, blaming instead the size of external shocks, combined with variations in economic structures. Criticizing the resource misallocation argument, he contends that the economic policies taken prior to the external shocks were quite appropriate, given the negative real interest rates of the 1970s and the buoyant industrial country markets for the output of debt-financed projects. Criticizing conventional World Bank and IMF policy proposals, Singh suggests that successful development policy in the future will consist of a more appropriate industrial pattern, a more efficient state-enterprise sector, greater internal liberalization and greater trade among small developing countries. Openness does not imply free trade, and efficient import substitution can still play an important role. Singh concludes that the proper set of policies can renew the development process during coming decades.

Jameson also examines differential development performance: the contrast within developing countries between macroeconomic performance and experience at the grassroots. The two perspectives give very different impressions of development since World War II. In the unbalanced growth period, 1950–70, the impressive macro performance came at the cost of imbalance and disruption at the grassroots level; the period of unbalanced decline, 1970–1990, saw an overall deterioration at the macro level, with the grassroots becoming a refuge sector while gaining greater autonomy from macro influence. Jameson next addresses the role of grassroots development efforts in coming decades, by investigating three conceptions of grassroots development. The actual role of grassroots movements in development will be conditioned by international and national factors; he makes the case that constraints on grassroots development have weakened considerably since the 1970s. As a result, grassroots efforts and processes have the possibility of moving development in a new and positive direction in coming decades, and he suggests a set of policies and changes which can facilitate and encourage this.

Finally, Griffin suggests an international development strategy for the 1990s. After reviewing the dismal development performance of the 1980s he argues that positive changes have occurred in the world economy which give grounds for future hope, provided that appropriate national and international development policies are pursued. Griffin's strategy calls for faster growth by increasing the rate of investment within developing economies and by increasing the efficiency of investment; for human development by increasing spending on education, health and housing; for direct measures to attack the problem of poverty; and for restraining the deterioration of the natural environment. He argues that this strategy can be seen as a world social contract which can benefit all nations, and discusses how the United Nations family can make it meaningful. Griffin's strategy combines the stress on capital accumulation characteristic of early post-war development economics, the neoclassical focus on efficiency, with a more radical emphasis on poverty and inequality, and a newer attention to environmental issues.

Amitava Krishna Dutt
Kenneth P. Jameson

1. Two Issues in the State of Development Economics

Amitava Krishna Dutt*

INTRODUCTION

In recent years a number of appraisals have appeared on the state of development economics.[1] The purpose of this chapter is to examine two important questions raised in these appraisals. First, is development economics declining? Second, is there a convergence of views among alternative approaches to the subject?

Interest in the first question was aroused by Hirschman's (1981) obituary of the subject, which drew a picture of a new subject slain by neoclassical and neo-Marxian attackers. Many of the initial responses to this essay accepted that the subject was on the decline, and debated whether this fate was deserved or not.[2] Surveys of recent contributions to the subject, however, reveal that the obituary was premature. It will be argued below that the earlier prognosis resulted from the peculiar definition of the term 'development economics' used by Hirschman and that attacks on the subject were to a considerable extent aided by this definition. The peculiarity of the definition springs in large part from a failure to take into account the existence of alternative approaches to the subject.

The second question turns to this issue of alternative perspectives and asks whether they are converging or diverging. The traditional view of those who admit the existence of legitimate alternative approaches to the subject is that the divisions are too strong to allow consensus.[3] Some recent appraisals, however, point approvingly to important convergences in views among the more sophisticated followers of the different approaches.[4] It will be argued here that some convergence is in fact taking place. While this is to be applauded as a sign of reduced dogmatism and as opening up the possibility of mutually beneficial exchange, it will also be argued that important differences still exist, and that these should be nurtured for the healthy develop-

---

* I am grateful to Jose Cordero and Keun-Young Lee for their research assistance.

ment of the subject. After examining some views on alternative approaches to the subject, it will be suggested that a proper discussion of divergences must be conducted at several different – although not unrelated – levels. Finally, differences in what we call method, vision, strategies, and meanings of development will be discussed.

THE DEMISE OF DEVELOPMENT ECONOMICS?

According to Hirschman (1981), after a period of remarkable growth in the 1940s and 1950s, development economics, the comparatively young subdiscipline of economics, experienced a decline: 'the old liveliness is no longer there, ... new ideas are ever harder to come by and ... the field is not adequately reproducing itself'.[5] Hirschman explained this decline in terms of the conjunction of attacks from mainstream neoclassical economists and neo-Marxian scholars.

In his discussion Hirschman characterized 'development economics' as a field of inquiry which: (i) viewed underdeveloped economies as being very different from developed economies and therefore requiring a non-traditional analysis (rejection of the 'monoeconomics claim'), and (ii) claimed that economic relations between developed and underdeveloped economies could be shaped to benefit both (the 'mutual benefit claim'). This characterization allowed Hirschman to distinguish the subject from the mainstream (which accepted the monoeconomics claim) and from neo-Marxism (which denied both the monoeconomics and mutual benefit claims), and to explain its demise in terms of the attacks by these approaches.

Contributors to the discussion provoked by Hirschman's analysis basically accept this definition of the subject, though they sometimes modify it to suit their purposes. Lal (1985) rejoices at the demise of the subject by attempting to expose its poverty, clearly directing his wrath at 'a particular school of thought on the economics of developing countries' which believes that: the price mechanism must be supplanted by direct government controls; the traditional concerns of orthodox microeconomics relating to resource allocation are of minor importance in comparison to macroeconomic concerns relating to aggregates such as saving and the balance of payments; the case for free trade is invalid, and massive government intervention is required for alleviating poverty and improving income distribution. He concludes that 'the demise of development economics is likely to be conducive to the health of both the economics and the economies of developing countries' (Lal 1985, p.109).[6] Others, while admitting shortcomings, have been more charitable towards the subject. Sen (1983) argues that traditional development economics (its major strategic themes being industrialization, rapid capital accumulation, mobilization of underutilized manpower, planning and an economically active state) was not very much off the mark 'and the time to bury it ... has not yet arrived'. He admits, however, that the subject has not been very successful in characterizing economic development, which he defines as an expansion of people's capabilities. Bhagwati (1984) admits that the market failure argument was overemphasized, and that the pessimism regarding trade opportunities which led to autarkic approaches was unjustified, but argues in favour of overall growth (without which there would be little to redistribute) and selective intervention by the government in favour of specific target groups for the alleviation of poverty. Lewis (1984) and Chakravarty (1987) are also supportive of development economics, but appear to shy away from the early overemphasis on market failures; they call for a development economics with greater emphasis on government, class formation and conflict, institutional arrangements and value systems, and with a greater integration of history and theory.

Hirschman's characterization of development economics, however, is problematic. While one may naturally define the subject as one which deals with the study of the growth and development of nations, especially those at early stages of development (and this is the sense in which we will use it hereafter, except where explicitly noted to the contrary), Hirschman's definition refers to a particular subset of development economics. To focus on *any* particular subset creates some problems, but Hirschman's specific definition of the subset raises further difficulties.

First, the focus on a subset fails to take account of the fact that development economics – even during what Hirschman calls its early days – was not a homogeneous subject, but a collection of different approaches and points of view. For instance, while there were those who stressed the importance of industrialization, there were others who emphasized the role of the agricultural sector; and while the majority favoured government intervention in the economy, some certainly stressed the value of free markets.[7] We will return to this theme of alternative approaches in subsequent sections of this chapter.

Second, the focus on a subset leads to endless and unilluminating attacks on the subject by selecting a set of theories and observations of which one disapproves. This is especially because it is difficult to agree on any specific criteria by which to define precisely the chosen subset of the subject.[8]

Third, the focus on a subset also makes it likely that important common features within the whole subject will be missed, yielding a myopic and distorted view of its history. Using our definition, development economics does not appear to be a new subject emerging in the post-war period, but one which has a long history with remarkable powers of resilience. Students of the history of economic thought have long recognized the subject's past (Robbins 1968, Lewis 1988); one can even detect a recent flurry of interest in establishing and analysing links between the less-developed economies of today and the history of currently-developed economies.[9] Although not identical, there may be important similarities in the problems facing, and the analytical approaches relevant for understanding, the two types of economies. This is not to claim that development economics has progressed in a linear manner. Quite the contrary; ideas on development were submerged after the marginalist revolution by the emphasis on resource allocation at a point in time, and interest in development was confined mainly to the followers of Marx, Schumpeter and some institutionalist writers, to scholars interested in colonial administration, and to some nationalist writers who drew on the work of precursors (such as List) from countries which had developed earlier.[10]

What thus appears to Hirschman to be the birth of a new subject is more appropriately seen as a return to prominence of an old one, caused by the conjunction of several powerful influences.[11] At one level the rise of Keynesianism paved the way for state intervention, for the development of analytical concepts such as unemployment, for the focus on macroeconomic aggregates, and generally for departures from neoclassical orthodoxy; the consequent development of growth theory by Keynesians and neoclassicals, input-output analysis and optimal programming also helped the growth of the subject. At other levels, the wartime experiences with active state intervention and planning; the experience of planning in the Soviet Union; the political independence of several less developed economies and the consequent desire of, and pressures on, new nationalist governments to prove themselves; the advent of international agencies fostering development, and the spectre of communism – all strengthened the need for development with active state intervention.[12] The combination of these factors helped to create a tremendous enthusiasm for the development of poor nations, prompting economists to study their specific problems. As they observed less developed economies closely they were struck by the enormous differences between them and the advanced economies (an opinion found earlier in Marshall (1920)), and this probably led many to reject the monoeconomics claim. But since the majority of economists were trained in neoclassical economics they did not travel far from its methods. Thus issues of market failure and planning were more prominent in their minds than the classical themes of economic evolution, growth and distribution. This probably added to the illusion of newness, making the subject appear quite different from what concerned classical economists.

Hirschman's particular characterization of development economics also raises some problems. First, he is inaccurate and imprecise regarding the mutual benefits claim of development economics.[13] Many development economists in his sense (including Nurkse (1956) who discussed the harmful international demonstration effects, and Myrdal (1957) in whose framework the negative backwash effects could overpower the positive spread effects of international linkages) thought that international interaction was actually harmful to poor countries in ways similar to neo-Marxists such as Baran (1957) and others, though they did not express such reservations in terms of Marxist notions of surplus transfer. Hirschman, however, defined the mutual benefit claim not in terms of what in fact happened, but what could be made to happen: North-South relations could be arranged for mutual benefit. But since he failed to define the precise terms and conditions under which this could happen (few would disagree if it meant a thoroughgoing restructuring of international economic relations and political frameworks of poor coun-tries), Lal (1985) had no difficulty whatsoever in bracketing development economists in Hirschman's sense with neo-Marxists and criticizing them together.

Second, Hirschman is not precise in defining the monoeconomics claim. Does it mean that rich and poor nations are similar in nature? Or that they can be understood in terms of the same theoretical models? Or that they can be analysed using the same method? These are quite different claims, and each one can have several interpretations. But whatever sense was intended, many development economists accepted the monoeconomics claim. Haberler (1959), Bauer and Yamey (1957) and Schultz (1964) saw the two types of economies as essentially alike. Even those who would fit Hirschman's defi-nition of development economists, such as Scitovsky (1954) and Bardhan (1964), used analytical approaches involving the concept of externalities, commonly applied to the economics of developed countries. The work of others, like Nurkse and Rosenstein-Rodan, was formalized using methods commonly applied to developed economies.[14] Even the dual-economy mod-els of Lewis (1954) – and, more so, those of Jorgenson (1961) and his followers which assumed away unemployment – were modifications of models applicable to rich countries, using profit maximizing, price-taking behaviour.

Hirschman's ambiguity regarding the monoeconomics claim allowed Lal (1985) to attack its supposed rejection by development economics in his sense: all markets may not exist in poor countries because of high transac-tions costs; important externalities and economies of scale may also be present. All of this could be adequately handled with the tools of 'modern welfare economics', using the model of perfect competition as a benchmark. But Lal's is not the only type of monoeconomics claim that can be made: concepts and theories developed for less developed economies have been fruitfully employed for analysing developed economies. For instance, as Hirschman himself notes, Lewis' (1954) ideas on dual economies have found echoes in the dual labour market theories of Piore and others; and structuralist models developed primarily for less developed economies have now found their way into the growth and distribution literature for developed economies. As Seers (1979a) and Streeten (1984b) point out, an economics emphasizing the similarities between developed and less developed economies seems to be emerging.

It is understandable that a subject recently rejuvenated should try to justify its existence by claiming to be very different from the rest of the discipline. Rejecting Hirschman's monoeconomics claim was only one way of making this claim, and one which could be easily criticized. Other differences have also been stressed. Sen (1988) has argued that development economics may be seen as concerned with the broad issues of poverty, misery and well-being, and enhancing the quality of life – themes from which the rest of the subject seems to have turned away. But it would be counterproductive to insist on a sharp divide on this score since it would imply that economics as a whole is not concerned with these basic questions. Toye (1985) argues that development economics can be different only if it departs from the unidisciplinary purity of orthodox economics and develops interdisciplinary aspects incorporating economic behaviour, technology, institutions and politics.[15] Again, to agree on this is to admit that the rest of economics has not been concerned with these 'non-economic' issues.

The existence of development economics as a separate subject does not require that it should be very different from the rest of economics. As Sen (1988, p. 11) points out, it is important not to make too much of this divide, 'nor to confuse separateness with independence. Tools of standard economics may have much fruitful use in development economics as well, even when the exact problems addressed happen to be quite specialized.' The study of development economics may raise new issues and questions not previously considered very important for developed countries – such as those relating to market imperfections, externalities and increasing returns, particular forms of agrarian institutions, and those concerning the interdependence of social, political and technological factors. These may then be incorporated into and explained in terms of economic theory devised primarily for developed economies, or which may require the enunciation of new theories.[16]

Despite such questions about Hirschman's analysis, the tremendous enthusiasm that characterized development economics in the early days of its rejuvenation may admittedly have diminished. The reasons for this have to do partly with some of the same factors which explained its upswing, and partly with some issues internal to the subject itself. In the first category, in economics as a whole neoclassical orthodoxy was regaining lost ground at the expense of the Keynesian challengers. Neoclassical scholars provided interpretations of development experiences which appeared to negate the types of factors – such as state intervention – emphasized by some influential development economists. There were also some examples of 'development debacles' (Hirschman 1981), and more generally it came to be realized that no easy panacea existed for removing the problems of less developed economies (Streeten 1984b). In the second category, mainstream neoclassical theory began to incorporate some of the issues highlighted in the post-war contributions to development economics, so that they did not appear so novel; as the novelty of the study of less developed economies wore off they appeared to be not unlike the models mainstream economics provided to study them. Of course attacks on the nature of the subject also came from other directions: from the left it was claimed that development economics was preoccupied with growth rather than distribution, and with mathematics rather than socio-economic reality (see Seers 1979a); others – including those outside the traditional boundaries of the subject – criticized the common neglect of non-economic factors, such as anthropological ones (Hill 1986).[17]

Though the early excitement noted by Hirschman may now have waned, there is no evidence that the subject as a whole is undergoing decline. As Lewis (1984) points out, it may be losing American Ph.D. students because the best jobs are not in that subject (due to cuts in foreign aid and the changed priorities of international agencies), but development economics continues to be taught in American universities, particularly to students from the Third World. Moreover, even though there are probably fewer *pure* development economists of great reputation than before, practitioners of other subdisciplines – labour, international, industrial organization, and economic theory in general – from mainstream and other perspectives are working on issues which were previously the sole domain of development economics (though this is clearly no substitute for a group working solely on less developed economies). Indeed, in recent years there has been an outpouring of research on development economics, especially in the new neoclassical literature on agricultural institutions, and in the new structuralist macroeconomics literature on growth, distribution, stabilization and trade, not to mention the steady flow from neo-Marxian quarters.[18] In Lewis' words, '[d]evelopment economics is not at its most spectacular, but it is alive and well' (1984, p. 10).

ALTERNATIVE APPROACHES TO DEVELOPMENT ECONOMICS

In development economics, perhaps more than in any other branch of the discipline, a number of different approaches are generally recognized. This is not to say that those partial to one particular approach have not attempted to minimize unfairly the importance of alternatives;[19] moreover, as we have seen, the subject has sometimes been defined so as to exclude alternative approaches, a tendency that we have argued to be problematic. Accepting their existence, however, we now turn to our second question: has there occurred a convergence of views amongst those of different approaches? The answer naturally hinges on definition. We therefore begin our analysis by examining a variety of these approaches and their implications for the convergence question.

One division often made in the subject as a whole has found its way into development economics: between the right and left in political terms (see Seers 1979b). The right is assumed to support free markets while the left is taken to focus on equity issues, to be generally critical of free market forces and supportive of government control. The former is usually associated with the neoclassical approach, the latter with Marxism. Lal (1985) seems to draw a similar distinction, between the neoclassical approach which examines the world in terms of the neoclassical general equilibrium model with optimizing agents, and all other approaches which favour state intervention and equity issues (including not only Marxists but also Hirschman's 'development economics'). While most observers feel that the twain shall never meet, Seers (1979b) finds that there has occurred a convergence of views. As an example he cites the work of Warren (1973) who, although in the Marxist camp, agrees with neoclassicals like Bauer on matters of policy, believing that global capitalist development has actually benefited the majority of the world's population and that Third World poverty could be alleviated by incorporating the poor economies more fully into the capitalist system. Recognizing that not many Marxists would agree with Warren's views, Seers also contends that Marxists and neoclassicals share many other preoccupations: stress on material incentives, an interpretation of history as progress, stress on material progress (economism), an emphasis on capital accumulation, a belief in modernization, and a general disinterest in ethnic, religious and linguistic issues. To appropriately distinguish different viewpoints, Seers suggests that the left-right axis be supplemented by a nationalist-antinationalist axis by which different approaches to development economics can be adequately distinguished: thus neoclassicals would be antinationalist and on the right, dependency theorists would be nationalist and on the left, and those like Warren would be antinationalist and on the left.

A two-way division along roughly similar left-right lines is also suggested by Wilber and Jameson (1979). They use the Kuhnian concept of paradigms (defined as a world view shared by a group working on or thinking about a particular topic) and distinguish between orthodox and political economy paradigms. The former take the goal of development to be material prosperity in the sense of high mass consumption; this type of development is assumed to occur primarily with the use of free markets and as a result of individual choice, although some state intervention and planning may be necessary if the smooth functioning of markets is hindered by distortions (market or state-imposed) and non-maximizing behaviour, or if development does not solve the problems of poverty and inequality within and between nations. The political economy paradigm surveys the process of development – which is a means rather than an end – and examines the control and use of the surplus produced in the economy, with the Marxist variant focusing on internal class structure and internal dissipation of the surplus, and the dependency school focusing on relations between nations and the external dissipation of surplus of poor nations. According to Wilber and Jameson, these two paradigms are distinct, offering little apparent room for convergence.

Several three-way classifications have also been advanced, such as that seemingly suggested in Hirschman's distinctions between 'development economics' and the neoclassical and neo-Marxist approaches in terms of their positions on the monoeconomics and mutual benefit claims. Arndt (1987) distinguishes the mainstream of development economics, with its emphasis on material growth (with variants stressing capital formation, human capital, and trade as an engine for growth) and its subsequent shift to social objectives, from the leftist radical counterpoint (including neo-Marxists and structuralists) which is preoccupied with the need to change the existing inequitable social order with revolution and redistribution, and from the rightist radical counterpoint which in varying degrees is opposed to Western-style modernization for LDCs (including Boeke and Frankel, Gandhi and Khomeni, and also, surprisingly, Viner and Bauer).

Chenery (1975) distinguishes between neoclassical, Marxist and structuralist approaches: the first two attempt to adapt systems of thought initially applied to developed economies to less developed economies, whereas the last 'attempts to identify specific rigidities, lags and other characteristics of the structure of developing economies. ...' (p.310). He identifies the neoclassical approach with models without 'rigidities', allowing for smooth substitution. Since the role of structural rigidities can be studied by incorporating them into neoclassical models, Chenery predicts that

> [t]he simplifying assumptions of the models currently in use tend to exaggerate the differences between neoclassical and structuralist prescriptions. As statistically determined relations replace *a priori* hypotheses, it is predictable that these differences will be reduced. A similar process can be hoped for when neo-Marxist theorists will turn their attention to verifying their hypotheses (p. 314).

Bardhan (1988) partitions the subject in a similar manner, distinguishing between neoclassical, Marxist and structuralist-institutionalist approaches (although he recognizes that each is a portmanteau category). Neoclassicals analyse economic behaviour in terms of maximizing individuals; Marxists emphasize structural constraints and the importance of class; and structural-ists stress the structures of particular economies (for instance, the impor-tance of oligopoly and sectoral divisions) and structural differences between economies. Comparing the Marxists and the neoclassicals, Bardhan finds the former strong in recognizing the role of history and the importance of collective action and classes, but weak in spelling out causal mechanisms; the latter is strong on causal mechanisms based on individual behaviour, but weak on history and institutions. He points out, however, a convergence between the two approaches, reflected in the work of the new neoclassicals and rational choice Marxists who combine the strengths of both approaches (the former recognizing the importance of property relations within neoclas-sical theory and the latter introducing individual optimization into Marxian analysis). Bardhan argues:

> [W]ith the lines of mutual communication between contending schools largely blocked by years of misunderstanding and jargon-mongering, easy 'victories' are often unilaterally claimed and hailed after setting up essentially a straw man to represent the opposing viewpoint and comfortably shooting it down. I happen to believe that the differences between the more sophisticated versions of alterna-tive approaches, even though substantial, are narrower than is generally per-ceived (p. 40).
>
> [T]he differences between alternative approaches are narrower now than gen-erally perceived and there is some scope for culling valuable insights from all of them, without underplaying their still substantially different perspectives (p. 67).

Stiglitz (1988) also makes a tripartite division, but between the neoclassical approach which assumes that agents are rational maximizers and markets function reasonably well; the information-theoretic approach (which we will call, following Bardhan, the new neoclassical approach) which also considers maximizing agents but assumes that information is costly, causing agents to behave very differently than if they had perfect information, and allows institutions to adapt, perhaps with lags, to changes in information costs; and the historical-institutional view which takes agents (like peasants) to be irrational and their behaviour dictated by customs and institutions which are not explained by the approach. The boundaries here are rigidly drawn, and there seems no sign of convergence.

A final division we may consider is that suggested by Griffin (1989) who, in examining strategies of development, distinguishes between six alternative approaches. A monetarist strategy focuses on the efficiency of resource allocation and depends heavily on free markets; an outward-looking strategy also emphasizes free markets and production according to comparative advantage, but promotes foreign trade and capital flows which sometimes require an active state for removing price distortions; an industrialization strategy, with an active state, emphasizes growth which is claimed to have trickle-down effects; a green revolution strategy focuses on agricultural growth through technological change; redistributive strategies seek to improve income distribution directly by asset redistribution and other means; and, finally, socialist strategies emphasize state ownership and planning rather than markets.

Rather than comment in detail on each of these points of view, it will suffice to note here that these alternative divisions of the subject and related views on the convergence question can be linked to two main factors. First, in some cases the categories may be interpreted as being dictated by some particular agenda on the part of those promoting them. Some divisions – which attempt to show the wide divergences between different approaches – are drawn to protect one group from the domination by others; for instance, there have been attempts to distinguish sharply non-neoclassical from neo-classical approaches, given the dominance of the latter in the profession and a desire by some to protect the former. Other classifications are related to efforts to show why one preferred approach is better than the alternatives which are defined so as to appear unsatisfactory: Stiglitz's (1988) division seems designed to reveal the strengths of the new neoclassical approach, Lal's (1985) to criticize all non-neoclassical interpretations, while Bardhan's (1988) discussion of convergence reveals rational choice Marxism in the most favourable possible light. In the presence of such a partisan agenda, some scepticism regarding the classifications (and their implications for convergence) could perhaps be forgiven. Second, the different divisions may be related to different criteria. Thus, Arndt (1987) is concerned with the meaning and objectives of development, Chenery (1975) with method, and Griffin (1989) with strategies of development. However, as we shall argue more fully later, the precise criteria for various approaches are not carefully spelt out, and sometimes different criteria appear to be related but we are never told exactly how. Despite all these reservations, however, these classifications will serve some useful purposes in our subsequent discussion.

In the next four sections we will examine more carefully whether there is a convergence of views between different approaches to development economics by distinguishing between alternative approaches at four different levels – in what we will call differences in method, in vision, in strategies and in the meaning of development. The following sections will attempt to make these expressions more precise, to distinguish alternative approaches to development at each of these levels, and to argue that particular approaches at one level are not necessarily linked to particular approaches at others. Finally, for each level we will examine to what extent and in what sense convergence is occurring, and to what extent this is desirable.

DIFFERENCES IN METHOD

The first level at which we distinguish alternative approaches is that of method, by which we mean method of explanation, or what we call organizing principles of analysis.[20] Organizing principles are taken here to mean ways in which explanations are structured in a particular approach; they are logical devices which make no statement about the real world.[21]

It is fairly difficult to partition the field in this way because practitioners of different approaches are seldom explicit on what organizing principle they use; it may also be possible to impute to particular development economists a variety of different organizing principles. We will attempt to overcome this difficulty by taking as our starting point the tripartite division according to method – between neoclassicals, Marxists and structuralists – suggested by Chenery (1975), and by trying to discover what organizing principles economists in each approach (as usually and roughly perceived) actually use in their analysis.[22]

Neoclassicals usually see themselves as grounding all explanation in terms of individual optimizing agents; in formal analysis this implies specifying the objectives and constraints of individual agents and deriving behavioural rules from optimization exercises. The distinguishing characteristic of neoclassical economics is the use of such optimizing techniques: anything not explained in terms of such techniques is no explanation at all.[23] A second organizing principle commonly used by neoclassicals is the Walras-Arrow-Debreu general equilibrium model not only with optimizing individuals, but also with assumptions about technology, preferences and markets which are required for the two fundamental theorems of welfare economics relating competitive equilibrium to Pareto optimality. According to this approach, all real-world 'imperfections' and 'distortions' can be explained as deviations from one or more of the assumptions of the model; the analysis can also show how to remove the effects of the distortions and make the economy more efficient. Lal (1985) seems to argue that this is the only form of rigorous economic analysis. This second approach is becoming less popular among neoclassicals (interpreted as those who reduce all explanation to the optimizing individual), who are increasingly turning to simpler partial equilibrium approaches which introduce information imperfections more carefully into the analysis (see Stiglitz 1988): in the 'benchmark' models of this approach, the equilibrium is Pareto inefficient.

The organizing principle of the Marxists may be taken to be the reduction of all explanation to a struggle between classes as defined by the social relations of production. Thus explanation is organized around such issues as which are the important social classes, how do they relate to each other, how are their interests opposed, how can their struggle be characterized and how does this affect the behaviour of economies.[24] In broader informal analysis this is usually accompanied by an awareness of the interaction between factors of a narrowly economic kind on the one hand, and sociological and political factors on a broad interdisciplinary canvas on the other, although the explicitness of the latter aspect is missing in more formal analysis. The value-theoretic framework which dominated much of Marxist analysis in the past can also be treated as an organizing principle,[25] but is gradually losing ground as many Marxists are beginning to question the usefulness of labour values.

For structuralists the organizing principle is probably the most difficult to identify, given the relative newness of the approach. We will focus on the way new structuralists (see Taylor 1983, in particular) have conducted their analysis; that is, by starting with aggregative accounting relations involving different factors of importance and then, using 'stylized facts' regarding these factors, developing complete models which can determine the variables of interest in terms of accounting identities, behavioural and other relations and some givens of the analysis. Although our description here is formal, the approach is not necessarily so: the use of aggregative accounting relations refers to an 'overall' view;[26] the use of given relations refers to given 'structures'; and the focus on stylized facts refers to specific characteristics relevant to the particular system being analysed.[27]

We now make several comments – not all unrelated – about these organizing principles and the methodological approaches that use them.[28]

First, these organizing principles are not mutually exclusive, so that the approaches based on them are not necessarily contradictory. For instance, the existence of classes can be rationalized in terms of individual optimization given the differential ownership of the means of production (Roemer 1982, Eswaran and Kotwal 1986), and class conflict can be interpreted as the result of bargaining between optimizing groups or agents (Roemer 1985); thus the way in which neoclassicals conduct their analysis using their own approach does not necessarily conflict with that of Marxists. Moreover, as Chichilnisky (1984) points out, structuralist analysis can be made sense of in terms of neoclassical general equilibrium models using optimizing behaviour with distortions and imperfections. Furthermore, structuralist approaches usually do introduce differences in behaviour between classes and class conflict into their analysis *if* this is considered important in terms of stylized facts. The difference between the approaches (as we have here defined them) has to do with the methodological dictates that accompany the way in which the analysis is actually conducted. Structuralists would not insist on using optimization to derive their behavioural relations, nor necessarily emphasize class issues; Marxists would not require class to be explained in terms of optimizing decisions. To the extent that the so-called rational choice Marxists (see Roemer 1986, Bardhan 1988) insist that class and class conflict *must* be explained in terms of optimizing principles in rigorous analysis, their approach can be said to be neoclassical rather than Marxian.

Second, our use of the terms neoclassical, Marxist and structuralist is different from the way in which these terms are often used. The neoclassical approach is often identified with the neoclassical general equilibrium model as a description of reality; this is not what we mean. The structuralist approach is often equated with the view that rigidities – such as technological ones (reflected by fixed coefficients) and behavioural ones (showing low price responses of individuals) – are important in reality (Bardhan 1988); this is not how we define the structuralist approach.

Third, as already mentioned above, the organizing principles discussed here are merely methods of analysis and not intended to be descriptions of the real world. Since there appears to be much confusion over this issue in the literature, the point requires some discussion. Regarding the neoclassical approach it may be argued that the assumption of optimizing behaviour is actually a view of the world – that is, the view that individuals are rational. Although this has been the interpretation of many neoclassically-inclined economists (we have referred to Stiglitz's (1988) views above), the connection between optimization and rationality – however defined – is tenuous. As Boland (1981) has noted, the assumption of optimization cannot even be tested in principle because it does not specify what is actually being optimized and under what constraints. If individual agents are made to optimize ignoring important real-world constraints, or if their objective functions are inconsistent in some way, few would call such behaviour rational. Or if individuals are assumed to use rules of thumb and not optimizing behaviour, this cannot be called irrational. First, these rules of thumb may easily be derived from optimization exercises. Second, and more important, in a complex environment it may be rational for individuals to fall back on rules of thumb and satisfice, and not incur the high costs of gathering information and of actually computing the optimum. Indeed, since agents cannot know *a priori* how much information to gather, they must in effect be following rules of thumb all the time.[29] Regarding Marxian analysis there is no empirical claim being made that class struggle is the most important determining phenomenon, or is even present in a given society; only that analysis must be reduced to classes (even analysis of why separate classes do not exist, or why class struggle is not important). Regarding structuralist analysis, there is no claim being made that particular structures, however defined, are given;[30] while for one analysis a particular characteristic of the economy may be taken to be given (say the mark-up rate set by oligopolistic firms), this is not an intrinsic characteristic of the structuralist approach (since another model can consider how the mark-up rate is determined in terms of other stylized facts which take other stylized characteristics – such as the state of the class struggle and the degree of monopoly – as given; see Dutt 1990b).

Fourth, and as implied in the previous point, no approach can be said to be right or wrong, or (intrinsically) better or worse than its alternatives, and it is futile to argue otherwise. Stiglitz's argument that the neoclassical (and his preferred new neoclassical or information-theoretic) approach is better than the alternatives, because it assumes individuals to be rational, is open to question given our argument about the tenuous link between optimization and rationality. By the same token, the neoclassical approach cannot be criticized for assuming that individuals *are* rational by arguing that this is an unrealistic assumption. Neither can Marxian or structuralist analyses be criticized because they do not explain classes and structures rigorously for various reasons: (i) because this criticism is based on a particular notion of what rigorous explanation means (that is, in terms of optimizing behaviour); (ii) because no theory can explain *everything* and particular Marxist and structuralist theories may not wish to explain particular institutions and structures; and (iii) because it seems possible to explain almost all structuralist and Marxian givens in terms of optimizing behaviour without adding much to the analysis and often leaving a great deal out.[31] An argument in favour of the neoclassical approach – that the use of optimization makes for a 'consistent' analysis of behaviour – does not state what 'consistent' means and is empirically of doubtful validity.[32] As a final example, the neoclassical approach cannot be criticized for not taking an aggregative view and ignoring the societal determination of individual behaviour, since neoclassical models with optimizing behaviour can and have been constructed to encompass (for instance) the endogeneity of preferences and the determination of a firm's behaviour by aggregate demand.

Fifth, although no one approach enjoys overall superiority, it may be the case that one may have more advantages in dealing with particular issues than another, partly due to its intrinsic characteristics. Moreover, because historically certain approaches have been used in certain ways, *specific* analysis using different approaches may yield different implications. The adoption of the neoclassical approach seems to have led many analysts to conclude that equilibrium is efficient: Lal's (1985) adoption of the neoclassical approach seems to have led him – without adequate justification – to attack various types of state interventions. More subtly, there may be a tendency to view distortions as optimal choices in the presence of externalities: interlinked transactions over several markets in underdeveloped agriculture have often been interpreted in this way in neoclassical analysis (Bardhan 1988, Stiglitz 1988), though this may not be the only explanation consistent with the neoclassical approach. More generally, though this is not intrinsic to neoclassical analysis, the approach may tempt one to assume that there is more choice available to individuals than is often really the case. Many structuralist models may produce particular results because of the specific assumptions made, such as fixed coefficients of production and the exogeneity of certain parameters which are not in fact unrelated to some of the other variables of the model. More generally (and again, there is no intrinsic reason for this), there may be a tendency on the part of practitioners of this approach to minimize the choice open to individuals and assume that institutions are less flexible than they really are. What all of this discussion implies is that although there may ultimately be little reason to choose one approach over the other, it is important to nurture all the alternative approaches so that various views of the world can be examined and their implications adequately considered.

DIFFERENCES IN VISION

By differences in vision we mean differences in opinion regarding the key characteristics of the economy being examined. Since this definition is rather vague, we will illustrate the meaning of differences in vision by considering one of the most important issues in development economics: the determinants of growth and distribution.[33]

In this context alternative visions refer to alternative ideas as to what factors primarily determine growth and distribution in the economy. One useful way to give this idea precision is to use the structuralist approach and the two following accounting relations for a closed economy:[34]

$$1 = a_0 C + (K/X)g \qquad (1.1)$$

and

$$1 = a_0(W/P) + (K/X)r. \qquad (1.2)$$

Here a_0 refers to the given labour-output ratio (assuming for simplicity a fixed-coefficients production relation), C is consumption per worker, K the stock of capital, X the level of output, g the rate of growth of the capital stock, W the money wage, P the price level and r the rate of profit.[35] The first equation states that (assuming away fiscal variables) output equals consumption plus investment, and the second states that income either goes to wages or to profits. In addition, if we assume for simplicity that all wage income is consumed and a given fraction s of profits is saved,

$$g = sr. \qquad (1.3)$$

These three relations are insufficient to determine the values of the five variables of this system – g, W/P, r, C and K/X – which include growth (g) and distributional (W/P, r) variables. Alternative visions can then be represented by alternative 'closures' which introduce two additional relations each to 'close' the model.[36] A neoclassical closure assumes full capacity utilization due to competition, so that $K/X = a_1$ where a_1 is the technologically-fixed capital-output ratio, and assumes that growth occurs with full-employed labour so that $g = n$, where n is the fixed rate of growth of labour supply. A neo-Marxian closure also assumes full-capacity utilization but takes the real wage to be fixed by the state of class struggle.[37] A neo-Keynesian closure assumes full-capacity utilization but introduces a desired accumulation function, $g = g(r)$, relating desired accumulation by firms positively to the rate of profit. Finally, a Kalecki-Steindl closure assumes that firms set prices according to a mark-up on prime costs in a situation of excess capacity utilization, so that $P = Wa_o(1 + z)$ where z is the given mark-up rate depending on the degree of monopoly; firms' accumulation plans depend positively on the rate of capacity utilization in addition to the rate of profit, so that $g = g(r, X/K)$.

Several comments are in order regarding this. First, while the framework has focused on a few issues, it can be made more complex by incorporating additional ones such as technological change.[38] Second, although we have made some specific assumptions such as that of fixed coefficients, our analysis does not require them.[39] Third, although we have used the structuralist approach (in the sense of starting with aggregative accounting identities and filling in other relations), the models and their underlying visions could have been shown using other approaches as well (for instance the neoclassical approach, allowing for optimizing behaviour as much as possible).[40] The basic point we wish to make is that the characteristics of economies can be distinguished according to what primarily determines their rates of growth: for neoclassicists labour supply growth (and the rate of technological change[41]), for neo-Marxians class struggle and hence distribution, for neo-Keynesians aggregate demand and animal spirits and hence the accumulation plans of firms, and in the Kalecki-Steindl vision the degree of monopoly and aggregate demand.[42] Fourth, these alternatives have remarkably different implications: for instance, the relationship between the rate of accumulation (g) and distribution (W/P) is negative in all but the last. Fifth, these visions do not exhaust all possible ones. For instance, an open economy extension of the model which assumes that output requires some imported intermediate inputs and has an upper limit to exports and available foreign exchange can be constrained by foreign exchange.[43] Finally, while what we have discussed are 'pure' visions, actual economies can perhaps often be best described in a manner which combines a variety of their features. For instance, models of inflation have been developed which combine neo-Marxian and demand-constrained features in a one-sector model.[44] Further, multisector models can distinguish sectors by adopting different closures for different sectors:[45]

models of dual economies developed by Lewis (1954), Jorgenson (1961) and Kaldor (1977) can all be interpreted in this way.[46]

Differences in vision exist regarding the determinants of overall growth and distribution, but also on how one examines particular parts of less developed economies. One issue on which much has been written in recent years is the structure of underdeveloped agriculture. Here there seem to be three divergent points of view (Stiglitz 1988).

One view adopts what we may call a neo-Marxian vision, which generally takes (as in the case of the macromodels discussed above) distributional parameters or class positions and power as exogenously given and examines their consequences for accumulation and technological change. In this view the market mechanism is understood as one of surplus transfer which Bhaduri (1986) calls 'forced commerce'. Bhaduri (1983) and others have developed models which show how given class structures (involving classes such as landlords, moneylenders and workers) and often given distributional parameters (such as the share rent) result in and maintain or even worsen inequalities of income and wealth in agriculture, often serving to retard the rate of accumulation and technological change.

A diametrically opposed view is the neoclassical one which takes peasants to be optimizers (thus following the neoclassical approach) and also takes all markets to clear and result in a Pareto-optimal outcome, irrespective of the distribution of income and wealth (Schultz 1964). The assumption of market-clearing – including that of full employment of labour (Schultz, 1964, argues that even disguised unemployment does not exist) – gives this viewpoint a neoclassical vision in addition to a neoclassical approach.

A third view is critical of both these, arguing, first, against the neo-Marxist approach for not assuming that agents are optimizers, and for taking institutions, class relations and distributional parameters as given and hence unexplained; and, second, against the neoclassical approach for allowing all the assumptions to result in the Pareto-optimality of equilibrium. This view, which introduces market imperfections in the form of imperfect information, actually combines elements from neoclassical and neo-Marxian visions; not surprisingly, it has found support both among some neoclassically-oriented economists (Stiglitz 1988) and those with Marxist leanings (Bardhan 1988).

We have commented on the issue of optimization in the previous section, but some reference to other points of comparison between this view (which we call the new neoclassical view) and the neo-Marxian view is in order. First, although neo-Marxian models often leave institutions and distributional parameters unexplained, it is not clear that the 'explanation' (even in terms of individual optimization) put forward in some of the new neoclassical contributions is the only possible one. Thus different visions may well exist between the two groups which both endogenize institutions. To take one

example, interlinked market transactions can be viewed as a rational response to market failures and risks in credit, land and labour markets and to
costly monitoring of worker efforts (Bardhan 1984a, Stiglitz 1988), and, by
internalizing externalities, raising efficiency; however, they may alternatively
be explained as a method of increasing the appropriation of surplus from
peasants by landlords and moneylenders (Hart 1986). In another example
(Basu 1984, pp. 141–42) optimizing models of interest-rate determination
by Bhaduri (1983) and those in the new neoclassical tradition differ according to what they assume about the restrictions faced by the lender – whether
they are restricted in adopting a price strategy or whether they face no such
constraint and can push the borrower to the 'reservation utility'.

Second, the similarity in the results obtained by the neo-Marxians and
new neoclassicals should not be overlooked. Since the latter allow for important market failures in underdeveloped agriculture (incomplete markets,
information asymmetry, moral hazard problems, etc), there is no presumption
of the efficiency of resource allocation, making the latter crucially dependent upon the nature of property relations, a result similar to that shown by
neo-Marxists. Thus Braverman and Stiglitz (1986) show that in some cases
productivity-raising innovations may be resisted by individual landlords
who fear an exacerbation of the incentives problem, a result similar to
Bhaduri's (1973) where the landlord does not allow technological change
because of the loss of interest income, although for very different reasons.[47]
There is a need for a better understanding of the similarities and differences
between these conflicting visions and for going beyond the spurious criticisms
based on rationality and exogeneity of institutions.

We thus find a variety of competing visions or views on the functioning of
actual economies which are not intrinsically linked to particular methodological approaches. However it is difficult, if not impossible, to choose between
these alternative visions on objective grounds: the problems with hypothesis
testing and falsification are well known to those who have cared to read and
think on the subject. Development economists have been as unsuccessful in
choosing between alternative visions as have other economists.[48] The choice
between visions is thus made for subjective reasons, often related to the
majority view held by leading scholars whose approach one follows. Our
analysis implies that a more honest, informed judgement can be made about
how an economy functions (and hence on what vision is appropriate) if each
vision is taken seriously and its analysis carefully explored.

ALTERNATIVE STRATEGIES

As mentioned above, Griffin (1989) has distinguished strategies of development by identifying several mutually-exclusive identifiable strategies and by
trying to spotlight their main features. While this is useful for some purposes
of classification, we will proceed differently, by commenting on three important debates in development economics: those regarding free markets
versus state intervention, outward-looking versus inward-looking strategies,
and agriculture versus industry. Our comments will be made in terms of five
observations, which we illustrate with examples drawn from these three
debates.

First, there is no clear connection between alternative methodological
approaches to development and the position taken on these strategies, however contradictory this may seem. In the early days of the rejuvenation of the
discipline, development economists generally favoured government intervention and planning, stressing indivisibilities, increasing returns and externalities (Rosenstein-Rodan 1943, 1961; Scitovsky 1954). In this period there
was also general support for inward-looking, import-substituting strategies,
based on the view that export prospects were limited, and that the terms of
trade were turning against poor countries. Finally, there was a general focus
on industrialization – especially through the fostering of heavy industries –
often at the expense of agriculture. Neoclassically-oriented development
economists who were critical of this mainstream instead usually supported
markets, free trade and an emphasis on agriculture (Bauer 1971, Viner 1953,
Schultz 1964 and Johnson 1958). The resurgence of the neoclassical approach
in general and in development economics in particular was accompanied by
a shift towards markets and free trade, as reflected in the views expressed by
Lal (1985). Marxists, on the other hand, have usually been identified with
state intervention and a heavy industrialization strategy and with the inward-
oriented approach (especially because of the writings of the dependency and
development-of-underdevelopment views). Since structuralists have often
been identified with the views of the mainstream development economists of
the early days, their views have generally been supposed to be similar.

However, the neoclassical approach, whether in the form that uses the
perfect market model as a benchmark or simply the optimizing form, does
not necessarily provide a case for free markets or free trade. With the
neoclassical approach, a large number of distortions can make the case for
state intervention: Stern (1989) provides a comprehensive list, including
imperfect competition, externalities, increasing returns to scale and missing
markets. Even the early arguments of Rosenstein-Rodan and others have
been rigorously formulated using the neoclassical approach, emphasizing
distortions due to increasing returns to scale or imperfect competition (Basu

1984, Murphy, Shleifer and Vishny 1988a and 1988b).[49] An attempt to 'prove' the superiority of free markets using the neoclassical approach – by claiming that the existence of government controls causes productive resources to be used up in influencing controls through directly unproductive activities (Bhagwati 1982) – is not entirely convincing because in the presence of distortions such activities can sometimes be shown to be welfare improving! The new neoclassical approach, which departs from the perfect market model benchmark by introducing imperfect information from the start but which works with optimizing agents, is quite agnostic on the issue of market-versus-state. With imperfect information, market equilibrium will not be constrained Pareto optimal, although some information problems of moral hazard and adverse selection are present for regulatory and planning bodies as well (Stiglitz 1988). Regarding trade, it is well known that in the presence of distortions free trade may not be the best policy: the infant industry argument is a well-known exception, as is that for increasing returns (see Bhagwati and Srinivasan 1983).[50] The existence of risk may imply that a particular sector may produce less than what is socially desirable unless it is protected (Newbery and Stiglitz 1984). All those using the Marxist approach need not be in favour of state intervention or inward-looking policies. We have already referred to the views of Warren (1973) regarding the beneficial aspects of the international spread of capitalism. Some Marxists may identify the state with the interests of some dominant class which may not be in the social interest. A sophisticated Marxist analysis (see Bardhan 1984b) sees the state as a strategic actor which interacts with various classes. This analysis is applied to the case of India where a heterogeneous collection of dominant classes with multiple veto powers uses the state to fritter away, in the form of public subsidies, investible surplus which retards industrial growth; this may be contrasted with the case of South Korea where the state is able to promote development through activist measures. Thus the superiority of state intervention in the market hinges here on the characteristics and relative power of the dominant classes and the nature of the state. Finally, our interpretation of the structuralist approach implies that it has no necessary implications for these questions.[51]

Second, though there is some relation between economic vision and strategies adopted, this link is not always clear-cut. If by the neoclassical vision we imply economies which fully employ their labour, this does not provide a case for free trade. If certain sectors show increasing returns to scale or stronger learning effects which may have spinoffs in other sectors, there is a case for changing the sectoral composition of output towards these sectors (usually identified as the industrial sector which makes this also an argument in favour of industry) by protection.[52] The support for free trade in the neoclassical vision typically emphasizes the inefficiencies due to intersectoral misallocation of resources caused by distorted price structures, but the empirical importance of such losses has often been questioned. Myint's (1987) support of free trade is made not in terms of this neoclassical vision, from which he clearly dissociates himself, but on the basis of vent for surplus (which assumes resources to be unemployed) and productivity effects, following the approach of Adam Smith.

One implication of this observation is that those with a particular vision must often look more carefully at the empirical details before they support a particular strategy. For instance, demand-constrained and foreign exchange-constrained economies can both be used to support an outward-looking approach based on export promotion. But, if an empirical judgement can be made that the possibilities of export promotion are remote, these same visions would support an import-substitution policy. It should also be pointed out in this context that whereas North-South models have often been taken to support the case of import substitution (by showing the unlikely possibilities of export promotion, with the South experiencing declining terms of trade and undergoing relatively lower growth), these results do not arise from the particular visions representing the Northern and Southern economies, but from specific additional behavioural relations that are incorporated into them. Thus these models do not necessarily imply either terms of trade deterioration or uneven development.[53] Consider another example, regarding the choice between agriculture and industry. One way to address this question is to examine in which sector additional capital should be invested (on the margin) to raise the overall balanced growth rate of the economy. The choice of a particular 'closure' of a dual economy model, however, is not usually sufficient to decide on this issue: for instance, it may be shown that in the influential Kaldorian model (Kaldor 1977), the answer to this question depends on the specific parameters of the model.

Third, the view taken regarding one strategic issue may not be clearly related to the view taken on another. Thus in an outward-oriented view, where the economy seeks to grow rapidly by promoting exports, it may do so through strong export incentives and government regulations (which allocate investment towards export sectors) and by developing industry as an export sector at the expense of agriculture.

Fourth, there has been a tendency to think in terms of polar opposites, and not much effort devoted towards combining the best features of divergent strategies. In the case of market-versus-state, the new neoclassical view implies that neither markets nor state is always better; this approach provides some guidance on the conditions under which one or other system may be more effective, as well as suggesting how intermediate systems can be developed incorporating some elements from both. Regarding the export-promotion/import-substitution divide, the choice has been presented in an either/or form, overlooking the fact that in an economy with unemployed resources (that is, economies other than ones with a neoclassical vision[54]), it may be possible to pursue both policies, pushing up exports as well as imports.[55] In fact, it can be argued that by reducing industrial growth, technological change (of a learning by doing variety) and consequently the attractiveness of exports, import liberalization can result in slowing down export growth. Regarding agriculture-industry choices it may also be argued that there has been too much emphasis on the choice between sectors at a point in time, rather than the dynamic interaction between the two sectors, stressing their complementarity (Kaldor 1977, Rao and Caballero 1990).[56]

Finally, despite many efforts, discussions regarding the merits of different strategies based on actual country experiences are not very conclusive. The successes of Taiwan, South Korea, Hong Kong and Singapore have been linked to their laissez-faire policies and their outward-orientation in trade, while it is argued that the highly interventionist and inward-looking experience of India explains its poor performance. But this interpretation is highly controversial: the successful economies have been highly interventionist too, with substantial government direction of the investment process, restrictions on imports for industrial promotion, and with public enterprises often leading the way (Wade 1985, Pack and Westphal 1986, Bardhan 1988). Moreover, India's interventionist and protectionist policy has been considered responsible for the development of India's technologically advanced industrial base (Singh and Ghosh 1988).

Our observations imply that there is very little reason to be dogmatic about recommending specific strategies for developing economies to adopt. Finding suitable strategies not only requires a clear idea of what theoretical vision is appropriate for a particular economy at a particular point in time, but also detailed knowledge (and wisdom) about the empirical characteristics of the particular economy. One response to these uncertainties is to follow the rule of thumb of supporting those strategies one usually associates with the methodological approach one is partial to, but our analysis suggests that the chances of making incorrect decisions by following this approach are extremely high.

THE MEANING OF DEVELOPMENT

The final level at which we distinguish alternative approaches to the subject is what is meant by economic development. If asked to identify a single measure of development, which implies an improvement in the average standard of living or well-being, probably the majority of development economists would point to a rise in per capita GNP. But few would wish to think of this as the sole indicator. Development is also taken to imply an improvement in distribution (which is ignored in GNP) and the removal of poverty. Moreover, much more is implied in standard of living than average product or income, since poverty can be defined as the failure to meet certain levels of consumption of such important commodities as food, clothing and education, and since individual well-being depends also on intangibles such as freedom. Sen (1983, 1988) has linked well-being to the ability to do certain things and to attain certain types of 'being' (such as being educated, being free from avoidable morbidity, being well-nourished, etc) which he calls the 'functionings' of a person. Development refers to an increase in the achievement of functionings by individuals, which depend not only on income and the public provision of goods, but also on the characteristics of goods to achieve particular functionings of individuals. Moreover, the list of functionings that are considered important can be extended to include such vague achievements as 'liberation' (Goulet 1971). An alternative approach, though less widespread, is to steer away from individual functionings and emphasize collective goals like self-reliance, cultural independence, national sovereignty and the cooperative spirit. These do not exhaust all possibilities. Some, mainly non-economists, have defined development as modernization along Western lines, whereas others have denounced Western civilization and interpreted development as the flowering of traditional societies.[57]

Clearly, therefore, differences in opinion on what development means will significantly affect the focus of development economics and the strategies chosen for development. However, it is easy to overemphasize these differences, as we shall argue below.

First, there does appear to be a considerable narrowing of opinion amongst development economists regarding what is meant by economic development. Several collective goals (as opposed to instruments in achieving other goals) have become less popular and seem to be increasingly confined to those dogmatically wedded to certain social arrangements. Others, such as Western-style modernization or its negation, raise a variety of issues which economists – but not necessarily social reformers – have tended to shy away from. Relatively fewer economists are willing to forget about equity and focus only on efficiency questions.

Second, what often appears to be a debate on the meaning of development is actually a debate on the correct vision of economic development. As Bhagwati (1984) has argued, the switch from the emphasis on growth to equity in the 1970s did not reflect a change in the meaning of development. In the early years growth was not seen as an end in itself, but rather as a means to improving well-being and removing poverty. Whatever its validity the later view that growth did not achieve these ends led to the emergence of the 'basic needs' approach as a reaction against particular strategies to alleviate the problem of poverty through growth (Streeten 1984a).

Third, what are often thought of as contradictory objectives of growth may often not be so. In earlier sections we have discussed several examples in which growth and equity are positively related: first, in macroeconomic models of growth and distribution where improved distribution can expand markets and accelerate the rate of growth of the economy; and, second, in models of underdeveloped agriculture of neo-Marxian and new neoclassical variants where improved distribution of property and power can encourage accumulation and technological change and remove inefficiencies. Rising per capita incomes often make it easier for individuals to achieve higher functionings.

Fourth, even with conflicting and different meanings of development it may be possible to obtain at least a partial ordering over economic states. Sen (1988) notes that different people may have different opinions on how much weight to attach to the achievement of different functionings ('value heterogeneity'), and with development itself (however defined) these weights may change over time ('value endogeneity'). The approach of dominance provides a minimal partial ordering in the presence of value heterogeneity when there is an agreed list of which functionings are considered to be valuable. But Sen (1988) argues that one may go further: the relative values can be specified as belonging to particular ranges, and corresponding to these, an overall ranking (which is a partial ordering more extensive than the minimal dominance order) can be obtained. Even in the case of value endogeneity, an intersection technique can be used by which a 'change' can become an 'improvement' if it is so judged according to values both before and after the change.

Fifth, even if some cultures and nations appear to favour a particular meaning of development, they should nevertheless study other theoretical frameworks which also emphasize the determination of what they believe are unrelated matters. Thus, the rejection of growth as an objective should not be associated with a lack of interest in what determines growth, since growth may be causally linked to factors considered important for development, and also because it may be worth knowing what the costs of following particular objectives are in terms of other possible objectives.

Finally, a strong case may be made that there should be no *final* goal or definition of development, since goals will change during the process of development in an unknowable way.[58] Thus one should focus on marginal improvements – defined, for instance, by greater achievements in 'functions' as currently understood. This is one interpretation of an approach that emphasizes the means of development rather than ends, and does not worry too much about the meaning of development.

CONCLUSION

In this paper we have been concerned with two questions that have been raised in a number of recent appraisals of the state of development economics.

Regarding the supposed demise of development economics, although there have been periods of rise and fall in the popularity of the subject, and perhaps a decline in enthusiasm, there is no evidence that the subject is undergoing decline. Quite the contrary, it is experiencing remarkable growth in several directions.

Regarding the convergence of views among different approaches, it no longer appears possible to consider the subject as comprised of two (or more) monolithic blocks divided according to how they view development, what methodological approach they use, what vision they have about the functioning of the economy and what strategies they recommend. Development economists do have differences of opinion about the meaning of development, but these are probably less significant than often believed. They also have different methodological approaches and although this need not necessarily separate economists (regarding what should be done for development), we have argued that the subject would benefit from nurturing different methodological approaches since some historical links appear to exist between methods of analysis and views of the world. We have also argued that adherence to alternative methods does not always dictate how economists actually view particular economies or what strategies they recommend for their development; thus non-dogmatic economists of different approaches have considerable scope for agreement on what to do in a particular context. Complete convergence in this sense is unlikely, however, because of the difficulties in distinguishing empirically between alternative theories. This makes it all the more necessary to examine carefully alternative visions and examine their implications, to be able to make more informed and honest choices between them.

NOTES

1. See, for instance, Hirschman (1981), Little (1982), Sen (1983), Lewis (1984), Bhagwati (1984), Lal (1985), Chakravarty (1987) and Bardhan (1988).
2. See Sen (1983) and Lal (1985), for example, for opposing views.
3. See Wilber and Jameson (1979), for instance.
4. See Bardhan (1988).
5. Hirschman (1981, p. 1).
6. Lal's position is not very far from Little's (1982), although the latter provides a more balanced and less acerbic evaluation.
7. See below for references.
8. To a large extent this is how Lal (1985) attacks the subject: by criticizing specific theories involving the use of two-gap and North-South models, and by criticizing specific observations

such as the declining Southern terms of trade, uneven international development and the existence of surplus labour. While the criticisms of each element may have some validity, attacking a subject after defining it to include elements which one disapproves of, is not particularly helpful. Unenlightened defences of the subject can be made in the same way. We will return to other issues raised by Lal in later sections.

9. This is not only relevant for those who have dealt with broad questions relating to growth, stagnation and income distribution in the past, such as Smith, Malthus, Ricardo and Marx; but also for mercantilism (Wiles 1987) especially in relation to foreign exchange constraints, state intervention and planning, and protection; and the pre-Smithian French economists such as the Physiocrats (Vaggi 1989) and Turgot, especially in relation to agrarian structure and the relation between agriculture and industry.

10. See Arndt (1987) for a discussion of this literature.

11. Many of these were pointed out by Hirschman to explain his conception of the birth of the subject.

12. See Hirschman (1981) and Meier (1984).

13. See also Streeten (1984b).

14. See Basu (1984), Murphy, Shleifer and Vishny (1988a and 1988b).

15. This sentiment is also to be found in Lewis (1984) and Chakravarty (1987).

16. A different type of opposition follows from the observation that all developing economies are different: thus there should be no general development economics, but the economics of India, Brazil, Mexico, etc. While it may well be legitimate to study the economics of particular countries or particular regions within them, this does not imply that nothing can be learned by studying developing economies comparatively, or that the study of different economies does not raise similar issues.

17. Hill criticizes some of the broad generalizations on underdeveloped agriculture made by development economics which are, according to her, at variance with the facts revealed by anthropological case studies. Her criticism of neoclassical writers for conducting analysis based on common-sense generalizations (using the concept of the representative peasant and ignoring class distinctions) is particularly severe; note that such economists are not criticized by Lal.

18. See especially the surveys in Chenery and Srinivasan (1988, 1989), Ranis and Schultz (1988), Stern (1989), and *Journal of Development Economics*, 22(1) June, Symposium on New Direction in Development Theory. Terms such as 'new neoclassical' and 'new structuralist' will be defined below.

19. By excluding Marxian approaches completely and relegating the discussion of structuralist approaches to a few issues, Stern's (1989) survey makes it seem that the neoclassical approach is (almost) the only one.

20. There are several other issues usually related to methodology which have caused much controversy, including those concerning *a priori* theorizing versus detailed description of the real world; formal mathematical versus verbal analysis; and empirical testing or falsification. Much has been written on these issues and our position may be simply stated. On the first two of these issues, the controversy appears to be misguided. While theorizing must necessarily keep an eye on reality if it is to be relevant for the real world, it is difficult to understand how one can look at reality and describe it without having – explicitly or implicitly – *some* theoretical framework. Both verbal and mathematical analysis are useful in certain ways: the former probably having a comparative advantage in creativity, while the latter in clearly examining the implications of the interaction of a number of interdependent forces. Regarding the last issue, economists from different traditions have fallen prey to the fetish of positivism without much thought to Duhem-Quine and other problems, greater awareness of which would be good for economics. While particular approaches in the sense to be described in the chapter have often taken specific positions on the three issues discussed here, there is no necessary connection between the approaches and the positions.

21. Some realists would argue that there is no need to have such organizing principles, but only statements about the real world. We would dispute this claim and confine our attention to those development economists who do have identifiable organizing principles.

22. These three groups – neoclassical, Marxists, and structuralists – obviously do not include all development economists, since there are probably others who would not see themselves as fitting into any one of these categories as defined below. The institutionalists, for instance, are not included as comprising a separate approach because we have found it difficult to find a clear common organizing principle in their work; see below.

23. Clearly, everything in a model cannot be derived on the basis of individual optimization. But neoclassical economists usually think that a model is unsuccessful if something is exogenously specified; they think a modification of the model would be better if it explained this given in terms of optimizing behaviour.

24. This is not to imply that Marxists do not consider the role of other categories such as nations (for example, Frank, Amin and others in the 'dependency' tradition) or the presence of non-class relations (see Resnick and Wolff 1987), but that class and class relations are the object of focus.

25. It plays a role roughly similar to that of the neoclassical general equilibrium model: where in the neoclassical approach the focus is on efficiency (ignoring distortions due to market imperfections), in the Marxian approach the focus is on exploitation (ignoring the details due exchange and competition).

26. The focus on aggregates is in contrast to the focus on individuals or other subsets of the aggregates. Note that the aggregate refers to the whole system under analysis, which may, but need not necessarily, refer to a whole nation or the entire world economy (so that the structural approach can be applied to issues other than macroeconomic ones, as usually understood).

27. We prefer this as the defining characteristic of the approach over one which starts from a more general social science perspective of structuralism. The latter path has been taken by Jameson (1986), who links structuralism in economics to that in psychology, linguistics and anthropology and finds its defining characteristics, among others, to be a focus on an organized set of interdependent elements (which is similar to our interpretation), and a focus on 'deep structure' lying behind directly-observable surface phenomena (which has no counterpart in our interpretation). Criticizing the structuralist approach, Jameson argues that there is no clear notion of the deep structure of single economies (unlike the centre-periphery notion that exists for the analysis of world economies). The mathematical models of neo-structuralists for the analysis of North-South trade are similar to closed economy two-sector models of dual economies, and it is therefore not clear in what sense there is a deep structure embedded in one and not in the other.

28. As mentioned above, we may have excluded some who do not appear to belong to any one of these three schools. We mentioned institutionalists earlier. But some institutionalists, who favour optimization or the transactions cost approach could be classified as neoclassicals in our terminology; those emphasizing classes would be in the Marxist category; and those focusing on macroeconomic relations and particular stylized facts (which may represent institutional givens) could be called structuralist. A case may be made that institutionalists comprise a separate group of those who reduce all explanation to institutions, but since there is no agreement as to what precisely is meant by institutions (with Veblen's focus on prevailing methods of thought and Commons's on methods of collective control), it is difficult to distinguish this as a coherent approach separate from the other three discussed.

29. See Elster (1979) for a discussion of these issues.

30. Contrary to the suggestion of Ruccio (1991).

31. For example, the assumption of a given real wage in Marxian models can be, and has been, explained in terms of the efficiency wage model by introducing optimizing behaviour (see Bowles 1985, Akerlof and Yellen 1986). The assumption of a given mark-up in structuralist models has similarly been explained in terms of optimizing models with firms with given perceived elasticities of demand (see Dutt 1990b). These 'explanations', however, exclude reference to several other important determinants of these given parameters, for instance political issues relating to class struggle in both cases.

32. A well-known example from development economics – the Lewis (1954) model – should give us cause for doubt. Lewis' capitalist firms do optimize and set their real

wage equal to the marginal product of labour. But as Basu (1984) argues, this implies inconsistent behaviour on their part, because they invest all their savings and do not take into consideration the fact that by doing so they will be squeezing future profits – which is perhaps why less developed economies do not grow in the manner discussed by Lewis. The problem here is not with optimization, but with the fact that long-run issues and market imperfections are ignored. The point remains that the use of optimization is no safeguard against introducing implausible or inconsistent behaviour.

33. There is clearly no unique way to distinguish between key characteristics of the economy. The discussion here focuses on one method which appears to have been quite useful.

34. See Dutt (1990b) for details.

35. K/X is the actual capital-output ratio and satisfies $K/X \geq a_1$ where a_1 is the technologically-given capital-output ratio; a strict inequality implies the existence of excess capacity of capital.

36. See Marglin (1984) and Dutt (1990b) for a fuller exposition.

37. It may have been preferable to use other terms for these closures (so as not to confuse these visions with the neoclassical and Marxian approaches discussed above), but we have conformed to common usage.

38. See Dutt (1990b, chapter 5).

39. See Dutt (1990b, chapter 3). Note that we have not identified a structuralist vision, only a structuralist methodological approach. It has sometimes been suggested that the structuralist vision relates to models which have rigidities (fixed coefficients production functions, fixed saving propensities, etc). But since these rigidities are not the primary causes of the differences between the economic functioning of alternative models (see also Marglin (1984) on this point), it is more useful to think instead of the visions in the sense discussed in the text.

40. See Dutt (1990b, chapter 3). This confirms the point made in the previous section that alternative methods and alternative visions are not necessarily linked.

41. This has particularly been emphasized in recent models using the neoclassical approach (an optimizing framework) and a neoclassical vision (growth with fully-employed resources) such as those of Romer (1986, 1987) and Lucas (1988).

42. Demand-constrained models were dismissed as irrelevant for less developed economies in early discussions (Dasgupta 1954, Rao 1952), but have recently been argued to be relevant for some less developed economies (Taylor 1983, Dutt 1984, Rakshit 1982 and 1989).

43. This is shown by two-gap models. Note that contrary to what is often suggested (see Little 1982), this vision does not require the extreme rigidities assumed in simple two-gap models (see Findlay 1971) which are called 'structuralist' because of the presence of structural rigidities.

44. See Marglin (1984, chapter 20) and Dutt (1990b, chapter 4).

45. See Dutt (1990b, chapter 6).

46. See Dutt (1990a). North-South models showing the interaction of developed and less developed economies also distinguish the two economies according to visions in the sense discussed here. See Dutt (1989) for a survey.

47. Consider also two other examples where what can be called 'new neoclassical' contributions come close to the neo-Marxian view on the link between distribution and efficiency: inefficiencies in sharecropping due to the moral hazard problem can sometimes be eliminated by providing land to tenants or providing them with credit to buy the land (Stiglitz 1988); and a more equitable distribution of assets can reduce malnutrition and raise aggregate output in the economy (Dasgupta and Ray 1986).

48. See Jorgenson (1961), Marglin (1966) and Dixit (1973) for debates on how to choose between classical and neoclassical dual-economy models.

49. The defence that in the presence of such distortions the appropriate response is tax-subsidy policies and not planning is not entirely convincing because such policies which tinker with individual market failures may, according to the theory of the second best, aggravate the situation.

50. Increasing returns to scale and imperfect competition may, of course, result in benefits

from free trade due to greater specialization, as has been shown in models of intra-industry trade (Helpman and Krugman 1985).

51. Taylor (1983, 1988) has usually taken a stand which is anti-market and anti-trade, but this has more to do with vision than approach. We may also draw here on another strategy debate, that over stabilization policy. Here, too, we find that views on strategy need not be linked with approach. Taylor and his colleagues (see Swedish International Development Authority 1989), who use a structuralist approach, recommend what appears to be a monetarist stabilization policy involving cuts in government expenditure and money supply growth in Nicaragua. At the same time those following a neoclassical approach, with optimizing agents, have sometimes argued for stabilization policies of the non-monetarist variety.

52. Following the trade theory literature it may be argued that this does not provide a case for trade intervention, only for domestic government taxes and subsidies; however, on grounds of administrative feasibility and budgetary constraints, protection through import taxes may be called for.

53. See Dutt (1989, 1990b), which introduces additional factors, such as inelastic demand for Southern products and international demonstration effects, to neo-Marxian and Kalecki-Steindl visions.

54. In such economies shifting incentives to the import sector implies turning them away from the export sector and moving along the production-possibilities curve; this is not so if one is inside the frontier, with unemployed resources.

55. In some cases protecting imports may create disincentive effects for exports by raising the prices of intermediate goods, but such problems can be taken care of with tax exemptions for exporters.

56. This overemphasis on polar opposites is perhaps a legacy of the way development economics reemerged – as an attack on marginalism – and the manner in which marginalism has responded to the attack.

57. See Arndt (1987) for an historical discussion of these alternative objectives.

58. This is different from Sen's value endogeneity problem since it makes the nature of endogeneity intrinsically unknown.

REFERENCES

Akerlof, G. and Yellen, J. (eds) (1986), *Efficiency Wage Models of Labor Markets*, Cambridge: Cambridge University Press.

Arndt, H.W. (1987), *Economic Development*, Chicago: University of Chicago Press.

Baran, P. (1957), *The Political Economy of Growth*, New York: Monthly Review Press.

Bardhan, P.K. (1964), 'External Economies, Economic Development, and the Theory of Protection', *Oxford Economics Papers*, **16**, March.

Bardhan, P.K. (1984a), *Land, Labor and Rural Poverty: Essays in Development Economics*, New York: Columbia University Press.

Bardhan, P.K. (1984b), *The Political Economy of Development in India*, Oxford: Basil Blackwell.

Bardhan, P.K. (1988), 'Alternative Approaches to Development Economics', in Chenery and Srinivasan (below).

Basu, K. (1984), *The Less Developed Economy*, Oxford: Basil Blackwell.

Bauer, P.T. (1971), *Dissent on Development: Studies and Debates in Development Economics*, London: Weidenfeld & Nicholson.

Bauer, P.T. and Yamey, B.S. (1957), *The Economics of Under-developed Countries*, Chicago: University of Chicago Press.

Bell, C. and Zusman, P. (1976), 'A Bargaining Theoretic Approach to Cropsharing Contracts', *American Economic Review*, **66**, September, 578–88.

Bhaduri, A., (1977), 'A Study in Agricultural Backwardness under Semi-Feudalism', *Economic Journal*, **83**, 120–37.

Bhaduri, A. (1983), *The Economic Structure of Backward Agriculture*, London: Academic Press.

Bhaduri, A. (1986), 'Forced Commerce and Agrarian Growth', *World Development*, **14**(2), 267–72.

Bhagwati, J.N. (1982), 'Directly Unproductive Profit-Seeking (DUP) Activities', *Journal of Political Economy*, **90**(5), October, 988–1002.

Bhagwati, J.N. (1984), 'Development Economics: What Have We Learnt?' *Asian Development Review*, **2**(1), 23–38. Reprinted in J.N. Bhagwati (1985), *Wealth and Poverty*, Oxford: Basil Blackwell.

Bhagwati, J.N. (1988), 'Poverty and Public Policy', *World Development*, **16**(5), 539–55.

Bhagwati, J.N. and Srinivasan, T.N. (1983), *Lectures on International Trade*, Cambridge, Mass: MIT Press.

Boland, L.A. (1981), 'On the Futility of Criticizing the Neoclassical Maximization Hypothesis', *American Economic Review*, December, **71**(5), 1031–36.

Bowles, S. (1985), 'The Production Process in a Competitive Economy: Walrasian, neo-Hobbesian, and Marxian Models', *American Economic Review*, 75(**1**), March, 16–36.

Braverman, A. and Stiglitz, J. (1986), 'Landlords, Tenants and Technological Innovations', *Journal of Development Economics*, **23**, 313–32.

Chakravarty, S. (1987), 'The State of Development Economics', *Manchester School*, June, 125–43.

Chenery, H.B. (1975), 'The Structuralist Approach to Development Policy', *American Economic Review*, Papers and Proceedings, **65**(2), May, 310–16.

Chenery, H.B. and Srinivasan, T.N. (eds), (1988), *Handbook of Development Economics*, **1**, Amsterdam: North Holland.

Chenery, H.B. and Srinivasan, T.N. (eds), (1989), *Handbook of Development Economics*, **2**, Amsterdam: North Holland.

Chichilnisky, G. (1984), 'Review of "Structuralist Macroeconomics" by Lance Taylor', *Journal of Economic Literature*, December, **22**(4), 1641–43.

Dasgupta, A.K. (1954), 'Keynesian Economics and Underdeveloped Countries', *The Economic Weekly*, 26 January.

Dasgupta, P. and Ray, D. (1986), 'Inequality as a Determinant of Malnutrition and Unemployment: Theory', *Economic Journal*, **96**, December, 1011–34.

Dixit, A. (1973), 'Models of Dual Economies' in J.A. Mirrlees and N.H. Stern (eds), *Models of Economic Growth*, London: Macmillan.

Dutt, A.K. (1984), 'Stagnation, Income Distribution and Monopoly Power', *Cambridge Journal of Economics*, **8**(1), March, 25–40.

Dutt, A.K. (1989), 'North-South Models: A Critical Survey', unpublished, University of Notre Dame.

Dutt, A.K. (1990a), 'Sectoral Balance in Development: a Survey', *World Development*, **18**(6), 815–30.

Dutt, A.K. (1990b), *Growth, Distribution, and Uneven Development*, Cambridge: Cambridge University Press.

Elster, J. (1979), *Ulysses and the Sirens. Studies in Rationality and Irrationality*, Cambridge: Cambridge University Press.

Eswaran, M. and Kotwal, A. (1986), 'Access to Capital and Agrarian Production Organization', *Economic Journal*, **96**, June, 482–98.

Findlay, R. (1971), 'The "Foreign Exchange Gap" and Growth in Developing Economies', in J.N. Bhagwati (ed), *Trade, Balance of Payments, and Growth*, Amsterdam: North Holland.

Goulet, D. (1971), ' "Development" ... or Liberation', *International Development Review*, September.

Griffin, K. (1989), *Alternative Strategies for Economic Development*, New York: St Martin's Press.

Haberler, G. (1959), *International Trade and Economic Development*, Cairo: National Bank of Egypt.

Hart, G. (1986), 'Interlocking Transactions: Obstacles, Precursors or Instruments of Agrarian Capitalism?', *Journal of Development Economics*, **23**, 177–203.

Helpman, E. and Krugman, P. (1985), *Market Structure and Foreign Trade*, Cambridge, Mass: MIT Press.

Hill, P. (1986), *Development Economics on Trial: The Anthropological Case for a Prosecution*, Cambridge: Cambridge University Press.

Hirschman, A.O. (1981), 'The Rise and Decline of Development Economics', in A.O. Hirschman, *Essays in Trespassing: Economics to Politics and Beyond*, Cambridge: Cambridge University Press.

Jameson, K.P. (1986), 'Latin American Structuralism: A Methodological Perspective', *World Development*, **14**(2), 223–32.

Johnson, H.G. (1958), 'Planning and the Market in Economic Development', *Pakistan Economic Journal*, June.

Jorgenson, D. (1961), 'The Development of a Dual Economy', *Economic Journal*, **71**(282), 309–34.

Kaldor, N. (1977), 'Equilibrium Theory and Growth Theory' in M. Boskin (ed.), *Economics and Human Welfare*, New York: Academic Press.

Lal, D. (1985), *The Poverty of 'Development Economics'*, Cambridge, Mass: Harvard University Press.

Lewis, W.A. (1954), 'Economic Development with Unlimited Supplies of Labour', *Manchester School*, **22**(2), 131–91.

Lewis, W.A. (1984), 'The State of Development Theory', *American Economic Review*, **74**(1).

Lewis, W.A. (1988), 'The Roots of Development Theory' in Chenery and Srinivasan (1988).

Little, I.M.D. (1982), *Economic Development*, New York: Basic Books.

Lucas, R.E. (1988), 'On the Mechanics of Economic Development', *Journal of Monetary Economics*, **22**, 3–42.

Marglin, S.A. (1966), 'Comment on Jorgenson' in I. Adelman and E. Thorbecke (eds), *Theory and Design of Economic Development*, Baltimore: Johns Hopkins Press.

Marglin, S.A. (1984), *Growth, Distribution and Prices*, Cambridge, Mass: Harvard University Press.

Marshall, A. (1920), *Principles of Economics*, 8th ed, London: Macmillan.

Meier, G.M. (1984), 'The Formative Period' in Meier and Seers (1984).

Meier, G.M. (ed.), (1987), *Pioneers in Development, Second Series*, New York: Oxford University Press.

Meier, G.M. and Seers, D. (eds), (1984), *Pioneers in Development*, New York: Oxford University Press.

Murphy, K.M., Shleifer, A. and Vishny, R. (1989a), 'Income Distribution, Market Size and Industrialization', *Quarterly Journal of Economics*, **104**(3), August, 537–64.

Murphy, K.M., Shleifer, A. and Vishny, R. (1989b), 'Industrialization and the Big Push', *Journal of Political Economy*, **97**(5), October, 1003–26.

Myint, H., 'The Neoclassical Resurgence in Development Economics: Its Strength and Limitations', in Meier (1987).

Myrdal, G. (1957), *Rich Lands and Poor*, New York: Harper and Brothers.

Newbery, D.M.G. and Stiglitz, J. (1984), 'Pareto Inferior Trade', *Review of Economic Studies*, **51**(1), 1–12.

Nurkse, R. (1956), *Problems of Capital Formation in Underdeveloped Countries*, Oxford: Basil Blackwell.

Pack, H. and Westphal, L.E. (1986), 'Industrial Strategy and Technological Change: Theory versus Reality', *Journal of Development Economics*, June.

Rakshit, M. (1982), *The Labour Surplus Economy*, Delhi: Macmillan.

Rakshit, M. (ed.), (1989), *Studies in the Macroeconomics of Developing Countries*, Delhi: Oxford University Press.

Ranis, G. and Schultz, T.P., (1988), *The State of Development Economics. Progress and Perspectives*, Oxford: Basil Blackwell.

Rao, J.M. and Caballero, J.M. (1990), 'Agricultural Performance and Development Strategy: Retrospect and Prospect', *World Development*, **18**(6), June, 899–913.

Rao, V.K.R.V. (1952), 'Investment, Income and the Multiplier in an Underdeveloped Economy', *Indian Economic Review*, February.

Resnick, S.A. and Wolff, R.D. (1987), *Knowledge and Class. A Marxian Critique of Political Economy*, Chicago: University of Chicago Press.

Robbins, L. (1968), *The Theory of Economic Development in the History of Economic Thought*, London: Macmillan.

Roemer, J. (1982), *A General Theory of Exploitation and Class*, Cambridge, Mass: Harvard University Press.

Roemer, J. (1985), 'Rationalizing Revolutionary Ideology', *Econometrica*, **53**, 85–108.

Roemer, J. (ed.), (1986), *Analytical Marxism*, Cambridge: Cambridge University Press.

Romer, P.M. (1986), 'Increasing Returns and Long-Run Growth', *Journal of Political Economy*, **94**, 1002–37.

Romer, P.M. (1987), 'Growth Based on Increasing Returns due to Specialization', *American Economic Review*, Papers and Proceedings, **77**, 56–62.

Rosenstein-Rodan, P.N. (1943), 'Problems of Industrialization in Eastern and South-Eastern Europe', *Economic Journal*, **53**, 202–11.

Rosenstein-Rodan, P.N. (1961), 'Notes on the Theory of the Big Push' in H.S. Ellis and H.C. Wallich (eds), *Economic Development in Latin America*, New York: St Martin's Press.

Ruccio, D.F. (1991), 'When Failure becomes Success: Class and the Debate over Stabilization and Adjustment', forthcoming, *World Development*.

Schultz, T.P. (1964), *Transforming Traditional Agriculture*, Chicago: Chicago University Press.

Scitovsky, T. (1954), 'Two Concepts of External Economies' in M. Abramovitz (ed.), *The Allocation of Economic Resources*, Stanford: Stanford University Press.

Seers, D. (1979a), 'The Birth, Life and Death of Development Economics', *Development and Change*, **10**, 707–19.

Seers, D. (1979b), 'The Congruence of Marxism and other Neoclassical Doctrines', in A Rothko Chapel Colloquium, *Toward a New Strategy for Development*, New York: Pergamon Press.

Sen, A.K. (1983), 'Development: Which Way Now?', *Economic Journal*, **93**, December, 745–62.

Sen, A.K., 'The Concept of Development', in Chenery and Srinivasan (1988).

Singh, A. and Ghosh, J. (1988), 'Import Liberalisation and the New Industrial Strategy: An Analysis of Their Impact on Output and Employment', *Economic and Political Weekly*, **23**(45–47), Special Number, November, 2313–42.

Stern, N. (1989), 'The Economics of Development: a Survey', *Economic Journal*, **99**, September, 597–685.

Stiglitz, J.E., 'Economic Organization, Information and Development', in Chenery and Srinivasan (1988).

Streeten, P. (1984a), 'Basic Needs: Some Unsettled Questions', *World Development*, **12**(9), 973–79.

Streeten, P. (1984b), 'Development Dichotomies' in Meier and Seers (1984).

Swedish International Development Authority (1989), *Nicaragua: The Transition from Economic Chaos toward Sustainable Growth*, SIDA.

Taylor, L. (1983), *Structuralist Macroeconomics*, New York: Basic Books.

Taylor, L. (1988), *Varieties of Stabilization Experience. Towards Sensible Macroeconomics in the Third World*, Oxford: Clarendon Press.

Toye, J. (1985), 'Dirigisme and Development Economics', *Cambridge Journal of Economics*, **9**, 1–14.

Vaggi, G. (1989), 'A Two-Sector, Four-Class Model' in S. Chakravarty (ed.), *The Balance Between Industry and Agriculture in Development, Vol 3*, London: Macmillan.

Viner, J. (1953), *International Trade and Economic Development*, Oxford: Clarendon Press.

Wade, R. (1985), 'The Role of Government in Overcoming Market Failure: Taiwan, South Korea and Japan' in H. Hughes (ed.), *Explaining the Success of East Asian Industrialization*, Cambridge: Cambridge University Press.

Warren, B. (1973), 'Imperialism and Capitalist Industrialization', *New Left Review*, **81**, September-October.

Wilber, C.K. and Jameson, K.P. (1979), 'Paradigms of Economic Development and Beyond' in K. Jameson and C.K. Wilber (eds), *Directions in Economic Development*, Notre Dame: University of Notre Dame Press.

Wiles, R.C. (1987), 'The Development of Mercantilist Economic Thought' in S. Todd Lowrey (ed.), *Pre-Classical Economic Thought*, Boston: Kluwer Academic Publishers.

2. Structuralist and Competing Approaches to Development Economics

Lance Taylor

Structuralist economists take a national economy's institutions and own patterns of change as their bases for analysis, recognizing the historical nature of their craft. They act on the principle that theory in economics has to take the form of common sense generalizations from broadly similar developments at different places and times. Neoclassical rituals to the contrary, useful theory inevitably follows observed experience. Its true foundations cannot be abstract models based on 'first principles' of optimization by demon agents subject to mathematically tractable constraints. Indeed, as Pasinetti (1981) eloquently argues, responding to ideas raised by structuralists and redraping them in the latest optimization styles is what most neoclassical theorizing is all about.

From this perspective, I want to take up two areas in the macroeconomics of development where structuralists have been active for some time: the analysis of income distribution and growth on the one hand, and money and finance on the other. I will draw in stylized fashion on the history of economic thought, to point out contrasts between structuralist and mainstream ideas relating to these broad areas of concern. I will then close with some observations about how the structuralist models that we review may bear on the severe problems facing developing countries in the decade to come. The details are spelled out at length in Taylor (1991).

THEORIES OF ECONOMIC GROWTH

Chakravarty (1980) distinguishes what he calls the Mill-Marshall and Marx-Schumpeter traditions in the theory of economic growth – the first author in each pair representing a watershed from the classical models of Smith and Ricardo. To these strands, we can add an underconsumptionist or stagnationist tradition which extends naturally to deal with issues such as external constraints on growth, the agricultural/non-agricultural terms of trade and, finally, the models proposed in Cambridge (England) after World War II which built on the work of Kalecki and Keynes to deal with distribution and growth.[1]

Neither Mill nor Marshall fits with complete comfort into Chakravarty's box (Mill was well aware of class and gender conflict, while Marshall had much to say on the importance of historical processes and economies of scale, as well as anticipating many of Keynes' insights into the trade cycle). Nonetheless, their approach to growth theory leads ultimately to the optimal saving and overlapping generations models that dominate mainstream macroeconomics today (Blanchard and Fischer, 1989).

According to his writings gathered by Whitaker (1975), the young Marshall followed Mill in setting out a growth model stressing the steady accumulation of physical capital and dropping the classical population theory via which demand for labour (from the wage fund) controls supply via Malthusian checks. Both Englishmen largely ignored the implications for growth of increasing returns, the potential contradiction between technical change and the real wage or employment brought out by Ricardo in his famous chapter 'On Machinery' (which greatly influenced Marx), and indeed all macro aspects of class conflict and cumulative processes besides the productive use of saving. The gist of their model can be summarized in the form of three hypotheses:

1. There is an aggregate production function incorporating substitution between capital and labour. Production takes place under constant returns to scale.
2. The labour force grows in 'natural' units, but per worker 'efficiency' in production also rises due to technical progress and greater skills (the latter in part resulting from more education).
3. Saving comes from desires for deferred consumption and to assure inheritance; both motivations underlie thrifty 'waiting'. Output not consumed is directly transformed into new capital formation, and as the stock of capital goes up the rate of interest (or profit) falls.

In a few words, growth results from saving generated by forces of productivity and thrift, plus exogenous technical change.

As Solow (1956) and subsequent neoclassical work based on Ramsey's (1928) optimal saving and Diamond's (1965) overlapping generations models have shown, these hypotheses support an analytical engine of considerable power. However, it is still a generalization based upon the English capitalism of thrifty family firms that was ceasing to prevail even in Victorian times. Factors the model omits include the following:

1. The links that exist between growth of money and credit institutions and industrialization; one thinks of Gerschenkron's (1962) emphasis on the role of commercial banks in guiding German industrial expansion last century.
2. There are different rates of technical change (not to mention wage and profit rates) across sectors, suggesting that non-competitive market structures endure.
3. Risk pooling and reduction advanced greatly in Marshall's day due to the growth of financial intermediation and the corporate business form.
4. The state intervened at many levels to speed economic growth, creating labour skills by education, imposing worker discipline and pursuing an activist commercial policy – in sharp disagreement with the tenets of 19th (and 20th) century neoclassical theories of trade.
5. Investment projects undertaken by firms were essential both to create aggregate demand and to embody new techniques. In both developing and now industrialized economies, public investment played an essential complementary role.
6. Investment and saving can also get out of gear, creating inflationary or contractionary tendencies depending on which is potentially greater. The question about how investment injections are made equal to saving leakages is simply not addressed by the neoclassical model, whereas structuralists give it prominence in their scenarios for growth.
7. As opposed to the utility maximization that dominates Ramsey-style optimal saving models, consumer choice in Marshall's time and now appears to be rather passive. Households may dissave to switch to inno-vative products as entrepreneurs make them appear: how many staples of the 1990 advanced economy consumption baskets (VCRs, Fax ma-chines, shopping centre sushi bars) even existed ten years before? As Pasinetti (1981) emphasizes, the genius of capitalism resides in fore-stalling an unemployment crisis by inventing new products to replace old ones as demand for them subsides.

No existing theory of growth deals adequately with all these issues, although some structuralist constructs go part way. In so doing, they utilize insights into the growth process that can be gleaned from Schumpeter and Marx.

To summarize Marx's views on growth (or anything else, for that matter) in a way acceptable to all his readers is impossible. Following Chakravarty, all we can do here is set out a number of points that he raised which can be inserted into simple, formal models; these unfortunately fall well short of capturing the complexity and internal contradictions of his perceptions of growth under capitalism and other modes of production:

1. Indeed, the first thing to note is that Marx emphasized that economies change in irreversible historical time in an overall institutional framework such as 'capitalism', 'feudalism' or 'oriental despotism'. Any such mode of production can be characterized by specific social devices for appropriation of surplus product over necessary consumption. This classical insistence on the primacy of processes determining the income distribution is adopted by most structuralist authors.

2. Marx concentrated on the capitalist mode, in which growth results from both accumulation and endogenous technical change. Producers adopt new methods to edge out competitors or because rising labour power can wipe out surplus value, thereby wiping out capitalists as well.

3. Competition among capitalists tends to equalize profit rates across sectors. However, sectoral demand and supply levels may not mesh, giving rise to a 'disproportionality crisis'. Similarly, aggregate demand may not equal supply. Money provides a vehicle for hoarding purchasing power, which can lead to a 'realization crisis' or slump.

4. Both kinds of crises interact in a cyclical theory of growth, well described by Sylos-Labini (1984). At the bottom of a cycle, the real wage is held down by a large 'reserve army' of unemployed workers, and capitalists can accumulate freely. However, as output expands the reserve army is depleted and the real wage may rise. Capitalists search for new labour-saving technologies and also invest to build up the stock of capital and reduce employment via input substitution. Excessive funds tied up in machinery, sectoral imbalances and lack of purchasing power on the part of capitalists to sustain investment (or of workers to absorb the output that new investment produces) can all underlie a cyclical collapse.

    Lewis (1954) translated Marx's story of cyclical upswing into a long-run theory of economic growth, with 'surplus labour' replacing the reserve army. More recent, explicitly Marxist authors such as Glyn and Sutcliffe (1972) and Bowles, Gordon and Weisskopf (1986) stress the fall in investment that may occur in response to a profit squeeze as labour gains in bargaining power over a sequence of cycles.

5. Accumulation and growth may occur as these processes unfold, perhaps accompanied by a falling rate of profit, increased immiserization of the working class, or both. Both Marx and some recent authors see cyclical profit squeezes culminating in a steadily declining rate of profit over time.

Schumpeter took over much of Marx's supply-side vision and combined it with a provocative analysis of how the economy responds to technical innovation in forging his own defence of capitalism: he called his teacher Böhm-

Bawerk a 'bourgeois Marx' but could have applied the label equally to himself. His *Theory of Economic Development* (German version 1912; American edition 1934) resembles Marx in emphasizing technical advance under a given set of institutions, but also is very Keynesian (or Wicksellian) in building the growth process around the supply of credit and macro adjustments to changes in investment demand. Following Taylor and Arida (1988), a sketch of the theory goes as follows:

The starting point is rather like Mill-Marshall-Solow steady growth, which Schumpeter calls 'circular flow'. An economy in circular flow may be expanding, but it is not 'developing' in his terminology. Development occurs only when an entrepreneur makes an innovation – a new technique, product or way of organizing things – and shifts production coefficients or the rules of the game. He gains a monopoly profit until other people catch on and imitate, and the economy moves to a new configuration of circular flow.

The invention or insight underlying the innovation need not be the entrepreneur's: Schumpeter's 'new man' simply seizes it, puts it in action, makes his money, and (more likely than not) passes into the aristocracy as he retires. Ultimately, his innovation and fortune will be supplanted by others in the process of 'creative destruction' that makes capitalist economies progress.

The key analytical question about this process refers to both the financial and real sides of the economy: how does the entrepreneur obtain resources to innovate? An endogenous money supply and redistribution of real income flows are required to support his efforts.

To get his project going, the entrepreneur must invest – an extra demand imposed upon an economy already using its resources fully in circular flow. To finance investment, he obtains loans from the banks; new credit and thereby money are created in the process. The bank loans are used to purchase goods in momentarily fixed supply. Their prices are driven up, so that real incomes of other economic actors decline. The most common examples are workers receiving temporarily fixed nominal wages or the cash flows of non-innovating firms. There is 'forced saving' as workers' lower real incomes force them to consume less; groups which receive windfall income gains are assumed to have lower propensities to consume so that overall aggregate demand declines. Meanwhile, routine investment projects may be cut back.

The transition between states of circular flow is demand-driven from the investment side (though, of course, the innovation may involve production of new goods or increases in productivity), and short-run macro adjustment takes place through income redistribution via forced saving with an endogenously varying money supply. In a longer run, there can be a cyclical depression due to 'autodeflation' as bank loans are repaid; workers can regain real income via falling costs. In later versions of the model, Schumpeter emphasized that bankruptcy of outdated firms can also release resources for innovators, but the essentials are the same.

Finally, it is clear that Schumpeter is describing a 'punctuated' growth process (Eldredge 1985), as firms and their innovations rise and fall in creative destruction; the analogy to stasis suddenly interrupted by disappearances and arrivals of species as described by Eldredge (1985) and Gould (1989) is clear. Schumpeter's methodological perspective is identical to that of Marx and the paleontologists: both economic and biological growth can only be analysed in chronological, not logical, time. Formal models of these processes must allow the existence of multiple equilibria or diverse 'basins' and 'attractors' for the trajectories of the differential equations describing the evolution of the economy over time. Switching attractors is a mathematical metaphor for transforming the nature of circular flow.

Like other theorists of his 'post-Wicksellian' generation,[2] Schumpeter characteristically assumed that resources are fully employed: under such circumstances, forced saving is the mode of macroeconomic adjustment *par excellence*. However, if output can vary to equate saving with investment, one arrives at a class of 'stagnationist' growth models which underlie much discussion of the economic development process (for instance, Lustig 1980 and Chakravarty 1987). In rich countries, Kalecki (1971) is by far the most distinguished exponent of this tradition.

To understand the issues, it is useful to begin with possible stagnation as a result of regressive income redistribution in a model with one sector, and then bring in multisectoral complications. Suppose that investment responds to increased capacity utilization as in an accelerator (but not so strongly as to give rise to Harrodian stability problems of the type discussed below). Then a distributional shift against high-consuming wage earners can lead to lower investment and growth: a higher profit share or lower real wage reduces consumption demand and capacity utilization, and capital formation may slow down. With reduced enterprise cash flows, the profit rate (the product of the profit share and the output/capital ratio) may also decline along with the real wage. Dutt (1984) provides the details of how all this works out.

Now suppose that instead of modifying the economy-wide marginal propensity to save, income redistribution alters only the pattern of consumer purchases by sector, while leaving aggregate demand unchanged (that is, all sectors have identical wage and profit shares, and workers and capitalists have the same marginal propensities to consume). The wealthy may prefer to buy more services and sophisticated manufactures at the margin, for example, and the poor, simple industrial products and food. If redistribution occurs and sectoral demand patterns change, and *if* investment demand by sector responds, the economy may switch to another configuration of circular flow.

These results may not be heartening for proponents of progressive redistribution. The change in sectoral demand composition may create jobs, but only slow overall growth if investment in the favoured sector is not strongly stimulated by its own output increases. Bringing aggregate demand movements back into the story can further complicate its plot, especially if differences in saving rates between classes interact with sectorally differing profit shares as demand patterns change.

Stagnationist logic lies behind many redistribution proposals that have appeared over the years. The French-Swiss reformer Sismondi (1815) recommended progressive redistribution in the wake of the Napoleonic Wars to stimulate French industrialization: more prosperous workers would demand clothing and textiles and propel investment in those sectors. The same theme appeared in the writings of last century's Populists in Russia and is debated in India today. Causality was reversed by Latin American structuralists like Furtado (1972) and Tavares (1972). If industrialization beyond production of simple goods like food and textiles is to occur, they said, then under present social conditions income concentration is necessary to sustain demand for more sophisticated commodities since their production is likely to be subject to minimum cost-effective size requirements due to economies of scale.

These ideas suggest that demand changes can stimulate processes that cumulate over time to alter the nature of supply. For example, will redistribution and/or state intervention raise demand enough to initiate profitable production processes with fixed overheads that have constant marginal but decreasing average costs? Alternatively, is public intervention required to guide 'make or buy' choices in an economy which has potential economies of scale but also is imperfectly open to trade in the sense that import and export prices are not equal? Finally (following the Latin structuralist lead), will investment respond to consumer demand for 'luxuries' and lead to creation of a middle class which in turn buys more luxuries and stimulates further investment and growth?

Under appropriate circumstances, distributional shifts or public policy can create affirmative answers to questions of this sort, triggering changes (often involving decreasing costs) that can have profound economy-wide effects of the sort invoked by Young (1928) and his student Rosenstein-Rodan (1961) with his 'big push'. Once again, we are talking about discrete jumps in the character of circular flow.

These last examples also suggest that stagnationist analysis can overlap with distributional changes like those underlying forced saving. Scenarios involving multiple flows of supply and demand lie close at hand. Two are particularly relevant in the Third World: limitations on growth imposed by shortages of foreign exchange, and interactions between sectors adjusting to excess demand via changes in output and a flexible price respectively.

The ever-present danger of 'external strangulation' in developing econo-mies is an old theme in structuralist thought, dating to the work of the Economic Commission for Latin America in Santiago in the 1950s at least. The notion was formalized by Chenery and Bruno (1962) in the two-gap model incorporating separate foreign exchange and saving restrictions on growth.

The saving constraint follows naturally from Harrod-Domar algebra of the sort discussed below: investment has to be financed either by national saving or by capital inflows from abroad. But the inflows also cover the trade deficit. Industrialization via import substitution (the only way to build up local production capacity that has been discovered so far) means that the economy becomes dependent on imports of intermediate goods – without which local factories cannot work. At the same time, import substitution rarely extends to capital goods, so that up to half of investment spending takes the form of purchases from abroad. There is a sharp trade-off between current production and capital formation, which only additional foreign exchange can relieve. If domestic output is limited by scarcity of convertible dollars or yen, inflationary forced-saving macroeconomic adjustment often occurs.

The saving and foreign gaps have been extended in recent work (Bacha 1990, Taylor 1990a) to take into account two important fiscal effects. First, after the debt crisis many governments nationalized foreign obligations: the state is liable for external payments on debt. At the same time, econometric work in the 1980s typically showed that there is a strong 'crowding-in' effect of public on private capital formation (contrary to the crowding-out of private by public spending through rising interest rates in financial markets that is frequently presumed). The consequence is a 'fiscal gap' limiting growth because public (and therefore total) capital formation is cut back. Attempts to relieve fiscal burdens by relying on forced saving or the infla-tion tax (discussed below) became ever more frequent in the 1980s. The multiple interacting problems posed by saving, foreign exchange, fiscal and inflation gaps are a source of much current policy concern.

Turning to models with two broad commodities domestically supplied, a frequently used specification is based upon one sector where output is lim-ited by available capacity and the price adjusts to clear the market, plus a second sector in which production meets demand. This specification blends forced saving, Engel demand effects and output adjustment in an illuminating fashion. It can be applied in various contexts; for instance, to analyse the agricultural terms of trade, to discuss 'Dutch disease' problems (when a traded goods sector has its price fixed from the world market and a non-traded sector has an adjusting price), and to examine global macroeconomics between a 'North' exporting industrial goods and a 'South' selling primary products. The basic nature of the model can be illustrated with the first interpretation here.

Suppose that the terms of trade shift towards agriculture, say due to a reduction of food imports. Industrial output can either rise or fall. It will be pushed up by increased demand from higher agricultural income, but also held down by reduced real non-agricultural spending power (real wages drop due to forced saving from dearer food). The latter effect will be stronger insofar as Engel's Law makes food demand income-inelastic, so that the loss in workers' spending power primarily forces down their demand for industrial goods. Under such circumstances, letting more imports into the economy will doubly benefit the industrial sector – food prices will fall and output expand. Although he used a different model to argue his case, this outcome is consistent with Ricardo's advocacy of repealing the Corn Laws.

The alternative view was espoused by Malthus in his *Principles of Political Economy*, where the argument can be interpreted in terms of distributional effects on aggregate demand. Agriculture is responsible for a big proportion of income and consumer spending. Farmers (or landlords for Malthus) hit by adverse terms of trade will cut their purchases, reducing economic activity overall. Whether a Ricardian or Malthusian distributional configuration applies in developing countries today is highly relevant for policy; according to applied computable general equilibrium models (Taylor 1990b), the answer seems to go either way.

Besides import policy, other state interventions can affect the terms of trade. Fiscal expansion or increased investment, for example, will bid up the flexible price to generate forced saving to help meet the increased injection of demand. Ellman (1975) argues that food price-induced forced saving supported the Soviet industrialization push of the 1930s, in contrast to Preobrazhenski's (1965) suggestion that the terms of trade be shifted *against* agriculture by a monopsonistic state to extract an investable surplus.

Two final questions about fix-price/flex-price models[3] are how to use them to describe inflation and growth. Determination of the growth rate depends crucially on how causality in the macroeconomic system runs. If saving-investment balance in the North, for example, regulates expansion of the world economy, then the primary export terms of trade and capital formation in the South will tag along as adjusting variables. Contrariwise, slow growth in a dominant fixed-supply sector can determine behaviour of the whole system.

With regard to inflation, we can begin by observing that structuralist theory typically attributes steadily rising prices to conflicting income claims. Using the capitalist/worker story – a favourite of theorists but not necessarily the most relevant to developing economies – suppose that prices are set as a mark-up over wages and costs of imported intermediate goods. If the mark-up rate or import cost rises, prices follow and the real wage declines. Workers counter by pushing up money wages – the instrument over which they have a degree of control. But then prices go up further through the mark-up, wages follow, and so on. In Joan Robinson's (1962) phrase, there is an 'inflation barrier' below which the real wage cannot fall before a money wage inflation is set off. It will run more rapidly insofar as the distributional conflict is sharp and 'propagation mechanisms' (such as contract indexation) work fast.

The conflict can be over the price of food. This is where flex-prices enter the inflation process in a model popular in Latin America that was first proposed by Noyola (1956) and Sunkel (1960) after Kalecki (1976) had sketched an inflationary terms-of-trade model in lectures in Mexico City in 1953. These structuralist authors suggested land reform as a solution. It would shift out the agricultural supply function and thereby alleviate wage pressure resulting from a limited supply of food. Success of such an 'agriculture first' strategy depends heavily on the terms of trade: if they drop sharply when supply increases, then farm incomes will decline and the strategy can come to naught.

Cambridge growth theory – our final topic in this section – took off from Keynes, Kalecki and Sraffa (1960) in several directions. Despite coming from Oxford, Harrod (1939) produced the first model in the tradition. It demonstrated potential macroeconomic instability from two contradictions inherent in a stagnationist interpretation of Keynes. The first was between 'natural' (population increase plus labour efficiency gain) and 'warranted' (investment equals saving) rates of growth. Solow (1956) bypassed the possibility that the rates might not equalize by postulating full employment and letting saving determine investment along Mill-Marshall lines to make the warranted and natural rates the same.

Harrod's second contradiction (which Solow implied he resolved but really just swept under the rug by having saving drive capital formation) hinged on a stronger response of investment than saving to higher output. If the accelerator is very strong, a small positive output shock along the warranted 'knife edge' growth path would make injections increase more than leakages, so that output would rise further, and so on. For demand-determined real GDP in a stagnationist model, this sort of instability is unlikely on empirical grounds, but it can underlie a plausible model of hyperinflation when supply limitations bind (Taylor 1991).

After World War II, Kaldor (1957), Pasinetti (1962) and Robinson (1962) followed Marx, Schumpeter and the stagnationists in setting up models emphasizing interactions between income distribution and growth in historical time. Kaldor's and Pasinetti's growth analysis used forced saving as the macroeconomic adjustment mechanism under an assumption of full employment; the latter's explicitly class-based model gives rise to interesting possibilities for multiple equilibria (Darity 1981).

Cambridge economists, Robinson and Kaldor especially, also criticized facile neoclassical distribution theories. Kaldor's (1956) doubts centred on over-determination of macroeconomic equilibrium. He argued – correctly – that an independent investment function is inconsistent with full employment and marginal productivity rules for income distribution. Not surprisingly, he jettisoned the latter in favour of forced saving.

Harcourt (1972) ably summarizes the reswitching controversy which Sraffa and Robinson (1953–54) effectively launched. Their Cambridge (in England) defeated the Cambridge in Massachusetts (that is, MIT) in the debate about reswitching, but the victory had no effect on subsequent mainstream practice. Well-behaved aggregate production functions continue to rule the neoclassical growth roost, despite their conspicuously absent empirical foundations.

Finally, Kaldor (1957) like other dissident economists emphasized the importance of economies of scale and the endogeneity of technical change. His 'technical progress function', which tied increases in labour productivity to capital accumulation, was the initial influential attempt to deal with endogenous technical advance. Very recent neoclassical models that link productivity levels to available stocks of physical or human capital (Romer 1986, Lucas 1988) are a belated reinvention of a well-oiled Kaldorian wheel. Great originality rarely characterizes mainstream model design.

MONEY AND CREDIT

How does money affect macroeconomic equilibrium? This question has been hotly debated among both economists and non-economists for the past 300 years. It can be posed from at least three angles:

1. Does money largely control, or just respond to, developments elsewhere in the economy. In other words, is it 'active' (exogenous and determined prior to other variables) or 'passive' (endogenous) most of the time?
2. Do changes in the money supply mostly affect the volume of activity or the price level? What are the channels via which money has its impacts on quantities and prices?
3. Should we concentrate analysis on changes in 'money' (banking system liabilities) or 'credit' (banking system assets)?

Over the long sweep of economic analysis, one can find eminent partisans of all eight analytical positions implicit in this three-way classification. Table

Table 2.1   Positions of different monetary analysts

| Causal status of money/credit | Main effects of money/credit | | | |
| | On prices | | On quantities | |
	via money	via credit	via money	via credit
Passive	Hume	Thornton Wicksell Schumpeter	Malthus Banking school	Marx Kaldor Real business cycle school
Active	Ricardo Currency school Mill Monetarists	'Caps'	Keynes	'Hats' Law Minsky

2.1 presents an outline. We will go through the entries to sketch informally the theoretical views underlying each position, roughly in chronological order. Lessons for practical models will also be drawn.

The earliest participants in the Table are two political parties – the 'Hats' and the 'Caps' – which appear in the active/quantities/credit and active/prices/credit slots. These rather obscure historical groupings flourished in a parliamentary democracy for a few decades between Divine Right despots in Sweden in the mid-18th century. As their names suggest, the parties represented the big and small merchant bourgeoisie respectively and were among the first proponents of distinctively 'structuralist' (Hats) and 'monetarist' (Caps) positions in financial theory (Kindleberger 1985).

The Hats were policy activists, urging credit creation to spur Baltic trade. The Caps countered with arguments that excessive spending could lead to inflation, payments deficits and related ills. The Hats took power after a period of slow Cap growth and (as often happens with expansionist parties), pushed too hard – they lost power in an inflation and foreign-exchange crisis in 1765. Despite their respective policy failures, the intellectual points raised by the politically warring Swedes carry down through the years.

Both parties were fundamentally mercantilist. Their basic macro model can be summarized by the following equations: $J = I + B = J(credit)$; $S = S(population, unemployment, real wage)$; and $J - S = 0$, where J stands for demand injections (investment I and the trade surplus B) and S represents saving leakages. Various policy instruments and social processes were assumed to regulate the variables in the equations; namely, Malthusian checks for population, the poorhouse for unemployment, forced saving for the real wage (not much discussed), and tariffs and export subsidies for trade balance.

Investment could also be spurred by credit creation, a point stressed by John Law, a Scotsman who sought to stimulate French growth early in the 18th century by setting up development banks. That his scheme led to the Mississippi Bubble – one of the earliest speculative booms – has echoes in the financial instability theories of Hyman Minsky (1975, 1986), a contemporary economist who also emphasizes that by actively creating credit banks can have a strong influence on output via 'Keynesian' channels. Indeed, Minskyian interactions between production and finance can be so strong as to lead to macro instability or shifts between steady state equilibrium points: there is a degree of financial determination in real-side circular flow. John Law's fortunes might have fared better had he been able to hear what his distant analytical descendant Minsky had to say.

Caps, Hats and Law all argued as if money and credit could be controlled by the relevant authorities. Part of the intellectual reaction against mercantilism took the form of making money (or 'specie') as well as the trade surplus endogenous in the short run. David Hume (1752), a first-rate philosopher turning into a best-selling historian, is usually credited with this advance in economic analysis, although his contemporary Richard Cantillon (and Thomas Mun more than a century earlier) also set out the mechanics of price/specie-flow balance of payments adjustment.

Hume's location in the passive/prices/money slot follows from a model which might be written as

$$D = D(M) \qquad\qquad X = X(\text{employment})$$
$$MV = PX \qquad\qquad \dot{M} = X - D(PX/V) = B(P_w - P)$$

Aggregate demand D depends on the money stock M while (assuming full employment) output X is predetermined. The expansion in the money supply $\dot{M}$ ($= dM/dt$) is given by specie inflow resulting from the trade surplus $B = X - D$: in this sense money is passive or endogenous. Since money drives the price level P via the equation of exchange $MV = PX$, money expansion $\dot{M}$ is an inverse function of P. The last expression for $\dot{M}$ normalizes this response around a 'world' price Pw.

The story is simple, and well-known. A big money stock means that there is a high domestic price level and excess demand. The trade surplus becomes negative when D is high, meaning that specie flows out of the country and prices fall. Aggregate demand ceases to draw in imports and 'our' exports sell better – the trade deficit declines towards equilibrium. Policy-makers' attempts to stimulate output by monetary expansion (say by raising the banking system's money/specie multiplier) will backfire in this model; their attempt will simply drive up prices and worsen the trade deficit. Although they reasoned on different grounds and far less cogently, the Caps would have heartily approved of this conclusion.

The next major players in the Table are Malthus and Ricardo, who sit opposed in the northeast and southwest corners. We have already seen that the former argued along proto-Keynesian lines that food prices should be kept high by import restrictions, so that landlords (notoriously low savers) would spend on luxuries to support industrial demand. A precursor of the structuralist Banking School, Malthus thought that the money supply and/or velocity adjusted endogenously to meet demand, or the 'needs of trade'.

Ricardo, a superb monetary theorist, differed from Malthus in accepting supply-side determination of output or Say's Law (not necessarily a bad approximation in a period in which agriculture was still the dominant producing sector). He naturally followed the monetarist trail, most notably in 1810 when he attacked 'excessive' British note issue to finance the war against Napoleon. His evidence included a premium on gold in terms of notes within Britain, and a fall of the exchange value of sterling in Hamburg and Amsterdam. His logic was based on the quantity theory and purchasing power parity – standard components of all subsequent monetarist theory.

Ricardo's main policy recommendation was a Friedmanite rule called the 'currency principle', recommending that the outstanding money stock should be strictly tied to gold reserves. Money could not be created for frivolous purposes such as war finance, and its supply would only fluctuate in response to movements of gold. In effect, Ricardo sought to steer monetary policy along the trail blazed by Hume.

The Currency School, which took the monetarist side in British financial debates well into the 19th century, was founded on the basis of Ricardo's principle. Its greatest victory was Peel's Charter Act of 1844 for the Bank of England, which put a limit on the issue of notes against securities. Above this limit, notes had to be backed by gold. This triumph of principle was short-lived in practice, since there was a run against English banks in 1847. The Bank of England acted – correctly – as a lender of last resort (so described by Bagehot later in 1873), pumping resources into commercial banks in danger of collapse. To this end, the Charter Act had to be suspended.[4]

As the Currency School flourished, John Stuart Mill was putting together his own economic synthesis. Although he had some sympathy for the Banking School (see below), Mill is placed in the active/prices/money slot because he codified the doctrine of 'loanable funds' which underlies much mainstream thought, such as the latest twists on the Ramsey optimal growth model as expounded by Abel and Blanchard (1983). Following Henry Thornton, a contemporary of Ricardo, Mill let the interest rate adjust to erase any difference between aggregate saving and investment, thereby clearing the market for loanable funds. In effect, this theory *postulates* the full employment of the Mill-Marshall growth model, relying upon changes in the interest rate to attain macroeconomic balance.

Loanable funds is a non-monetary theory of the rate of interest of the sort later criticized by Keynes. It incorporates Patinkin's (1965) 'dichotomy' in that money can affect only the price (and presumably wage) level, without any influence on the volume of production. This is the ultimate monetarist position, with echoes in both Irving Fisher's suggestion that monetary policy should be actively deployed to control prices and Milton Friedman's argument against active policy because its effects on output are only visible with 'long and variable lags' while money rules the price level best in the long run.

The final entries in the broadly monetarist left columns of Table 1 are Thornton, Wicksell and Schumpeter (with respect to his short-run macro adjustment scenario, at least) in the passive/prices/credit niche. We concentrate on Knut Wicksell (1935) as the key player, even though much of his analysis was anticipated by Thornton almost 100 years before. It also bears mention in passing that the Keynes of the *Treatise on Money* (1930) was a stalwart post-Wicksellian along with Schumpeter. Only his revised views in the *General Theory* (1936) place him in the active/quantities/money cell.

Wicksell extended loanable funds theory by proposing that inflation is a 'cumulative process' based on the discrepancy between new credit demanded by investors and new deposit supply from desired saving (corresponding to a zero rate of inflation) at a rate of interest fixed by the banks. Suppose that the rate is set too low. Then an excess of new credits over new deposits leads to money creation; via the equation of exchange at presumed full employment, the consequence is rising prices. Inflation is the outcome of endogenous monetary emission, driven by credit creation.

The key analytical question is how saving and investment are brought together to secure macroeconomic equilibrium *ex post*. Forced saving provides part of the adjustment if wages are incompletely indexed to price increases. The rest comes from the 'inflation tax', a dynamic version of the well-known 'real balance effect', which states that people increase their saving to restore the real value of their money stock M/P which is squeezed when P rises. If output X and velocity V are assumed constant in the equation of exchange $MV = PX$, then the inflation tax interpretation rests on the equations

$$\dot{M}/PX = \dot{P}(M/P)/PX = \hat{P}/V$$

which follow from the growth rate version of the equation of exchange, $\hat{M} = \hat{P}$. After the first equality, $\dot{P}(M/P)$ is the instantaneous loss in real balances from price increases $\dot{P}$, which wealth-holders are supposed to make good by extra saving so that the 'tax' effectively cuts aggregate demand. The expression after the second equality shows that the tax base erodes as V rises when inflation speeds up (the monetarists' favourite stylized fact).

Wicksell thought that after a time, bankers would raise the interest rate to its 'natural' level to bring the cumulative inflation to a halt, but for present purposes this ending is not essential to his story. The key point is that through both the inflation tax and forced saving, a rising price level liquidates *ex ante* excess aggregate demand. Models illustrating this inflation theory appear in Taylor (1991). It is the monetarist alternative to the structuralist inflation model sketched at the end of the first section above.

Now we should turn our attention to the remaining entries in Table 1, beginning with the passive/quantities/money Banking School, the main rival of the Currency School in last century's British debate. The group is famous (or notorious, depending on one's perspective) for espousing the doctrine of 'real bills' which states that banks should discount all solid, non-speculative commercial paper – that is, true or real bills. How in practice a banker should identify paper tied firmly to the needs of trade was not spelled out; indeed Adam Smith (an early proponent of the doctrine) thought that banks should concentrate on real trade to avoid ratifying currency speculation. Extreme members of the Banking School finessed Smithian fears with a 'law of reflux' through which excessive lending would drive up activity and/or prices and lead the private sector to pay off loans and buy gold: there would be an automatic contraction of the money supply in response to too aggressive attempts to expand it! Hume's shade reappears in structuralist guise, although without his specie flow considerations.

Real bills ideas have downside implications as well. If credit needs are *not* satisfied by banks, then new, non-bank financial instruments are likely to be invented to meet the needs of trade. Such an outcome – along the lines of the highly neoclassical Coase (1937) theorem – sometimes happens, sometimes not, but it is implicit in Banking School views. Among structuralists, reflux notions show up in the 1959 report on the British monetary system by the Radcliffe Committee and in Kaldor (1982). The latter is worth quoting:

> If ... more money comes into existence than the public, at the given or expected level of incomes or expenditures, wishes to hold, the excess will be automatically *extinguished* – either through debt repayment or its conversion into interest-bearing assets. ...

One notes a certain affinity in structuralist positions across 150 years.

The final entries in the Table are the Real Business Cycle School and Marx, perhaps demonstrating that economic perceptions can unite strange political bedfellows. The former group is of recent origin, at the mainstream's neoclassical extreme verge. Its members argue that business cycles in advanced economies are due to strong substitution responses (labour versus leisure choices, and so on) to supply-side shocks to the macro system. They deem money unimportant because it is endogenous, subject to 'reverse causality' (Blanchard and Fischer 1989, Chapter 7). They are joined by Kaldor and the post-Keynesians Davidson and Weintraub (1973) in their view that typical Central Bank responsiveness to trade, plus the presence of inside money, render monetary aggregates endogenous: their leads and lags with output depend on institutions and contingencies beyond the analytical reach of Granger-Sims causality tests and similar econometric probes.

Marx, as always, is more complex. The existence of money was central to his view of capitalism, incarnated in the famous $M - C - M'$ sequence, in which exploitation arises as money M is thrown into circulation or capital C, which yields a money return M': surplus value is $M' - M$. *Access* to M gives capitalists an advantage in the economy, making their extraction of surplus possible.

At a more applied level of abstraction, Marx roughly adhered to Banking School ideas, at times arguing that velocity varies to satisfy the equation of exchange. This view is consistent with endogeneity of inside money; for instance, financial obligations created and destroyed by transactions among firms. Building on the reproduction schemes in Volume II of *Capital*, Foley (1986) has extended this approach to set up real/financial 'circuit of capital' models in which endogenous fluctuations can occur. His work neatly complements Minsky's in describing how financial crises are endemic to capitalism in both the developed and developing worlds.

PRACTICAL LESSONS FROM THE HISTORY OF THOUGHT

The marshalling of the model troops we have just completed suggests a number of areas in which structuralist ideas are of key relevance to developing countries today. They include the following:

First, development necessarily involves transformation of patterns of circular flow, not just through innovation, as Schumpeter proposed, but also due to realization of economies of scale, distributional changes, financial deepening and institutional shifts. Relevant theory has to recognize the possibility of bifurcations or other discontinuities in the growth process and provide broad guidelines about choices available at any time.

Second, barriers to change have to be recognized as well. Will the terms of trade move adversely enough to block an attempt at agriculturally-led growth? How binding is the foreign exchange restriction? Is it so tight that massive macroeconomic adjustment via forced saving and inflation tax increases will be required? Along Minskyian lines, is the fragility of the financial system likely to provoke massive speculation in local assets or foreign exchange, to be followed ultimately by a crash? An important strength of the structuralist tradition is its awareness – based on historical observation of similar events – of the manifold ways in which the macroeconomic system can fail.

Third, how can policy be designed to enhance the likelihood of growth and improved distribution? Financial restrictions on the state become important here, since they limit its capital formation in particular, as well as its capacity to guide change more generally. At the same time, it has to be recognized that interventionist policy is required: no economy has developed subject only to direction by the invisible hand. Creative solutions to this dilemma will be essential in the 1990s

Fourth in a shorter run, how are possibilities for macroeconomic adjustment limited by inherited patterns of response? Does progressive redistribution tend to stimulate or retard output growth from forces involving both supply and demand? Is the local inflationary process more monetarist or structuralist by nature? Answers to such questions can go either way, and one has to have a theory broad enough to comprehend them. Neoclassical macroeconomics often finds itself overly limited in this regard.

Finally, how is the capacity for flexible response to be built into policy-making, as well as the economic system more generally? In applied economics, one has to think about the possibilities at hand instead of how to fit local circumstances into the latest toolbox as advertized in *Econometrica* last year. Because it allows flexible models that can cope with diverse distributional and technical outcomes, structuralist theory has much to offer in this regard. Fully optimized solutions, by contrast, are limited by the constraints they so cleverly take into account.

Think of the panda – optimized to eat 15 hours a day to keep itself alive with an inherited carnivorous digestive track which evolution did its best to alter to let the beast subsist on bamboo. Without their cuddly good looks – a thoroughly random adaptation – pandas would surely be doomed as their bamboo forests shrink in the China of today. More flexibility might have helped forestall their fate. The same can be said about economic policy and theory more generally: as the times change in their unforeseeable fashion, an 'agent' who has previously optimized can easily find her/himself in an extremely uncomfortable box.

NOTES

1. Standard sources can be drawn upon to complement the capsule synopses of economic ideas presented here. Schumpeter (1954) is the classic reference on the history of economic analysis, and Kindleberger (1984 and 1985) is very good on different ideas regarding money and finance. Dobb (1973) emphasizes differences between neoclassical and dissident views about the relative importance of marginal productivity rules and class relationships in determining economic equilibrium. Blaug (1985) is the standard mainstream compendium – comprehensive, written with panache and only mildly reactionary. Unfortunately, these standard references are not very good on issues of economic development and growth. With an emphasis on the development literature, Taylor and Arida's (1988) survey complements the material here.
2. The term is due to Amadeo (1989); post-Wicksellian macroeconomics is discussed at length in Taylor (1991).
3. This terminology is due to Hicks (1965).
4. Dornbusch and Frenkel (1984) present a model of the 1847 bank run along (unacknowledged) Minskyian lines.

REFERENCES

Abel, Andrew B. and Blanchard, Olivier Jean (1983), 'An Intertemporal Model of Saving and Investment', *Econometrica*, **51**, 675–92.

Amadeo, Edward J. (1989), *Keynes's Principle of Effective Demand*, Aldershot, Hants: Edward Elgar.

Bacha, Edmar L. (1990), 'A Three-Gap Model of Foreign Transfers and the GDP Growth Rate in Developing Countries', *Journal of Development Economics*, **32**, 279–96.

Bagehot, Walter (1873), *Lombard Street*, Homewood IL: R.D. Irwin. Reprinted 1962.

Blanchard, Olivier Jean and Fischer, Stanley (1989), *Lectures on Macroeconomics*, Cambridge MA: MIT Press.

Blaug, Mark (1985), *Economic Theory in Retrospect*, 4th edition, Cambridge: Cambridge University Press.

Bowles, Samuel, Gordon, David M. and Weisskopf, Thomas E. (1986), 'Power and Profits: The Social Structure of Accumulation and Profitability of the Postwar U.S. Economy', *Review of Radical Political Economics*, **18**, 132–67.

Chakravarty, Sukhamoy (1980), *Alternative Approaches to a Theory of Economic Growth: Marx, Marshall, and Schumpeter*, R.C. Dutt Lecture on Political Economy, Delhi: Orient Longman.

Chakravarty, Sukhamoy (1987), *Development Planning: The Indian Experience*, Oxford: Clarendon Press.

Chenery, Hollis B. and Bruno, Michael (1962), 'Development Alternatives in an Open Economy: The Case of Israel', *Economic Journal*, **72**, 79–103.

Coase, Ronald (1937), 'The Nature of the Firm', *Econometrica*, **4**, 386–405.

Darity, William A. Jr. (1981), 'The Simple Analytics of Neo-Ricardian Growth and Distribution', *American Economic Review*, **71**, 978–93.

Davidson, Paul and Weintraub, Sidney (1973), 'Money as Cause and Effect', *Economic Journal*, **83**, 1117–32.

Diamond, Peter A. (1965), 'National Debt in a Neoclassical Growth Model', *American Economic Review*, **55**, 1126–50.

Dobb, Maurice (1973), *Theories of Value and Distribution since Adam Smith*, Cambridge: Cambridge University Press.

Dornbusch, Rudiger and Frenkel, Jacob A. (1984), 'The Gold Standard Crisis of 1847', *Journal of International Economics*, **16**, 1–27.

Dutt, Amitava K. (1984), 'Stagnation, Income Distribution, and Monopoly Power', *Cambridge Journal of Economics*, **8**, 25–40.

Eldredge, Niles (1985), *Time Frames: The Evolution of Punctuated Equilibria*, Princeton NJ: Princeton University Press.

Ellman, Michael (1975), 'Did the Agricultural Surplus Provide the Resources for the Increase in Investment during the First Five Year Plan?' *Economic Journal*, **85**, 844–64.

Foley, Duncan K. (1986), *Money, Accumulation, and Crisis*, London: Harwood Academic Publishers.

Furtado, Celso (1972), *Analise do 'Modelo' Brasileiro*, Rio de Janeiro: Civilização Brasileira.

Gerschenkron, Alexander (1962), *Economic Backwardness in Historical Perspective*, Cambridge MA: Harvard University Press.

Glyn, Andrew and Sutcliffe, Bob (1972), *Capitalism in Crisis*, New York: Pantheon.

Gould, Stephen Jay (1989), *The Burgess Shale*, New York: Norton.

Harcourt, Geoffrey (1972), *Some Cambridge Controversies in the Theory of Capital*, Cambridge: Cambridge University Press.

Harrod, Roy (1939), 'An Essay in Dynamic Theory', *Economic Journal*, **49**, 14–33.

Hicks, John R. (1965), *Capital and Growth*, Oxford: Clarendon Press.

Hume, David (1752), 'Of the Balance of Trade' in Richard N. Cooper (ed.), *International Finance*, Harmondsworth: Penguin. Reprinted 1969.

Kaldor, Nicholas (1956), 'Alternative Theories of Distribution', *Review of Economic Studies*, **23**, 83–100.

Kaldor, Nicholas (1957), 'A Model of Economic Growth', *Economic Journal*, **67**, 591–624.

Kaldor, Nicholas (1982), *The Scourge of Monetarism*, Oxford: Oxford University Press.

Kalecki, Michal (1971), *Selected Essays on the Dynamics of the Capitalist Economy*, Cambridge: Cambridge University Press.

Kalecki, Michal (1976), *Essays on Developing Economies*, London: Harvester Press.

Keynes, John Maynard (1930), *A Treatise on Money*, London: Macmillan.

Keynes, John Maynard (1936), *The General Theory of Employment, Interest, and Money*, London: Macmillan.

Kindleberger, Charles P. (1984), *A Financial History of Western Europe*, London: Allen and Unwin.

Kindleberger, Charles P. (1985), *Keynesianism vs. Monetarism and Other Essays in Financial History*, London: Allen and Unwin.

Lewis, W. Arthur (1954), 'Economic Development with Unlimited Supplies of Labor', *Manchester School of Economics and Social Studies*, **22**, 139–91.

Lucas, Robert E. Jr. (1988), 'On the Mechanics of Economic Development', *Journal of Monetary Economics*, **22**, 3–42.

Lustig, Nora (1980), 'Underconsumption in Latin American Economic Thought: Some Considerations', *Review of Radical Political Economics*, **12**, 35–43.

Minsky, Hyman P. (1975), *John Maynard Keynes*, New York: Columbia University Press.

Minsky, Hyman P. (1986), *Stabilizing an Unstable Economy*, New Haven CT: Yale University Press.

Noyola Vasquez, Juan F. (1956), 'El Desarollo Economico y la Inflacion en Mexico y Otros Paises Latinoamericanos', *Investigacion Economica*, **16**, 603–48.

Pasinetti, Luigi L. (1962), 'Rate of Profit and Income Distribution in Relation to the Rate of Economic Growth', *Review of Economic Studies*, **29**, 267–79.

Pasinetti, Luigi L. (1981), *Structural Change and Economic Growth*, Cambridge: Cambridge University Press.

Patinkin, Don (1965), *Money, Interest, and Prices*, New York: Harper and Row.

Preobrazhenski, Evgeny (1965), *The New Economics*, Oxford: Clarendon Press.

Ramsey, Frank P. (1928), 'A Mathematical Theory of Saving', *Economic Journal*, **38**, 543–59.

Robinson, Joan (1953–54), 'The Production Function and the Theory of Capital', *Review of Economic Studies*, **21**, 81–106.

Robinson, Joan (1962), *Essays in the Theory of Economic Growth*, London: Macmillan.

Romer, Paul M. (1986), 'Increasing Returns and Long-Run Growth', *Journal of Political Economy*, **94**, 1002–37.

Rosenstein-Rodan, Paul N. (1961), 'Notes on the Theory of the Big Push', in H.S. Ellis and H.C. Wallich (eds), *Economic Development for Latin America*, New York: St Martin's Press.

Schumpeter, Josef A. (1934), *The Theory of Economic Development*, Cambridge MA: Harvard University Press.

Schumpeter, Josef A. (1954), *History of Economic Analysis*, New York: Oxford University Press.

Sismondi, J.C.L. Sismonde de (1815), 'Political Economy', Edinburgh: *Sir J.D. Brewster's Edinburgh Encyclopedia*.

Solow, Robert M. (1956), 'A Contribution to the Theory of Economic Growth', *Quarterly Journal of Economics*, **70**, 65–94.

Sraffa, Piero (1960), *Production of Commodities by Means of Commodities*, Cambridge: Cambridge University Press.

Sunkel, Osvaldo (1960), 'Inflation in Chile: An Unorthodox Approach', *International Economic Papers*, **10**, 107–31.

Sylos-Labini, Paolo (1984), *The Forces of Economic Growth and Decline*, Cambridge MA: MIT Press.

Tavares, Maria da Conceição (1972), *Da Substituição de Importaçoes ao Capitalismo Financeiro*, Rio de Janeiro: Zahar.

Taylor, Lance (1990a), 'Foreign Resource Flows and Developing Country Growth', Helsinki: WIDER.

Taylor, Lance (1990b), 'Structuralist CGE Models' in Lance Taylor (ed.), *Structuralist Computable General Equilibrium Models: Socially Relevant Policy Analysis for the Developing World*, Cambridge MA: MIT Press.

Taylor, Lance (1991), *Income Distribution, Inflation, and Growth*, Cambridge MA: MIT Press.

Taylor, Lance and Arida, Persio (1988), 'Long-Run Income Distribution and Growth', in Hollis B. Chenery and T.N. Srinivasan (eds), *Handbook of Development Economics* Volume I, Amsterdam: North-Holland.

Whitaker, John K. (1975), *The Early Writings of Alfred Marshall*, London: Macmillan.

Wicksell, Knut (1935), *Lectures on Political Economy*, Volume II, London: Routledge and Kegan Paul.

Young, Allyn (1928), 'Increasing Returns and Economic Progress', *Economic Journal*, **38**, 527–42.

3. Alternative Tactics and Strategies for Economic Development

Joseph E. Stiglitz[1]

INTRODUCTION

Comments on Some Recent Experiences

There have been few events during the past several hundred years as momentous as those that occurred within Eastern Europe during 1989. They are momentous not only for those who live in these countries, but for others in less developed countries who are striving to find a road to economic development. It is as if, with a single voice, those who have lived under this alternative economic system have stood up and said: 'This – the socialist road – is not the way to economic progress. Our economic system is a failure, and the price we have paid, the loss of our freedom, would not have been worth any slight economic progress that we might have purchased.'[2] Thus, one of the largest-scale and one of the boldest social experiments of all times seems to be coming to an ignominious end.

But the sense of discontent with the role of government in economic affairs has not been limited during the last decade to the so-called socialist countries. Throughout the developed world, the decade of the 1980s has seen governments in retreat: privatization, deregulation and, if not the dismantling of the welfare state, a whittling down of its role.

The age-long question of the proper balance between the private and the public sector has once again been answered: and the universal answer seems to be that 'we' had gone too far, given the government too large a role, too much power, and that a new balance had to be attained.

Hirschman's Interpretation

Albert Hirschman, in his gem of a book *Shifting Involvements* (1982), has provided us with some insights into the process we may be observing: he suggests that our excessive expectations of what government can do lead to disappointments which, for a time, motivate us towards a more privately oriented society; but this too breeds its own discontent – as we increasingly confront major social problems which remain unresolved and as we seek a greater Good that extends beyond the fulfilment of our private desires.

If Hirschman is correct, then the 'retreat of government' that we are now witnessing is only temporary. Whether this is the case or not, it is important to try to extract from the experiences of recent decades certain basic lessons on the merits of alternative strategies for economic development and, in particular, on the role of government.

Two Shifts of Intellectual Perspectives

Intellectual movements are often swept along by the tide of events, sometimes at cross-currents. They have a life of their own, only loosely coupled with surrounding events. The past 15 years have seen two conflicting shifts in perspective on the role of government. One of these shifts in viewpoint may have as much to do with the waning role of government as the seeming failures of government – at least the failures of government to accomplish as much as its most ardent advocates had claimed. For, as I shall comment below, there were notable successes of government (Korea, Japan, and Singapore) mixed in with the failures; it often seems, at least within some circles, as if the failures have been given a selective emphasis over the successes.

The new market failures approach

The first change in perspective has resulted from a recognition of the importance of risk and information imperfections in the economy – market 'imperfections' which are even more pervasive within LDCs than in developed economies. With this recognition has gone a changed perception of the efficiency of a market economy. The 'Fundamental Theorem of Welfare Economics', the theorem which tried to give precision to Adam Smith's invisible-hand conjecture, has been shown to be far more restrictive than was previously realized: Greenwald and Stiglitz (1986, 1988)[3] have shown that the economy is essentially always constrained Pareto inefficient. Arrow and Debreu's great achievement[4] was to find that singular example – that peculiar array of assumptions – under which markets are efficient.

The Greenwald-Stiglitz theorem was not simply concerned with theoretical niceties: they and their co-authors established that both labour and capital markets worked in ways fundamentally different than conceived by the standard neoclassical model. For instance, the imperfections in risk markets were an inherent consequence of informational limitations; as a result, there was equity rationing; and as a result of that, firms acted in a risk averse manner, with profound consequences for the macroeconomic behaviour of the economy. It was shown that even with perfect competition, there could be credit rationing (Stiglitz and Weiss 1981, 1983, 1986) and equilibrium unemployment.[5]

These 'new market failures' were different from those that were the focus of discussion in the 1960s. The earlier failures, in particular, public goods and externalities, required only selective government intervention. Indeed, some argued that all the government needed to do, beyond financing public goods, was to impose certain 'corrective' taxes to deal with externalities.

As I shall comment later, within the socialist tradition considerable attention was paid to what in neoclassical terms we could call one further market failure[6] – the absence of futures markets. To correct this market failure, a more pervasive intervention of the government was required, either in the form of planning (possibly only 'indicative'; that is, providing firms with the information upon which they could base their plans) or, more frequently, the direct control of investment.

The consequences of the 'new market failures' were far more pervasive than those of the older market failures. Since almost all markets were characterized by imperfect information, and in almost all economic activities there were risks which could not be insured against on futures markets, the new market failures touched every market in the economy. There was, seemingly, a *potential* role for government intervention almost everywhere.

Of course, when the central theorem of economic analysis stated that no government, no matter how efficient and how benevolent, could improve upon the market's allocation of resources, there was little need to spend much time analysing how governments actually behaved and, in particular, in assessing whether they could or would actually improve the economy's resource allocations. But once the presumption of the efficiency of markets is removed, more careful attention needs to be paid to the nature of government. This is precisely the concern of the second major strand of research to which I want to call attention.

Developments in political economy
While the intellectual underpinnings of our faith in the market economy were being swept aside, there was another movement that attacked our confidence in the ability of government to correct these and other pervasive market failures. Scholars like George Stigler, James Buchanan and, within the development literature, Ann Krueger and Jagdish Bhagwati, called attention to rent-seeking behaviour and other political economy problems which suggested that the frequent failure of government to maximize social welfare (using essentially any reasonable social welfare function) was no accident, but a consequence of natural economic forces.[7]

Perhaps nowhere is the discrepancy between public rhetoric and government actions so great as in programmes 'designed' to redistribute income. In traditional discussions, the role of government in redistributing income and wealth was emphasized. It was noted that the distribution of income which emerged from market forces might be 'socially unacceptable'. There seemed to be a presumption that the government, reflecting the interests of the 'people', could and would redistribute income from the wealthy to the poor.

The experience of the past 15 years has cast doubt on that presumption. The beneficiaries of government programmes in many LDCs are urban workers, who are much wealthier than the poor rural peasants from whom revenues are collected, often through export taxes; the beneficiaries of loan programmes are often the large wealthy farmers who have 'good collateral' as well as political connections. Such issues arise in the US as well: while the farm programme may help the small farmer who, in popular rhetoric, is supposed to be its beneficiary, it helps the large farmer even more.

It is curious that the second movement (emphasizing the limitations of government) largely ignored the first (which had emphasized the limitations of markets): the former called for less government and a greater role for markets. The call for less government was based partly on ideology – the selective drawing of lessons from certain cases – and partly on a theory of government which perhaps exaggerated the importance of rent-seeking activities.

Objectives of this Chapter

My objective in this chapter is to identify what I see as some of the most important lessons to emerge both from recent development experiences and the recent development of ideas. Together, the lessons I draw do not constitute a formula for success, nor even a formula for avoiding disaster. But I do believe that learning these lessons will at least improve the chances for progress and reduce the likelihood that – in the name of economic development – untold misery is once again visited upon those who have already been dealt not the best of hands by fortune.

FREEDOM AND GROWTH

I should begin my discussion with a lesson that extends beyond the narrow technical limits of economics. If one picked up a principles of economics textbook of 15 or perhaps even 10 years ago, one 'learned' that the socialist economies were growing faster than the capitalist economies. There seemed to be a trade-off: 'growth' versus 'freedom'. Markets and free enterprise were luxuries which rich countries like the US could afford, but for those who were desperately poor, who had no time to waste in frivolities, centralized government control was required. (The reasoning paralleled the experience of many countries in war-time: government seized the reins and markets were put under strict control.)

From our current perspective, the countries participating (voluntarily or involuntarily) in the socialist experiment seem to have had *less* political freedom and *less* economic progress. Did these texts make a sign error? Could it be that political freedom and economic progress are, at least at some stages of development, complements (not substitutes), to use the jargon of economics? I believe they are, partly for reasons which I hope to make clear by the end of the chapter. For now, we need only observe that the historical record certainly does not reveal the kind of trade-off that once was a part of conventional wisdom.

A look at the successes and failures of the socialist economies makes it clear that they have been able to attain high rates of savings – not necessarily higher than those obtained voluntarily in countries like Taiwan and Japan – but certainly higher than obtained in most other societies. They can repress consumption.

But governments do not have the power to make the economy efficient. Indeed, we now realize that to a large extent the high savings rate was necessary to offset massive inefficiencies. There is a growing consensus, for instance, that total factor productivity in, say, Chinese agriculture may actually have decreased for the quarter century from 1955 to 1980.

There is a Role for Government

Yet it would be wrong to conclude from these experiences and from its more general retreat that government is not only not the solution (to the difficulties of economic development), but is actually the problem itself. Such critics suggest that, were it not for the interference of government, natural economic forces would have led to a burst of economic energy, lifting the billions in the Third World out of the mire of poverty in which they have lived for millennia. This contention flies in the face of two virtually incontrovertible facts: first, many economies seem to have done a perfectly fine job of stagnating, without any assistance from the government. Gavin Wright (1986) has provided an excellent account of the post-war South which, in spite of free trade with the North, in spite of free capital mobility and no legal barriers to immigration, trailed far behind the rest of the country until, in Wright's interpretation, the government interventions of the New Deal.

Secondly, government has played a vital role in the development of most major countries. In the US, there was massive government assistance to establish the railroads; in Japan, most observers assign a central role to MITI; in Korea, government is similarly given credit for its central role. In each of these cases, critics may suggest that what the government did was not vital (the development of the US would have been delayed only slightly had railroads not been developed) or possibly even perverse (Japan without MITI would have been an even greater economic power). But these are merely exercises in counterfactual history; interesting as they are, they do not contradict the basic fact that we have few instances of major countries growing without government playing a seemingly vital role.

A CLOSER LOOK AT THE ROLE OF GOVERNMENT

The question is thus not 'whether' government should or must have a role in development: historical experience suggests that some government role is essential for the success of development efforts. Instead we need to ask, 'What are the unique advantages that the institution of government brings to development efforts; what are the *costs* of such government programmes and interventions; and how can we utilize the advantages at the least cost?'

To answer that, we need to have an understanding of government's comparative and absolute advantage. And that, in turn, requires an understanding of the distinctive aspects of government: how government differs, on the one hand, from conventional private enterprises and, on the other, from voluntary and self-generating associations formed to promote the welfare of their members (such as clubs and cooperatives). Elsewhere (1989a), I have attempted to spell out a general theory of the 'economic role of the state'.[8]

Here, as I have said, I want to combine some of the insights provided by that theoretical structure with observations concerning the development experience of the past 15 years, to enable us to formulate a clearer view of appropriate development strategies – in particular the role of government – and to understand better why some of the development strategies attempted in the past have failed.

On the Socialist and Market Socialist Perspectives

Development economics has evolved as a mixture of *hypotheses* about the salient characteristics of LDCs, in particular how they differ from developed countries;[9] *descriptions* of the stages of growth through which countries have passed on the road to development; and *prescriptions* of strategies and tactics to be pursued in the quest for successful development. The prescriptions are often of the form, 'since those who have successfully developed went through these stages and took these actions, these are the stages that must be followed'. The prescriptions also include both specifications of what functions the government is to perform and what directions government policies should take. In this chapter, my comments are directed mainly at the prescriptive aspects of development economics.

Keynes (1936) wrote that 'Practical men, who believe themselves to be quite exempt from intellectual influences, are usually the slaves of some defunct economist'. There is little doubt that the ideas of Marx and other socialist thinkers of the last century have had profound (whether intended or unintended) effects on the lives of us in this century. The evolution of development strategies in the 1900s has owed much to this socialist strand of thought, and to one other – that of market socialism. The latter emphasized the role of prices in coordinating *current* production plans, with state enterprises simply maximizing profits. Even imbalances between production and consumption could be handled, by confronting producers and consumers with different prices. The 'central planner' still had a distinctive role – in allocating investment.[10]

Market socialism seemed to offer the possibility of using prices – the centrepiece of market economies – within a socialist society, where the worst evils of capitalism (those associated with private property) would be avoided. These included the failure to direct investment in ways that were most socially productive; the failure to coordinate investment decisions, leading at times to excess capacity and at other times to insufficient capacity; and the failure to maintain the economy at full employment. (We need to recall that periodic episodes, such as the Great Depression, where the capitalist system seemed to fail 'to perform' – with massive unemployment of labour and underutilization of capital – have characterized capitalist economies until quite recently.)[11]

Even countries which did not follow the 'full' route of socialism – such as India – adopted many of its central features. There was a planning ministry; and while government did not control all of investment, it exercised enormous influence through its licensing powers, its control of imports, of foreign exchange and of the banking system.

Marxist ideology on the natural evolution of a society got reflected in the view that there was a natural sequence of steps in the development process: a transformation from agriculture to industry, with a strong emphasis on heavy industry in the early stages of development. Country after country adopted this as a paradigm for their growth. In addition, Marx's stress on 'capital' in capitalism lead many countries to emphasize the importance of capital accumulation in the growth process. The high rates of 'forced' saving in China and many of the other socialist economies are, from this perspective, hardly surprising.

The theorists of market economies – Walras and the other predecessors of Arrow and Debreu – are no less to blame for the success of the market socialist ideology. For *if* their models of capitalist economies had been correct (or, perhaps I should say, complete), then market socialism would have worked. But these models missed at least part of the essence of capitalist economies.

The Failure of Market Socialism

What is it that they missed? The answer is not simple: the vast literature which has developed during the past 15 years on the economics of information has been centrally concerned with answering that question. Let me here outline a few of the more important aspects.

Contracts and reputations

Economic relations are governed not just by prices, but by contracts and by reputations. 'Contracts' can be thought of as arising when there is an incomplete set of prices. There is no market price for a particular commodity to be delivered at a particular date at a particular location, with a contingency clause that, should there be a strike that commodity will be delivered 30 days later. Contracts spell out the obligations of both parties to the contract under the unique set of conditions which relate to the economic circumstances in which the parties find themselves.

'Reputations' are important because many of the circumstances surrounding an economic relationship cannot be adjudicated by a court, by an 'objective' outside third party. Even if it were possible, it would be prohibitively costly to think through all the contingencies which might arise, and to evaluate how, when they occur, they should be dealt with. A contract must necessarily be incomplete. The maintenance of economic relationships depends on the 'goodwill' of the parties concerned, on their desire to maintain their reputations. Anyone who has had the fortune or misfortune of being involved in construction knows exactly what I am getting at: there is no way that a contract could specify all of the possible contingencies which arise – subcontractors failing to deliver on time, work crew members being sick, particular 'parts' not arriving when scheduled, etc. And there is no way that a contract could specify the 'quality' with which each part of the construction should be fulfilled.

The simple example that we teach our first-year undergraduates, of the market for wheat, has had undue influence on much of our profession's thinking. If that comprised the whole of economic life, the simple markets of market socialism or of the Arrow-Debreu models might indeed work. But, unfortunately, much of modern industrial economics is not well described by such a model.

This brings me to the second major aspect that was missing from the earlier formulations.

Innovation
In the formulations of market socialism, Walras, Arrow and Debreu all assumed that technology was stagnant. They did not address the question of innovation: what motivates inventors to invent, and entrepreneurs to adopt and adapt the fruits of their inventive activity.

Planning at the micro level
The market socialist perspective recognizes the importance of the absence of a complete set of futures and risk markets for the traditional formulation of market economies. Market socialists thus stressed the need for government planning and/or government control of investment. But they failed to take adequate cognizance of the importance of planning at the micro-level. Thus, when at the turn of the century US Steel decided to construct a steel mill on the southern shore of Lake Michigan, there was extensive planning and coordination: of iron ore mines, shipping fleets, coal mines, railroads, marketing, etc. There was even coordination of housing and employment. Government does not have a monopoly on planning, or even planning in the absence of prices. The issue is not planning versus no planning, but the locus of planning.

Planning entails the gathering and processing of information. And information is just not like any other commodity; it cannot simply be 'purchased'. (I and others have written extensively on the reasons for this.) A central planner cannot even 'command' underlings to transmit 'all of the relevant information'. The planner may not know what information is relevant; moreover, the underling can supply a superabundance of information, confronting the central planner with an impossible signal extraction problem: what should he do with all the data that is received? (When there are uncertainties about the future, then the problems are, if anything, more difficult: a listing of the contingencies and their consequences without an indication of the relative likelihood of various contingencies may be of limited value; but how is the planner to assess the accuracy of any judgements concerning the likelihood of various contingencies?)

This brings me to the final issue.

Incentives
The problem of incentives was essentially completely ignored by market socialism. The managers of state enterprises maximized profits because they were good socialists: that was what they were supposed to do. Since the analytics of market socialism never formally took into account the possibility of uncertainties, the question of how the managers were supposed to respond to uncertainties was not (to my knowledge) formally discussed. In situations where objective, relative-frequency probabilities could not be formed, what loss function was to be employed in the formulation of subjec-

tive probabilities? What kinds of communication – besides prices – between the planner and the enterprise were contemplated? And more fundamentally, why should the enterprise manager pursue social objectives rather than his private objectives? How, for instance, was the central planner to know whether the manager of the telephone monopoly was being inefficient? What discipline devices were there to replace those provided by the market?

Critics of socialist experiments, such as Kornai, emphasize the problems posed by the lack of incentives: the soft budget constraints (the possibility of government subsidies) eliminating the kind of incentive provided by the threat of bankruptcy;[12] and the shortages created by having prices set at below market clearing levels giving managers discretion in the allocation of their output, which they can use to increase their own private welfare.[13]

Even when socialist economies have allowed some 'entrepreneurial' activity, incentives have been attenuated by two factors: (i) the lack of commitment (and the lack of ability to commit) that the policy will continue. Thus, incentives to invest in building up customer relations will be limited if the government responds to success by imposing confiscatory taxes;[14] (ii) the lack of a system to enforce contractual arrangements.

On the Importance of Ownership

Thus we have come to realize that ownership and control of enterprises does make a difference, though often for reasons other from those commonly assumed a quarter or half century ago. It is not that socialist or state-run enterprises necessarily act more in the interests of society or that they are more effective in taking externalities into account. The most unsafe atomic energy plants in the country are run by the defence department, while the record of state enterprises on pollution is hardly enviable anywhere in the world.

While managerial discretion may characterize private bureaucracies no less than government bureaucracies, there are two critical checks on the former which are often lacking in the latter: the threat of bankruptcy (the hard budget constraint versus the soft) and the threat of competition.[15] Competition provides a basis for judging how well each unit is performing, and this information allows both the design of more effective incentive structures and the singling out of good managers from those less competent.[16]

Some Mistaken Concepts in Development Strategies

In the last few pages I have provided a list of some of the more fundamental conceptual failures in market socialist economists' understanding of how market economies function. We could make another long list of the consequences of these basic 'conceptual' failures. Let me mention a few of the more important.

Central planning

Whether in India or in the Socialist economies, central planning has been a dismal failure. The coordination issues on which it focused – the material balance equations (ensuring that the supply of various goods was adequate to the demand) – are of secondary importance in open economies, where shortfalls can be met out of imports.

The level of aggregation at which central planning must necessarily be conducted is of little use to the more important issues, such as: What kind of steel should be produced? What kind of steel mill should be constructed? *Who* should manage the steel mill? How can we provide the manager with the right incentives? If these *microeconomic* questions are not answered correctly, macroeconomic planning will be of limited use. When projects are not well executed, we can obtain incremental capital output ratios in the order of 10 or 15 – as Venezuela managed to do – rather than the 2 or 3 that we normally expect.

To put it another way, the differences in returns among projects within the same industry are undoubtedly greater than the differences in average returns across industries. It makes more sense to focus on competition for resources among projects than on competition among industries.

The distinction is important because it shifts the focus from what are the attributes of success to such details as what are the particular skills required for the project?

Capital accumulation and allocation

The development literature has stressed the importance of capital accumulation. The experience of the past decade has shown that even more important than the level of capital accumulation is how capital is allocated. We have seen massive squanderings of capital. High rates of saving seem neither necessary nor sufficient for success. I have already cited the socialist countries as examples where high rates of capital accumulation bore only enough fruit to offset the intrinsic inefficiencies of their system; the oil-rich countries provide further examples where high absolute savings (e.g. relative to non-oil income) yielded low returns.

While investment is undoubtedly important, to some extent the investment can be financed by borrowing rather than internal accumulation: Korea, like many other countries in the early stages of development, borrowed heavily at certain periods of its development process.[17]

High rates of growth may generate high savings rates, rather than the other way around, so that any observed correlations must be interpreted with caution.[18] (Indeed, it is curious how much trouble development economists have in explaining convincingly why markets in LDCs should save less than the 'socially' desirable levels. If rates of return were as high as they would be in typical models employing similar production functions in LDCs and development countries, given the relative capital shortage, then one might expect high rates of savings.[19] The lack of savings may be the result of the low return to savings – a microeconomic problem that should be solved *prior* to addressing the macroeconomic problem of increasing the savings rate. Given the low rates of return, it is not obviously socially desirable to save at much higher rates; while if the government were able to increase the rates of return, then government intervention to increase the savings rate might well not be needed.)

Once we recognize the importance of the *allocation* of capital, we come to appreciate the institutions in our economy which are designed to screen among loan applications and to monitor how those funds are allocated – our banks and other credit institutions.[20]

There seems an almost universal under-appreciation of the importance of the role played by these institutions in our society. I referred earlier to the fact that high in any socialist government's list of priorities is the nationalization of the financial institutions (witness France's actions in the early days of the Mitterand government). Even in more avowedly capitalist economies such as the US, government has taken an ever-increasing role in credit markets, to the point where in one recent year, half of all funds in the US capital markets were either raised by the government or guaranteed by it.

Recent work on the economics of information has led us to understand better that what used to be thought of as 'capital market imperfections' are simply the reflections of the informational imperfections which are endemic – and which it is the social function of these institutions to address. However, the LDCs should be wary in concluding from these theoretical assertions that the government can do the job better. While the market allocations may well not be (constrained) Pareto efficient, there is little evidence that governments can – without considerable thought about the design of appropriate institutions – improve upon the allocations, and there is considerable evidence that it can do worse. What is more, the discretionary power resulting from charging below-market rates of interest gives those in the government assigned the task of allocating credit enormous power, which can and has been used either for the personal interests of these individuals or for the interests of the party in power (see Stiglitz 1989c).

Stages of economic growth
I referred earlier to the doctrine that there were certain stages of growth through which an economy had to pass on its way to successful development:

from agriculture to industry, and from heavy industry to a broader spectrum of industrial goods.

There are, I believe, stages to economic growth, but the traditional characterization (strongly influenced by the Marxist historical perspective) is probably not the correct one. The 'narrow' conception of the stages of growth is deficient on several grounds – most importantly, in that it fails to recognize that a changing economic environment induces changes in both comparative and dynamic comparative advantage. Thus, while agriculture might have been relatively stagnant at one time, this is no longer true. Rates of increase in productivity in agriculture compare favourably with those in industry. From the narrow perspective of static comparative advantage, a country's chance of increasing productivity may be no less from specializing in agriculture than from specializing in industry.

From the perspective of dynamic comparative advantage, what is important is the ability to capture rents. Innovation rents are collected by innovating countries. Thus, the returns to industrialization of the 'following' countries are different from those of the 'leaders'. (And, by the same token, since there may be lower profits associated with the followers, the observed advantages of industrialization in generating capital accumulation may not accrue to them.) Followers thus have a distinctly different problem from leaders. Seeing what contributed to the success of leaders may have limited value for followers. Nonetheless, we may attempt to make some generalizations concerning the sources of dynamic and comparative advantage for today's LDCs .

First, the possibility remains of some 'innovating rents' associated with being the leader in introducing new technologies and products into an environment with different factor prices. The first country (firm) to adapt modern textile manufacturing technology to the special conditions of LDCs, with their low wages and special problems, may be able to capture some rents. But the same argument that held that followers are not in the same position as leaders – and need to adapt their development strategy accordingly – also holds that followers of followers are not in the same position as the original followers: it may not pay other countries to follow blindly the patterns of development that led to the success of the NICs.

Secondly, rather than focusing on issues such as industry-versus-agriculture or exports-versus-imports, the essential element in determining comparative advantage may be one of *organizational complexity*. Modern economies are differentiated from simpler economies not so much in the broad sectoral classification of the goods produced, but in the complexity of the goods. Some kinds of production require much more interaction; there are more gains to specialization; quality control is more important – the acceptable tolerances are simply much lower. Less developed economies have a comparative disadvantage in these goods. Any process of economic development entails the build up of this organizational infrastructure.

One aspect of organizational complexity should be mentioned. Innovation, almost by definition, cannot be routinized. We can routinize the *procedures*, but we cannot routinize the responses. The control mechanisms best suited for running a Silicon Valley computer firm are markedly different from those that may work in running a steel mill or an automobile assembly line (in the absence of innovation.) The former requires individual autonomy and responsibility; there are also risks, which need to be evaluated and assessed.

It remains an open question whether *any* centralized bureaucratic society, in which individuals are denied political liberties, can develop the capacity to handle the organizational complexity across a wide spectrum of commodities that modern market economies evidence. Certainly, the socialist experiments of this century suggest a negative answer. The ability to respond to the myriad of circumstances which might arise requires more individual autonomy and initiative than those societies have traditionally tolerated. Hopefully, we will not have the occasion to witness any further such experiments.

There is another aspect in which economic liberty is important: the right to enter a business and compete with the government or with other extant firms. Much of the inefficiency in the public sector can be traced to the lack of competition which it faces.[21] The prohibition on entry and other restraints of trade not only have deleterious effects in the short run, but further, in the long run, they reduce society's entrepreneurial ability, often diverting these talents into socially less productive channels (such as encouraging political entrepreneurship.)

When I presented this paper at Notre Dame, several participants in the audience, while agreeing with the thrust of my conclusion, nevertheless argued that at earlier stages of development, strong governments have played a vital role. The examples of Singapore and Korea were cited. These observations are not, I think, inconsistent with my thesis that at later stages in the development process, the tension between authoritarianism and economic success becomes greater. Nor do these examples establish that a strong government is required or is even necessarily helpful.

In all of this discussion, I have not been very explicit about defining either economic or political liberty.[22] For much of what I have to say, such precision is not necessary. As I have noted, one aspect of economic liberty that is important even in earlier stages is freedom of entry.

Industrial Policies

Although we argued earlier against giving central planning a major role in economic development, this does not mean that government should have no role. The successes of Korea and Japan are often attributed to the role of government in selecting certain areas for encouragement which we shall refer to as *industrial policies*. I first want to describe certain salient aspects of those policies and then to contrast current views on industrial policies with related policies which have been advocated in the past.

Big push theories and interlinkages

These are two popular theories of recent decades. The former emphasized the importance of coordinated expansion in many goods simultaneously, a coordination which (in Rosenstein Rodan's view[23]) would evidently require government intervention. There was no persuasive reason why this was so (though a modern theorist might make passing reference to diseconomies of scope). Sah and Stiglitz[24] have distinguished between externalities of the kind which can be internalized and externalities of the kind which cannot. The latter we refer to as *diffuse externalities*. They include the externalities associated with the organizational learning which arises in the development process, as well as network externalities which arise when a large number of individuals speak a common (technical) language and share a common know-how and a common set of standards.

These externalities are often associated with positive feedback mechanisms, and hence give rise to multiple equilibria: the return to being an inventor depends, for instance, on the number of innovating firms in the market which are looking for and receptive to new ideas. The return to being an innovator, to searching for new ideas to introduce, depends in part on the number of inventors and the supply of ideas to be appropriated.[25]

These are not the only important interlinkages in the economy: for those supplying finance, the perceived riskiness of providing capital for a new innovative project depends on one's experience with such projects; with experience grows the ability to judge, to differentiate between good and bad projects. But the supply of new projects depends on innovators' perceptions of the possibilities of obtaining finance.

Of course, any model that gives rise to multiple equilibria can be thought of as a 'Big Push' theory – the big push is simply the movement from the lower equilibrium to the upper equilibrium. Two other categories of models giving rise to multiple equilibria have been explored in recent years. In the first there are some increasing returns, often associated with learning by doing. The economy may be trapped in an equilibrium where it uses a technique of production with a low level of learning potential. Given its low level of income and associated high rates of interest, it simply does not pay to 'jump' – say to a more capital-intensive technique with higher learning (see Stiglitz 1988a).

The other set of models combines some form of non-convexities in a closed-economy model. The limiting factor in the low-level equilibrium is demand: at a low level of demand, output is low, so the economy cannot take advantage of scale economies. These models are less convincing in the context of modern open economies. To the extent that these economies of scale are important, they argue that smaller and poorer countries should specialize in more tradeable goods. Transport costs will result in such economies having a lower standard of living – just as transport costs (if not offset by some other locational advantages, such as the presence of some scarce natural resource) will result in lower standards of living of a physically isolated region within a country.

Dynamic comparative advantage
Part of the title of this chapter has to do with 'tactics and strategy'. I want to use the distinction to emphasize two different aspects of the development process.

Much recent discussion has emphasized the importance of countries pursuing their comparative advantage. This entails eliminating government-created distortions in the economy. With much of this I am very sympathetic. For many countries, this will entail concentrating on agriculture which has the advantage of 'organizational simplicity'. The green revolution has shown that it is capable of huge increases in productivity: an agriculturally-based economy need not be stagnating. Yet one senses that many LDCs are impatient with such a policy, which they perceive would leave them condemned forever to a second-class position. Moreover, success in agriculture will necessarily release huge numbers of workers who will have to be gainfully employed elsewhere.

The long-run programme designed to promote growth most effectively is what I refer to as the development strategy. And for development strategies, as I have said, the question may not be so much what *sector* in which to produce, but which enterprises to support or provide with credit. The focus is not current comparative advantage but long-run (or dynamic) comparative advantage. The concern is not only what can be learned, but whether production of any one commodity enhances the ability to learn (Stiglitz 1988a) and the ability to handle organizational complexity. There is no *a priori* reason why Switzerland should have developed a comparative advantage in watches – and no *a priori* reason why it should have retained its comparative advantage when the technology of watches changed. The particular commodities which a country develops a comparative advantage in may be arbitrary; but what this and other similar examples suggest is that when a country develops such a comparative advantage, there are often important 'external' learning benefits. (The diffuse externalities to be found today in Silicon Valley and that were also pervasive in the Ohio/Michigan area at the turn of the century, leading to the development of the mass-produced car and the invention of the aeroplane, surely account for much of the success of those two areas.)

There are other important diffuse externalities that should be taken into account in the design of industrial policies. Hoff (1989) has noted the value of information about what kinds of commodities and processes may be successful in a particular economic environment. The return to this kind of information is difficult to appropriate since the success of one product or process will be quickly imitated. There are also important marketing externalities: the discovery of a market where the products of a country will be appreciated is valuable information, but this too is difficult to appropriate. Moreover reputations established within a market frequently extend to other products and other brands of the country. There are thus a variety of diffuse externalities affecting the product market, the labour market (human capital) and financial markets.

While the presence of diffuse externalities is one set of factors to be taken into account in the design of an industrial policy for LDCs, there are other factors as well. Earlier, we stressed the importance of financial market imperfections. Firms may find it particularly difficult to borrow to finance R&D since the kind of capital acquired by R&D cannot, by and large, be collaterized. Similarly, with learning by doing, if a firm is ever to gain the experience to get its costs down to a level at which it can compete with foreign rivals, it will have to operate at a loss in the early stages of entry into a market (Dasgupta and Stiglitz 1988b).[26] Thus, in the absence of government intervention, financial constraints may pose a serious impediment to growth and development.

Export led growth and import substitution

While there has been some controversy in development economics about the appropriate role of agriculture (relative to industry), there has perhaps been even more controversy about *which* industries should be encouraged (assuming a government decides to pursue an 'industrial policy' of encouraging particular industries). Following a tradition that perhaps dates back to the Mercantilists, some have claimed that the best strategy is to focus on exports; others have concentrated on encouraging domestic industries to substitute for foreign imports.

To those who do not appreciate the large role that history plays in development economics – a central concern of the subject is to make inferences from past successes about what strategies are most likely to lend themselves to future success – this debate always seemed a bit strange. Shouldn't countries simply focus on their comparative advantage? If they do this, won't some of the products necessarily be exported; while if there are some products in which the country has a comparative advantage that it imports, won't there be some import substitution as well?

Yet the successes and failures of the past few decades suggest several lessons concerning aspects of development strategy which go beyond simple comparative advantage. First, governments have a difficult time ascertaining static comparative advantages; ascertaining dynamic comparative advantages would seem to be an even more formidable task. Whether for this or other reasons, industrial policies are subject to political pressures – the result being that the government may not improve upon the efficiency of the market's resource allocations. Export success provides some discipline upon firms in the industry: they have to compete (albeit with some government assistance). Import substitution has frequently resulted in a limited number of domestic producers relatively insulated from the forces of competition. Both Korea and Japan subjected many of the industries which they assisted through industrial policies to this kind of competitive test.

Secondly, for some commodities, particularly those which are more complex, the penetration into foreign markets may not be feasible unless a certain modicum of learning has occurred; that learning may only occur within a protected market. (The potential abuse to which such 'learning' arguments can be put by rent-seeking firms makes me hesitant to advance them; yet the fact that it may be difficult to distinguish instances where there are true learning benefits, particularly in the presence of financial constraints and diffuse externalities, from those where the argument is simply self-serving, does not deny some truth to policies concerned with developing home markets.)

THE ROLE OF GOVERNMENT: SOME FURTHER OBSERVATIONS

The role of the government in development strategies involving industrial policies will require care. The criticisms of government are not limited to how – through tariffs, regulations and taxes – they have interfered with the short-run efficiency of the economy. Rather they have rewarded political entrepreneurship at the expense of economic initiative. Worse still, they have stifled entrepreneurship altogether, encouraging many of the most talented youth to opt for the security of civil service jobs.

Yet the fact remains that government will almost surely need to play a central – though circumscribed – role in any successful development effort.

We do not, at this juncture, have a clear understanding of the circumstances that lead in some situations to destructive rent-seeking activity. While some popular expositions give credit to certain ethnic characteristics, this does not explain the vicissitudes within Korea, or indeed even in Japan, where certain forms of seeming political corruption occur, but not others. The checks provided by the export-oriented policies pursued by both countries may in fact be central.

Given the limited resources available, governments need to set priorities: what activities can they best undertake? In what ways can they most effectively channel and encourage private activity?

Traditional discussions have focused on the importance of government providing infrastructure – roads and buildings. But there is another form of infrastructure, no less important, if private activities are to be promoted: a legal system which allows the effective implementation of private contracts, as well as contracts between the state and the private sector. Many of today's LDCs are in a transitional phase. The social transformations associated with development have loosened traditional forms of contract enforcement, while effective legal forms have not yet developed.

Our earlier discussion referred to the central role of markets, contracts and reputations. Markets develop naturally; since government regulations often serve to impede their development, a first task of government policy is to remove such impediments. Contractual arrangements require a legal infrastructure with effective enforcement procedures. For reputations to develop, a stable economic environment is required which is more conducive to the persistence of firms and thus to the establishment of reputations. Again, with constantly varying government policies, regulations and taxes, as well as extensive government discretionary policy, survival may be more an indicator of political acumen and connections than of the economic efficiency of the firm.

Beyond these two basic elements of infrastructure, governments can make a contribution through industrial policies; an effective instrument – but one potentially subject to abuse, like any other powerful instrument – is credit policy. The endemic failures associated with financial markets provides a potential rationale for governments to concentrate on those markets (see Stiglitz 1989a).

CONCLUDING REMARKS

In closing, I want to return to some themes I introduced earlier. The fact that governments have not always succeeded in their development programmes – and may have made matters worse – should not blind us to the fact that some governments have made a positive difference; many if not all successful development programmes in major countries have entailed a significant role for government. The failure of markets, on their own, to deliver is by now a well-established theoretical possibility as well as an historical reality.

Secondly, there need not be a choice between political freedom and economic liberty on the one hand, and economic progress on the other. Indeed, in the long run – as part of a long-term development strategy – political freedom and economic progress are complementary. This is the great lesson of the events of the autumn of 1989.

NOTES

1. This paper is based on an AT&T Lecture delivered at Notre Dame, 2 April 1990. I am indebted to the National Science Foundation, the Hoover Institution and the Olin Foundation for financial support. The paper has been greatly improved as a result of helpful comments by A. Singh, Charles Wilber and other participants at the seminar at which the paper was originally presented.

2. As always, events can be interpreted in more than one way. In some of the countries, part of the reaction against socialism was against a form of government and an economic system imposed upon them in the aftermath of World War II. Whether right or wrong, the sentiment about the failure of communism is almost universal. As an illustration, see the Blue Ribbon Commission on Hungary, perhaps the best managed of the 'centrally planned' economies.

3. As well as a host of other studies, from Stiglitz (1972, 1982) to Newbery and Stiglitz (1981, 1982, 1984) to Arnott and Stiglitz (1985, 1986, 1989) to Geanakoplos, Magill, Quinzii and Dreze (1989). Each of these focuses on the special cases discussed in Greenwald and Stiglitz, such as incomplete risk markets, moral hazard, etc.

4. See K.J. Arrow (1951) and G. Debreu (1959).

5. The efficiency wage theory, originally developed in Stiglitz (1974, 1976a, 1976b), Mirrlees (1975) and Weiss (1980). For a more complete survey of this literature, see Stiglitz (1986, 1987), Yellen (1984) or Katz (1973). For more recent empirical work supporting the theory, see Kates and Summers (1989).

6. This was not necessarily the vocabulary used within the mainstream of the socialist tradition in either the East or the West.

7. Some of the conclusions of this literature – such as that all of the rents will be dissipated in rent-seeking expenditures – are not generally valid. Imperfect competition in rent-seeking implies that, with even small sunk costs, large 'profits' may be sustained. See, for instance, Stiglitz (1988a).

8. I attempted there to identify the *distinguishing* aspects of government: universal membership combined with its powers of compulsion. These powers enable the government to do things that the market cannot do; that is why governments, facing the same economic environment of costly information and costly transactions, can still, in principle, improve welfare. At the same time, the powers of compulsion give rise to potential abuses, and these potential abuses give rise to constraints imposed on government. These constraints in turn mean that the government is often at a marked disadvantage relative to markets. Ascertaining the circumstances under which government action (taking into account both its powers and the constraints under which it operates) might be welfare enhancing is a central question of modern welfare economics.

9. For a survey of some of the salient characteristics of LDCs, particularly as they relate to information and other market failures, see Stiglitz (1988b).

10. The fact that no country ever really tried market socialism – at least not in the form envisaged by Lange, Lerner or Taylor – does not detract from the influence that the idea has had.
11. Though we should also bear in mind that, until the Great Depression, most of the downturns were of relatively short duration.
12. It is worth noting that much of the recent literature on capitalist firms has emphasized the importance of the threat of bankruptcy as limiting managerial discretion, managers' ability to divert firms' resources to their private uses. This is alleged to be one of the important advantages of having a high debt-equity ratio. Robert Hall has referred to these as 'back-to-the-wall theories of corporate finance'. See also Jensen (1988).
13. In addition to these, the prevalence of effective tenure – the inability to fire workers – greatly attenuates incentives. Many of these problems arise in the government sector of non-socialist economies. See, for instance, Stiglitz (1988c, Chapter 10).
14. Litwack (1988) has emphasized this in his work.
15. In principle, of course, government enterprises could be organized competitively. However, this is seldom done.
16. The separation of ownership and control has been an important theme in market economies, at least since Knight's seminal work: the separation is by no means unique to socialist countries. A vast modern literature on the causes and consequences of the separation (the principal agent problem) has developed. For a brief survey, see Stiglitz (1989b).
17. This may be particularly true for infrastructure. For a variety of informational reasons (see, for instance, Stiglitz 1990), it may be difficult for any but the largest of firms to finance expansion by borrowing from abroad.
18. Theories of imperfect capital markets (based on imperfect information) provide a rationale for why this might be so.
19. Assuming that there is a positive interest elasticity to savings.
20. For an account of the importance of the development of financial institutions for the rise of modern capitalism, see Greenwald and Stiglitz (1990).
21. The classic study by Daves and Christensen (1980) of Canadian railroads showed that, when faced with private competition, the government railroad was fully as efficient as the private.
22. There are major difficulties in arriving at a precise definition. Governments can provide the form of economic liberty, but not the substance; distinguishing form and substance is, at best, difficult. Thus, systems of non-linear fines and penalties can be constructed which are essentially equivalent to direct government control. By controlling foreign exchange and access to credit, governments can often exercise enormous control over private enterprises – and not only over proposed new projects.

    Similarly, granting to private enterprises the 'right' to enter and compete against government enterprises may have little effect if the government uses its ability to control foreign exchange to deny them access to resources required for effective competition, or if the government uses its dominant role in industry to put new entrants at a marked disadvantage by refusing to purchase goods from them.
23. See Rosenstein Rodan and Eckaus (1973).
24. See R.K. Sah and J.E. Stiglitz (1989).
25. In Dasgupta and Stiglitz (1988a), we provide a fuller characterization of other consequences of learning by doing, learning to learn and localized learning.
26. Note that the standard objection to the infant industry argument is simply inapplicable. That objection holds that if it were socially worthwhile to enter an industry, it would pay any private firm to go ahead and enter the industry. That argument assumes perfect capital markets and competitive product markets (since the standard analysis also assumes that entry has no effect on consumer prices). But capital markets are never perfect, and product markets with learning by doing are never perfectly competitive.

REFERENCES

Arnott, R. and Stiglitz, J.E. (1985), 'Labor Turnover, Wage Structure and Moral Hazard: The Inefficiency of Competitive Markets', *Journal of Labor Economics*, 3(4), October, 434–62.

Arnott, R. and Stiglitz, J.E. (1986), 'Moral Hazard and Optimal Commodity Taxation', *Journal of Public Economics*, 29, 1–24.

Arnott, R. and Stiglitz, J.E. (1988), 'The Basic Analytics of Moral Hazard', *Scandinavian Journal of Economics*, 90(3), 383–413.

Arnott, R. and Stiglitz, J.E. (1989), 'The Welfare Economics of Moral Hazard', in Henri Louberge (ed.), *Risk, Information and Insurance: Essays in the Memory of Karl H. Borch*, Norwell, MA: Kluwer Academic Publishers.

Arrow, K.J. (1951), 'An Extension of the Basic Theorems of Classical Welfare Economics', *Proceedings of the Second Berkeley Symposium*, Berkeley: University of California Press.

Dasgupta, P. and Stiglitz, J. (1988a), 'Learning by Doing, Market Structure & Industrial & Trade Policies', *Oxford Economic Papers*, 40, 246–68.

Dasgupta, P. and Stiglitz, J. (1988b), 'Potential Competition, Actual Competition and Economic Welfare', *European Economic Review*, 32, May, 569–77.

Daves, D.W. and Christensen, L.R. (1980), 'The Relative Efficiency of Public and Private Firms in a Competitive Environment: The Case of Canadian Railroads', *Journal of Political Economy*, 88, 958–76.

Debreu, G. (1959), *Theory of Value*, Wiley Press.

Geanakoplos, J., Magill, M., Quinzii, M. and Dreze, J. (1989), 'Generic Inefficiency of Stock Market Equilibrium when Markets are Incomplete', *Journal of Mathematical Economics*, 19(1–2), 113–52..

Greenwald, B. and Stiglitz, J. (1986), 'Externalities in Economies with Imperfect Information and Incomplete Markets', *Quarterly Journal of Economics*, 101, May, 229–56.

Greenwald, B. and Stiglitz, J. (1988), 'Pareto Inefficiency of Market Economies: Search and Efficiency Wage Models', *American Economic Review*, May, 351–55.

Greenwald, B. and Stiglitz, J. (1990), 'Asymmetric Information and the New Theory of the Firm: Financial Constraints and Risk', *American Economic Review*, May, 160–65.

Hirschman, A. (1982), *Shifting Involvements*, Princeton, NJ: Princeton University Press.

Hoff, K. (1989), 'An Argument for Industrial Policy for Infant Industries Based on the Production and Transmission of Information', University of Maryland, mimeo.

Jensen, M. (1988), 'Takeovers: Their Causes and Consequences', *Journal of Economic Perspectives*, 2, Winter, 21–48.

Katz, L.W. (1973), *Analysis of Development Problems*, Amsterdam: North Holland.

Katz, L.W. (1986), 'Efficiency Wage Theories: A Partial Evaluation' in *NBER Macroeconomics Annual 1986*, Cambridge, MA: MIT Press, 235–76.

Katz, L.W. and Summers, L.H. (1989), 'Industry Rents: Evidence and Implications', *Brookings Papers: Microeconomics*, 209–20.

Keynes, John M. (1936), *The General Theory of Employment, Interest and Money*, New York: Harcourt Brace Jovanovich.

Knight, F. (1951), *The Economic Organization*, New York: A.M. Kelly.

Litwak, J. (1988), 'Coordination, Incentives, and the Ratchet Effect', Stanford University, mimeo.

Mirrlees, James (1975), 'A Pure Theory of Underdeveloped Economies', in L.A. Reynolds (ed.), *Agriculture in Development Theory*, New Haven: Yale University Press, 84–106.

Newbery, D. and Stiglitz, J.E. (1981), *The Theory of Commodity Price Stabilization*, Oxford University Press.

Newbery, D. and Stiglitz, J.E. (1982), 'The Choice of Techniques and the Optimality of Market Equilibrium with Rational Expectations', *Journal of Political Economy*, **90**(2), April, 223–46.

Newbery, D. and Stiglitz, J.E. (1984), 'Pareto Inferior Trade', *Review of Economic Studies*, **51**(164), January, 1–13.

Rosenstein Rodan, Paul and Eckaus, Richard S. (1973), *Analysis of Development Problems*, Amsterdam: North Holland.

Sah, R. and Stiglitz, J. (1989), 'Technological Learning, Social Learning and Technological Change' in S. Chakravarty (ed.), *The Balance between Industry and Agriculture in Economic Development*, Macmillan Press/International Economic Association, 285–98.

Stiglitz, J.E. (1972), 'On the Optimality of the Stock Market Allocation of Investment', *Quarterly Journal of Economics*, **86**(1), February, 25–60.

Stiglitz, Joseph E. (1974), 'Alternative Theories of Wage Determination and Unemployment in LDCs: The Labor Turnover Model', *Quarterly Journal of Economics*, **87**, May, 194–227.

Stiglitz, Joseph E. (1976a), 'Prices and Queues as Screening Devices in Competitive Markets', IMSSS Technical Report, No 212, Stanford University, August.

Stiglitz, Joseph E. (1976b), 'The Efficiency Wage Hypothesis, Surplus Labor and the Distribution of Income in LDCs', *Oxford Economic Papers*, **28**(2), July, 185–207.

Stiglitz, Joseph E. (1982), 'The Inefficiency of the Stock Market Equilibrium', *Review of Economic Studies*, April, 247–61.

Stiglitz, Joseph E. (1986), 'Theories of Wage Rigidities' in J.L. Butkiewicz, K.J. Koford, and J.B. Miller (eds), *Keynes' Economic Legacy: Contemporary Economic Theories*, New York: Praeger Publishers, 153–206.

Stiglitz, Joseph E. (1987), 'The Causes and Consequences of the Dependence of Quality on Price', *Journal of Economic Literature*, **25**, March, 1–48.

Stiglitz, Joseph E. (1988a), 'Technological Change, Sunk Costs and Competition' in N.N. Bailey and C. Winston (eds), *Brookings Papers on Economic Activity (3–1987) – Special Issue on Microeconomics*, 883–967.

Stiglitz, Joseph E. (1988b), 'Economic Organization, Information and Development' in H. Chenery and T.N. Srinivasan (eds), *Handbook of Development Economics*, Elsevier Science Publishers, 94–160.

Stiglitz, Joseph E. (1988c), *Economics of the Public Sector*, Second Edition, New York: Norton.

Stiglitz, Joseph E. (1989a), 'The Economic Role of the State' in A. Heertje (ed.), *The Economic Role of the State*, Amsterdam: Bank Insinger de Beaufort NV.

Stiglitz, Joseph E. (1989b), 'Principal and Agent' in J. Eatwell, M. Milgate and P. Newman (eds), *The New Palgrave: Allocation, Informaton and Markets*, London: Macmillan Press, 241–53.

Stiglitz, Joseph E. (1989c), 'Financial Markets and Development', *Oxford Review of Economic Policy*, **4**(4), 55–68.

Stiglitz, Joseph E. (1990), 'Banks versus Markets as Mechanisms for Allocating and Coordinating Investment', presented at the conference, 'Investment Coordination in the Pacific Century: Lessons from Theory and Practice', given at the University of Hawaii, January.

Stiglitz, J. and Weiss, A. (1981), 'Credit Rationing in Markets with Imperfect Information', *American Economic Review*, **71**, June, 393–410.

Stiglitz, J. and Weiss, A. (1983), 'Alternative Approaches to Analyzing Markets with Asymmetric Information: Reply', *American Economic Review*, **73**, 246–49.

Stiglitz, J. and Weiss, A. (1986), 'Credit Rationing and Collateral' in J. Edwards, J. Franks, C. Mayer and S. Schaefer (eds), *Recent Developments in Corporate Finance*, Cambridge: Cambridge University Press, 101–36.

Weiss, Andrew (1976), 'A Theory of Limited Labor Markets', Ph.D. Dissertation, Stanford University.

Weiss, Andrew (1980), 'Job Queues and Layoffs in Labor Markets with Flexible Wages', *Journal of Political Economy*, **88**, June, 526–38.

Wright, G. (1986), *Old South, New South*, New York: Basic Books.

Wright, G. (1987), 'The Economic Revolution in the American South', *Journal of Economic Perspectives*, **1**, Summer, 161–78.

Yellen, Janet (1984), 'Efficiency Wage Models of Unemployment', *American Economic Review*, **74**(2), March, 200–205.

4. The Actual Crisis of Economic Development in the 1980s: An Alternative Policy Perspective for the Future

Ajit Singh*

INTRODUCTION

The previous chapters in this volume have concentrated on the crisis in development economics and put forward different theoretical perspectives on the subject. This chapter is more concerned with the actual crisis of economic development which engulfed the Third World in the 1980s. It outlines the nature of this phenomenon and identifies the central theoretical and policy issues which it raises. It is argued here that the analysis of these issues by mainstream economists, and particularly by the international financial institutions, is seriously flawed; more importantly, the policy implications which follow from it are misleading and could deepen the developmental crisis of the poor countries, instead of resolving it. This chapter puts forward an alternative policy perspective which, it is suggested, is more appropriate for the developing countries in the conditions of the 1990s.

THE DEVELOPMENTAL CRISIS OF THE 1980s

In December 1980 the UN General Assembly, in its resolution on the International Development Strategy for the Third United Nations Development Decade, stated that the 'average annual rate of growth of gross domestic product for the developing countries as a whole during the Decade (1980s) should be 7 per cent.'[1] This was not an unreasonable ambition for the world community in the light of the respectable record of overall economic growth of about 6 per cent per annum which the Third World countries had achieved in the previous two decades.

* This is a revised version of a lecture delivered in the series on 'The Future of Development Economics' at the University of Notre Dame in April 1990

Table 4.1   Growth of population and of output in the Third World, 1971–
90, and of per capita income from 1980–89

	Growth of GDP (annual rate)		Growth of population (annual rate)	Index of per capita income in 1989[a] (1980 = 100)
	1971–80	1981–90	1981–91	
Developing Countries of which	5.6	3.2	2.1	107.0
1. Western Hemisphere	5.5	1.0	2.1	85.0
2. West Asia	6.5	–0.2	3.3	39.0
3. South and East Asia	5.8	7.0	2.2	153.0
4. Africa	4.9	0.5	3.1	70.0
5. Mediterranean	5.3	3.2	1.6	113.0

Note: [a]Per capita gross domestic product adjusted for changes in terms of trade and net factor payments.

Source: UN (1990); the above table has been adapted from Tables 1.2, II.1 & VII.2.

However, consider Table 4.1, which brings out the broad nature of the Third World's developmental crisis in the 1980s. It shows that instead of a rise, the last decade witnessed a steep fall in the trend rate of growth of production in developing countries, to about half the rate envisaged by the UN. As the population in the Third World increased in the 1970s at much the same pace as it did in the 1980s, the rate of growth of *per capita GDP* in the LDCs as a whole in the last decade fell to a third of the rate of the 1970s, to a little over 1 per cent per annum. Significantly Table 4.1 also suggests that in the Western Hemisphere (i.e. the Latin American and Caribbean countries) and in Africa, the *level* of per capita GDP fell in the 1980s – at an average rate of 1 per cent per annum in the former group of countries and at over 2.5 per cent per annum in the latter. When these per capita GDP figures are adjusted for changes in the terms of trade and net factor payments, the last column of the table shows that average per capita *income* in the Latin American countries was 15 per cent lower, and in African countries as much as 30 per cent lower, in 1989 than in 1980.

To put into perspective the implications of these aggregate figures of falling per capita production and income for the economies and people of the poor countries, consider the case of two specific nations, Mexico and Tanzania. In Mexico, between 1977 and 1981, in the years before the crisis, GDP was growing at a rate of about 7 per cent per annum. By 1981 the economy was creating nearly a million new jobs annually, just enough to provide employment to new entrants to the labour force which grew at a rate of 3 per cent per annum. However, in the years 1982 to 1988, there was no increase in GDP at all whilst population and labour force growth rates were much the same as before (population growth rate being about 2 per cent per annum).

In the second half of the 1970s, Mexican manufacturing production increased at a rate of 7.5 per cent per annum; however, following the debt crisis, industrial output in 1982 fell by 4 per cent and in 1983 by further 8 per cent. Overall in the 1980s manufacturing production hardly increased. Thus instead of rising employment in manufacturing and in other sectors of the economy to absorb at least the new entrants to the labour force, the experience of the 1980s for the Mexican people was one of reduced employment opportunities and a large deterioration in the already difficult employment situation. Moreover real wages in Mexico were estimated to have fallen by 50 per cent between 1981 and 1987.[2] Similarly in Tanzania, instead of industrialization and economic development, the 1980s brought about large-scale deindustrialization. Tanzanian manufacturing production *shrank* by well over 25 per cent over the period 1980 to 1985. Industrial capacity utilization was estimated to have fallen to about 20 per cent over this period, with extremely adverse consequences for employment and real wages.

Nevertheless Table 4.1 also reveals that despite the world economic crisis, the South and East Asian countries continued to do well in the 1980s. In sharp contrast to the situation in African and Latin American countries, the Asian economies on average managed to *increase* their trend rate of growth of GDP during the last decade. As one would expect, faster economic growth has been associated with further industrialization, growing real wages and employment, as well as significant falls in poverty levels in the countries of the region.

Table 4.2 outlines the trends in *sectoral* production performance in different regions of the Third World over the period 1965 to 1988.[3] The important point which emerges from this table is that the economic crisis of the 1980s has apparently affected industry and other sectors of the economy much more severely than agriculture. The table shows that for both low-

Table 4.2   Trends in sectoral production performance, 1965–88 (average annual percentage growth)

Country group	GDP		Industry		Agriculture	
	1965–80	1980–88	1965–80	1980–88	1965–80	1980–88
Low-income economies						
(exc. China and India)	5.5	2.0	10.0	1.7	2.3	2.3
Middle-income economies	6.1	2.9	5.9	3.2	3.2	2.7
Latin America	6.0	1.5	6.0	1.1	3.3	2.5
Sub-Saharan Africa	4.8	0.8	9.4	–0.8	1.3	1.8
South Asia (inc. India)	3.7	5.1	4.4	10.3	3.2	5.7
East Asia (inc. China)	7.2	8.5	10.8	10.3	3.2	5.7

Source: World Bank: *World Development Report 1990*, Washington, D.C. 1990, Table 2, 180–81.

income (excluding China and India) and middle-income economies, the trend rates of growth of GDP and industry from 1980 to 1988 were at best half those of 1965 to 1980, whilst agriculture growth fell at most by a quarter over the same period. Both in Latin America and sub-Saharan Africa, industrial as well as GDP growth rates collapsed in the 1980s; however, the fall in agriculture growth in Latin America during the last decade was relatively small, whilst in the sub-Saharan African economies agriculture recorded a trend increase in growth in the 1980s compared to the period 1965 to 1980.

ANALYTICAL ISSUES AND ALTERNATIVE POLICY PERSPECTIVES

The stylized facts summarized above concerning the Third World's economic crisis of the 1980s raise the following important analytical questions:

1. Why was there a trend decline in economic and industrial development in the South during the last decade?
2. Why was the performance of the Asian economies so vastly superior to that of Latin American and sub-Saharan African countries?
3. Why did agriculture fare so much better than industry or GDP as a whole during this crisis?

The answers to these questions are not merely of intellectual interest but have a direct bearing on the policy debate regarding future economic development in the Third World. An influential and important line of argument in this debate holds that, although general macroeconomic conditions associated with the world economic crisis may have adversely affected Southern economies during this decade, their setbacks are in large measure due to inefficient domestic utilization and allocation of resources and to myriad inefficiencies at the microeconomic level in the developing countries themselves. In this view, which is routinely put forward by international financial institutions (the World Bank and the IMF) and is shared by many mainstream economists,[4] the inappropriate policies of import substitution and inward orientation, excessive regulation of private enterprise leading *inter alia* to resource misallocation, rent seeking and corruption, the large role of state-controlled enterprises which are invariably poorly managed, have all greatly contributed to economic and industrial failure in the South.

A very important place is accorded in this thesis to the economic success of the East Asian NICs in the last decade. It is argued that the far superior performance of these countries relative to those in Latin America and Africa provides practical demonstration of the desirability of outward and more market-oriented economic policies. Apart from prudent macroeconomic management in line with Fund/Bank prescriptions, the developing countries are therefore urged in addition to undertake far-reaching structural reforms in order to achieve fast and 'efficient' industrial and economic development. These reforms involve measures such as import liberalization, encouragement of foreign investment, privatization of state-owned enterprises, deregulation of domestic product and financial markets. In short, in this policy programme, a substantial diminution in the role of the state in the industrial sphere and *pari passu* an expansion of that of the market are called for.

The second part of the chapter will analyse these policy issues. It will also outline a feasible alternative policy perspective which the developing countries could and should follow in the conditions of the 1990s. First, however, in the following three sections, we shall consider some of the analytical questions posed earlier.[5] Specifically we shall examine the impact of the world economic crisis on the developing countries in order to assess the extent to which their performance may have been adversely affected by external circumstances. In this context, we shall also consider the important issue why, despite the world economic crisis, the Asian countries continued to do well in the 1980s whilst the Latin American did so poorly.[6] The basic purpose of this analysis will be to explore the two main, but by no means mutually exclusive, hypotheses which can be put forward to account for the Third World's economic crisis in the last decade:

1. The South's economic and industrial setback in the 1980s was essentially due to world economic forces over which the developing countries had no control.
2. The economic and industrial decline was caused by domestic mismanagement, incorrect economic policies and microeconomic inefficiencies in the South.

THE WORLD ECONOMIC CRISIS: THE IMPACT ON THE DEVELOPING ECONOMIES IN THE 1980s

As a consequence of the world economic crisis, Third World countries were subjected to a series of historically unprecedented external shocks at the beginning of the 1980s. Equally significantly, a number of these adverse factors continued to operate throughout the decade (and into the 1990s) which has made full economic recovery in a large number of developing economies extremely difficult.

External Shocks: Channels of Transmission

The most important channels through which the slowdown in world economic activity, particularly in the early 1980s, affected economic and industrial development in Third World countries were the following:

1. a reduction in the demand for Third World products, including commodity and mineral exports;
2. as a consequence of (1), a fall in commodity prices and hence adverse movements in the terms of trade;
3. an increase in the real burden of interest and debt service payments partly due to (1) and partly due to an enormous increase in interest rates;
4. a reduction in the quantum of aid and other capital flows.

The end of the 1970s witnessed a far-reaching change in the domestic macroeconomic policies of industrial countries, heralded by the appointment of Paul Volcker as chairman of the Federal Reserve in the US in 1979. Following the second oil price increase, the US government embarked on a highly contractionary monetary and fiscal policy which was later emulated either willingly (as in the case of the UK) or unwillingly (through a process of competitive deflation) by other industrial countries.[7] The net result was a prolonged recession in the advanced economies whose real rate of growth of GNP fell from 4.2 per cent in 1978 and 3.3 per cent in 1979 to 1.2 per cent in 1980 and 1.4 per cent in 1981, to –0.4 per cent in 1982 at the bottom of the recession and to 2.6 per cent in 1983 (IMF 1986).

Marquez and McNeilly (1988) have estimated income elasticity of demand for South's exports to the industrial countries to be of the order of 1.4 to 1.9 for non-oil imports and 2.4 to 3.0 for manufactures. Reduced growth of economic activity in the North not only depressed Third World manufacturing exports, but also led to a sharp fall in commodity prices which are particularly sensitive to short-run changes in demand. According to IMF data, the prices of non-oil commodities exported by developing countries fell by 20 per cent in US dollar terms between 1980 and 1982. In the more relevant '*real*' terms (that is, deflated by the price index of manufactures exported by the industrial countries), the fall was about 17 per cent and brought commodity prices to their lowest level in the post-war period, 13 per cent below the previous nadir reached in 1975.[8] UNCTAD (1986) estimated that the cumulative loss of export earnings due to adverse changes in non-oil commodity prices in 1980–83 amounted to about $28 billion for 48 commodity-exporting developing countries. This accounted for almost one-third of the total current account deficits and nearly half the increase in indebtedness of those countries during that period.

The IMF data further indicate that although commodity prices improved in 1983 and 1984 as the world and particularly the US economy began to recover, they deteriorated again in 1985 and by the last quarter of that year, the index of real prices of non-oil commodities exported by developing countries stood at 78.1 (with 1980 = 100). Thus real non-oil commodities prices fell by over 20 per cent in the first half of the 1980s; compared with the high point of 1977, the fall was more than 40 per cent.

In addition to the demand shock and the commodity price shock, the developing countries at the beginning of this decade were also subject to an enormous interest rate shock. Federal Reserve Chairman Volcker's new monetary policy for the US, based on the quantitative targeting of monetary aggregates, led to an unprecedented rise in interest rates. The real interest rates, measured as the London Interbank Offer Rate (LIBOR) on three-month US dollar deposits less the rate of change of GDP deflator in the US, increased from an average of only 0.5 per cent during 1974–78 to more than 7 per cent in 1981, 1982 and 5 per cent in 1983. If real interest rates are defined more appropriately in terms of the difference between LIBOR and the rate of change of export prices of non-oil developing countries, the recorded increase in these rates was astounding. Reisen (1985) shows that the average real interest rate, so defined, on developing country floating rate debt increased from –11.8 per cent in 1977 to 15.9 per cent in 1983. Real interest rates on the external debt of developing countries continued to remain at a high level for most of the 1980s.

The three factors (1), (2) and (3) above (reduced rate of growth of demand for Third World exports, adverse movements in terms of trade and increased real interest rates) played havoc with the balance of payments situation of non-oil developing countries. Their combined current account deficit reached $174 billion in 1980, was $95 billion in 1981 and $73 billion in 1982. Even the latter figures are almost twice as high as the average annual level during 1978–79.

Cline (1984) has provided some rough and illustrative estimates of the impact of external shocks on the balance of payments position of the non-oil developing countries in 1981 and 1982. These are given below.

	Effect
Oil price increase in excess of US inflation, 1981–82	$119 billion
Terms of trade loss, 1981–82	$ 79 billion
Real interest in excess of 1961–80 average, 1981–82	$ 41 billion
Export volume loss caused by world recession, 1981–82	$ 21 billion
TOTAL	$250 billion

The total impact is far more than the deterioration in the current accounts of the non-oil developing countries during these years, implying that they had in fact undergone considerable domestic adjustment to the external shocks. For a slightly different period, the IMF Annual Report for 1983 reached a very similar conclusion on the effects of the external shocks:

> For the oil importing developing countries, *the entire deterioration of the combined current account balance from 1978 to 1981 can be ascribed essentially to these three adverse factors.* Indeed, the deterioration of their oil trade balance and their non-oil terms of trade together with the large excess of the rise in their external payments of interest over the increase in interest earnings on their reserves and other financial assets abroad, amounted to nearly $80 billion over these three years, against a cumulative increase of only $53 billion in their total current account deficit.[9]

Another extremely important shock to the foreign exchange and the balance of payments position of the developing countries, which is not often given adequate recognition in mainstream accounts, is that arising from a sharp reduction of capital flows to the developing countries during the 1980s. According to the UN (1986) estimates for 88 developing countries, there was a net resource transfer of $40 billion dollars per annum during the period 1978 to 1980.[10] However, in 1982, the year of the Mexican debt crisis, the net resource flows to developing countries fell to a mere $7.1 billion. In 1984 and in subsequent years there was a negative net transfer (that is, resources flowed from the developing to the developed countries rather than vice versa). The position was particularly serious in Africa and Latin America, the two continents which suffered most during the world economic slowdown in the 1980s, as the figures below show.[11]

	1977–78	1984–85
	(in billion US dollars per year)	
Africa	+8.6	−5.4
Latin America	+4.9	−39.0

In 1984–85, Latin American countries alone transferred annually $40 billion to rich countries. The corresponding negative transfer from the much poorer African countries was more than $5 billion in 1984–85, compared with the positive net transfer of more than $8 billion annually to these countries during 1977–78. The adverse implications of these changes in net resource flows to the foreign exchange-constrained developing countries in the 1980s cannot be exaggerated (see further below).

The Foreign Exchange Constraint and Economic Development

It is important to emphasize that the deterioration in the balance of payments position of the developing countries had far-reaching consequences for all spheres of the economy, real as well as financial. The effect on industrial production was direct and for many countries often immediate. The external payments' constraint often became so binding that countries had to curtail not only the imports of luxuries or other consumer goods, but also essential imports required for maintaining existing levels of domestic production. As the necessary complementary inputs in the form of industrial raw materials, spare parts, etc, could no longer be imported into countries like Tanzania, Mexico or Brazil, the level of industrial capacity utilization became very low so that industrial production declined sharply in the 1980s. Khan and Knight (1988) report that over the period 1982 to 1986 the volume of imports into the 15 most heavily indebted developing countries *fell* at an average rate of nearly 10 per cent; in the first two years of the debt crisis, 1982 to 1983, the decline in the volume of imports averaged about 19 per cent per year. The two authors suggest that though less pronounced, a similar pattern was evident in most other developing countries.[12] To illustrate, the dollar value of Mexico's imports fell almost 40 per cent in 1982 and 70 per cent from the first quarter of 1982 to first quarter of 1983. The fall in the dollar value of Brazil's imports was 12 per cent and 23 per cent in the corresponding periods, on top of an earlier fall in 1982 (World Bank 1984).

Agricultural production was affected both directly by the foreign exchange constraint and indirectly by reduced industrial production. Reduced imports, lower domestic production of fertilizers and other agricultural inputs, together with lower oil imports, hampered agricultural production directly. Indirectly, there was an unfavourable effect on production because of lower availability of so-called incentive goods for farmers (soaps, bicycles, etc).

Import compression not only threatened agricultural and industrial production but paradoxically it also reduced exports. The reason for this is not far to seek. Raw cotton may, for example, be produced in the Tanzanian hinterland, but an acute shortage of foreign exchange may mean that it cannot be processed (due to the lack of spare parts for operating the ginning mills) or transported to the port of Dar es Salaam for export abroad (because of the shortage of fuel etc for transportation). From their study of this phenomenon, based on a sample of 34 developing countries, Khan and Knight (1988) concluded that:

Broadly speaking, an exogenous real exchange rate shock that gives rise to a 10 per cent reduction in the volume of imports would, other things being equal,

lower the volume of exports in our model by about 2 percentage points in the
short run, and by over 5 percentage points in the long run. The fall in exports
would in turn reduce the volume of imports further.

Finally it is important to note that these disequilibria in the real economy
in turn generated inflation and disequilibrium in government finances. Since
in many developing countries, sales and excise taxes on industrial production,
as well as import duties, are a major source of government revenue, the
balance of payments constraint was both directly and indirectly responsible
for enormous increases in budget deficits or public sector borrowing requirements which these countries experienced. Again taking the Tanzanian example, it was estimated in the early 1980s that if industry were operating at a
normal level of capacity utilization instead of its then low level, sales and
excise tax revenues would have doubled, which would not only have eliminated the current fiscal deficit, but also made a sizeable contribution to the
capital account (see JASPA/ILO 1982).[13] Similarly Sachs (1987) has rightly
reminded us that for many heavily indebted countries, the balance of payments
crisis soon translated itself into an acute fiscal crisis, with serious consequences for economic, social and political stability, as well as for investment
and future growth (this point is developed further below).

THE CRISIS AND THE DIFFERENTIAL ECONOMIC
PERFORMANCE IN DEVELOPING COUNTRIES

It has been suggested above that world economic forces were wholly responsible for the serious deterioration in the balance of payments position of
non-oil developing countries. This in turn led to 'external strangulation' or
import compression, with extremely deleterious consequences for industrial
and economic development as well as for price stability and fiscal balance.
Apart from the enormous task of recovering from the economic disruption
caused by these huge external shocks[14] in the early 1980s, it is important to
note that for the developing countries many of the same adverse external
factors continued to operate throughout the decade. This was despite the fact
that since the trough of 1982 the OECD economies enjoyed a long period of
sustained expansion, albeit at a slower rate than during the Golden Age.
Commodity prices, which should normally have responded positively and
quickly to higher economic growth in the North, generally remained low for
most of the 1980s. Singh and Tabatabai (1990) note that the US dollar prices
of fruit and tropical beverages in 1988 were more than 30 per cent, and of
vegetable oils and oil seeds nearly 20 per cent, below their average prices in
1980. Moreover the 'real' prices[15] of non-fuel primary commodities exported
by the developing countries fell by 17 per cent between 1980 and 1982;

following the very fast growth of the US economy in 1983 and 1984, real commodity prices recovered somewhat, but by 1987 they were more than one-third below their 1980 level (and nearly 50 per cent below their previous peak reached in 1977). Similarly, despite some decline from the high point of the early 1980s, real interest rates on developing countries' external debt remained at a high level throughout the decade. Neither was there any significant improvement in the situation with respect to capital supply and external capital flows during the course of the decade.

Nevertheless, as noted earlier, notwithstanding the world economic crisis, South and East Asian countries continued to prosper and register relatively satisfactory economic development in the 1980s, whereas the Latin American and sub-Saharan African countries suffered retrogression or decline. How is this differential economic performance in the different regions of the South to be explained?[16]

The Comparative Performance of Asian and Latin American Economies

In a comparison of ten South and East Asian and nine Latin American countries, Singh (1986) found that over the period 1980 to 1985, only two countries in the former group had a growth rate of GDP of less than 5 per cent per annum (Philippines 2.3 per cent and Pakistan 4.4 per cent). In sharp contrast, *none* of the Latin American countries registered a corresponding GDP growth of more than 2 per cent per annum. Five of the nine Latin American countries (Argentina, Peru, Chile, Bolivia and Venezuela) actually recorded a fall in the level of the GDP (at constant prices) between 1980 and 1985. Similarly the inflation record of almost every Asian country in the first half of the 1980s was much better than that of every Latin American economy except Venezuela. Singh (1986) noted that this continental uniformity in economic performance is remarkable in view of the wide inter-country differences in economic structure, economic policy and even in the basic economic system. This is particularly true in Asia where countries like China, India and the Republic of Korea not only have different economic systems, but the two market economy countries (India and the Republic of Korea) have traditionally followed very different economic strategies.

The reasons for this differential economic performance of Asian and Latin American countries in the post-1979 world economic slowdown have been the subject of considerable controversy. (See Balassa 1984, Sachs 1985, Maddison 1985, Singh 1985, and Hughes and Singh 1988.) In the present context, treatment of this question will necessarily be brief.

A priori, there are three main factors which may help to explain the superior economic record of the Asian countries relative to those in Latin

America: (i) differences in economic structure; (ii) differences in economic policies pursued; and (iii) differences in the size of the economic shocks experienced by the countries on the two continents. Balassa (1984) and Sachs (1985) as well as the IMF and the World Bank suggest that a very important reason for the better Asian economic performance is that these countries have more open and export-oriented economic structures compared to those in Latin America. Differences in economic and industrial structures between the Asian and Latin American economies have been examined in detail in Singh (1985) and Hughes and Singh (1988). However, this analysis produces very little evidence in support of the Balassa-Sachs openness hypothesis. The least open Asian economies like China and India have been able to cope at least as effectively with the post-1979 world economic crisis as the highly export-oriented Korean economy.[17] Similarly, among the smaller Latin American countries, the more 'open' economies such as Chile (with a ratio of exports to GDP of 24 per cent) and Venezuela (with an exports to GDP ratio of 33 per cent) have a much poorer record of GDP growth over the period 1979–84 than the less open economy of Colombia (exports to GDP ratio of 17 per cent).[18]

Hughes and Singh (1988) and Singh (1986a) argue that certain exogenous shocks emanating from the post-1979 world economic crisis had a much greater impact on the economies of the Latin American countries than on those in Asia. First, it is suggested that the rise in interest rates had a far bigger effect on Latin American countries since a larger proportion of their debt was of the floating-rate variety. Moreover, the Latin American countries were starting from much less favourable initial conditions. In the period preceding the post-1979 world crisis (during 1973 to 1979), the median debt service-to-exports ratio of the Latin American countries was more than twice as high as that of the Asian countries – 22.9 per cent compared with 10.7 per cent (Hughes and Singh 1988).

Sachs (1985) suggests that with a few exceptions the impact of the rise in interest rates on the developing economies was not particularly significant. He writes: 'At the peak the measured US real interest rate rises by about 10 percentage points and is multiplied by a debt/GDP ratio of the order of 20 per cent, producing a peak annual loss of 2 per cent of GDP and an average annual loss of about 1 per cent of GDP'. However, this is not a valid argument since, as Hughes and Singh (1988) report, the median current account deficit in the Latin American countries was only about 3 per cent of GDP in the late 1970s. The impact of the increase in interest rates (whether measured in nominal or real terms) on the current balance of these economies was therefore highly significant. The dynamic consequences (particularly in terms of capital flows) of an increase (or decrease) in the current account deficit by nearly a third for a balance of payments-constrained economy cannot be exaggerated.

Secondly, Hughes and Singh emphasize that the Latin American countries were far more subject to capital supply shocks than the Asian economies (on this point, see also the excellent detailed analysis of Fishlow 1987). To illustrate the nature of these shocks, consider again Mexico. During the oil boom years, 1977 to 1981, the Mexican economy was growing at a rate of 7–8 per cent per annum with even non-oil GDP rising at a roughly similar rate. However, despite the enormous increase in oil exports, the balance of payments position had been deteriorating. The current account deficit rose from nearly $5 billion in 1979 to almost $7 billion in 1980 and to $11.7 billion in 1981. Notwithstanding this deterioration, the international banking community was happily willing to lend Mexico ever-increasing amounts to finance the deficits. Thus from 1978 to 1981, while international bank loans to developing countries as a whole increased by 76 per cent, they rose by 146 per cent to Mexico, already a large debtor in 1978. To meet the Mexican government's increased demand for foreign loans to finance the current account deficit, the international banks accelerated their lending in 1981, albeit with an increasing shortening of the term structure of the new loans (Ros 1986). In that year the capital account of the balance of payments indicates that Mexico's net public short-term liabilities rose by $12.7 billion (compared with $6 billion in 1980 and $1.7 billion in 1979). However, in the crisis year of 1982, these capital flows were abruptly halted; the capital account shows that Mexico's net public external short-term liabilities actually *decreased* by $614 million. Brailovsky and Barker (1983) rightly note that this capital supply shock had a devastating effect on the Mexican economy.

Most of the other Latin American economies were subject to similar capital supply shocks. These emanated from what Williamson (1985) has named the 'contagion effect' whereby, following the Mexican debt crisis in 1982, voluntary private capital flows to most Latin American countries were greatly reduced if not stopped altogether. The important point is that because of the 'contagion effect', capital flows were reduced much more to the Latin American than to the Asian economies. This in turn worsened the balance of payments constraint in the former more and *more suddenly* than in the latter.

Thirdly, it is suggested that reduced world economic growth and world trade during 1980–82 had a differential impact on the normal export markets for countries in the two continents. In particular the Middle Eastern market, which was expanding most rapidly during this period, was much more significant for many of the Asian countries than for Latin America. There are two important channels by which Asian countries have benefited from the economic prosperity in the Middle East: (i) workers' remittances, and (ii) the growth of merchandise exports.

Relative to Asian countries it is argued that the combination of the above three factors made the balance of payments constraint on Latin American economies much more severe, which in turn led to greatly reduced economic growth and higher inflation. In the institutional circumstances of the heavily-debted Latin American economies, a very important consequence of the balance of payments crisis was a fiscal crisis. In addition to the reasons given above in discussing the world economic crisis, this arose from the fact that the foreign debt was consolidated to become largely the liability of the government and there therefore comprised a huge burden of interest payments on the budget. Sachs (1987) provides data to show that in Argentina and Mexico in the mid 1980s, interest payments represented nearly a third of the governments' revenues. As the government in many Latin American countries has a direct and major role in undertaking or financing industrial activity and investment, the fiscal crisis led particularly to reduced industrial and infrastructural investment. A number of WIDER studies on macroeconomic adjustment in developing countries (see Taylor 1988) have shown that, in general in the South, public investment 'crowds in' rather than 'crowds out' private sector investment. This compounds the effects of the fiscal crisis on long-term economic development.

In view of all the direct and indirect effects of the foreign exchange constraint and the balance of payments crisis, it is not surprising to observe the poor industrial and overall economic record of Latin American relative to Asian countries.

MICROECONOMIC AND SUPPLY SIDE INEFFICIENCIES AND ECONOMIC DEVELOPMENT IN THE SOUTH

As against the view developed in the preceding two sections – that the deceleration in economic growth in the South during the 1980s was overwhelmingly due to external shocks and the associated foreign exchange constraint – it has been argued that microeconomic inefficiencies, misallocation of resources and supply-side deficiencies in the developing countries themselves have all played a major role in this process. It is clearly important to provide some assessment of the influence of these factors in relation to the current economic and industrial crisis of the developing countries.

Growth of Productivity and Efficiency of Capital Utilization

Lindbeck (1984, 1986) has drawn attention to the poor record of developing countries in 'speeding up the rate of productivity growth'. He notes that: 'While output in manufacturing in developing market economies increased by 5 per cent per year during 1960 to 1981, the accompanying increase in labour input was as high at 3.7 per cent, which implies that the increase in labour productivity was only about 1.3 per cent'.[19] The figures below provide information on the growth of manufacturing output, employment and productivity for the developed market economy countries and the developing countries over the periods 1963–1973 and 1973–1983.[20]

	Output	Employment	Productivity	Output	Employment	Productivity
	1963–73; % per annum			1973–83; % per annum		
Developed Countries	5.2	1.2	4.0	2.3	–0.5	2.8
Developing Countries	7.1	4.2	2.8	5.0	4.2	0.7

Both groups of countries recorded a decline in output and productivity growth after the 1973 oil shock. However the decline in productivity growth was greater in the South than in the North, mainly because manufacturing employment declined in the North while in the South it continued to grow at much the same rate as before. Nevertheless, from the standpoint of overall economic efficiency, it should be observed that a high rate of expansion of the manufacturing labour force in the labour surplus countries of the South raises productivity in the economy as a whole, since the level of productivity in manufacturing tends in these countries to be greater than in most other sectors. Similarly the North's relatively higher rate of productivity growth does not necessarily denote greater economic efficiency. This is because there was a decline in manufacturing employment; there is evidence that this reduced labour force in manufacturing was not redeployed elsewhere, but in fact contributed to an overall increase in unemployment in the North (Glyn and Rowthorn 1990).

Turning to the productivity of capital, the UN data on incremental capital output ratios (ICOR) in the world market economies during the 1960s and 1970s indicate that in the latter decade, the ICORs rose in all market economies, developing as well as developed. In the major industrial economies, the average ICOR rose from 4.7 in 1960–70 to 7.2 in 1970–80. The corresponding figures for the developing market economies as a whole were 3.0 and 4.6, and for the Latin American and Caribbean countries 3.5 and 4.9 respectively. In general the data suggest a much smaller rise in the value of ICORs in the 1970s for most groups of developing economies compared with the advanced countries. Again, however, all this by itself need not imply a growing inefficiency in resource utilization since an important reason for the increase in the ICORs in most countries during this period was clearly the world economic crisis, with its adverse impact on the balance of payments and domestic capacity utilization. As the advanced economies were more seriously affected by the first oil crisis than the developing countries, they showed a greater rise in the average value of their ICORs. However, in the case of developing countries, it is also necessary to consider the composition effect: a rise in aggregate value of the ICOR may also reflect structural changes in the economy towards, perhaps, heavy industry or infrastructural development.

Thus more disaggregated and microeconomic data as well as an examination of productivity trends over time, particularly of capital productivity at 'normal' levels of capacity utilization, are required to establish whether or not industrial resource utilization in the developing countries was becoming progressively more inefficient before the onset of the 1980s crisis. In this context it is instructive to study Tanzania (see Table 4.3), a country which the international financial institutions have often put forward as an example of unsuccessful industrial development because of the heavy involvement of the government in its economy and its socialist orientation. The table provides summary indicators of Tanzania's long-term industrial performance in the pre-crisis period 1971–72 to 1976–78. Bienefeld (1982) rightly assesses this record in the following favourable terms:

> In short the aggregate statistics present a picture of a healthy and positive *long-term* trend where substantial industrial growth had been achieved with an almost constant capital/labour ratio, and a falling real product wage (labour cost per worker deflated by implicit GDP wage deflator for manufacturing), together with a declining share of labour costs in value added. For a situation where labour absorption is itself an important objective, such a combination has much to recommend it and is in no sense necessarily inferior to a strategy which increases

Table 4.3　Summary of trends in Tanzanian manufacturing*

		1970–72	1976–78	Ratio 1976–78 1970–72
1.	Value added in constant (1966) prices (Shs m)	536.9	874.3	1.63
2.	Employment (000)	51,560.0	84,819.0	1.65
3.	Capital (Shs m) Constant (1966) prices	1,049.3	1,833.0	1.75
4.	Capital-Output ratio (3/1)	1.95	2.10	1.08
5.	Capital-Labour ratio	20.35	21.61	1.06
6.	Output per worker (2/1)	10,413.0	10,308.0	0.99
7.	Labour costs as share of value added (%)	41.3	34.3	0.83
8.	Real product wage (Shs per worker)	4,065.3	3,579.0	0.88
9.	Actual real rate of return on capital (%)	21.1	21.0	1.00

Note:　* Firms employing 10 or more workers.
Source:　Bienefeld (1982).

output per worker faster, but at the cost of higher wage costs.... At the macroeconomic level the role played by industry has been dynamic. It has helped to raise productivity in the economy as a whole, has produced substantial amounts of investible surplus, and has developed skills in Tanzanian workers and managers.

Similarly in a detailed disaggregated long-term study of Mexican industry in the period 1960 to 1979, Brailovsky (1981) has reported successful learning by doing and markedly improved trade balance coefficients over time for many Mexican industries, particularly the capital goods industries.

Allocation of Resources

In his comparison of East Asian and Latin American economic performances in the 1980s, Sachs (1985) has argued:

Latin American and Asian borrowers have differed not only in the amounts borrowed, but also in the uses to which the loans were applied. Simply put, the Latin American countries did not use the foreign borrowing to develop a resource base in tradable goods, especially exports, adequate for future debt servicing.

In relation to this kind of charge of resource misallocation in the Latin American and other developing countries, a number of observations are in order. These are briefly stated below.

First, during the middle 1970s, when the Latin American and other newly industrialized countries (NICs) contracted their enormous debts, they were no more than following market signals which were particularly favourable. Real interest rates were negative or very low. Secondly, as Fishlow's (1987) analysis of consumption functions indicates, the marginal propensity to save out of external borrowing was on the whole the same as, or greater than, domestic income. Fishlow (1987) notes: 'At the margin, therefore, there was an expected substitution for domestic saving. But there seems to be no difference in this respect between Indonesia and Korea, on the one hand, and Brazil and Mexico, on the other.'

Third, there was a marked increase in the rate of investment in the developing countries during the 1970s. Gross domestic investment as a proportion of GDP in these countries rose from 23.6 per cent in 1973 to 26.6 per cent in 1980. Moreover, this increase in investment was not just confined to the Asian countries, but was widespread in the South. World Bank (1988) data indicate that for the group of heavily indebted countries, the comparable increase in investment was from 21.8 per cent in 1973 to 25.2 per cent in 1980. For the sub-Saharan African countries the corresponding figures were 18.9 per cent and 20.4 per cent respectively.

Fourth, as far as the allocation of investment resources is concerned, it was not just Mexico or Brazil but also South Korea which used foreign borrowing in the 1970s to launch an ambitious programme of import substitution and development of heavy industries. Park (1986) observes with respect to South Korea: 'A massive investment programme in these industries financed largely by foreign loans and central bank credit was put in effect in 1973 and pursued vigorously until 1979. To the dismay of policy makers who had conceived this industrial restructuring, the development strategy ran into a host of financing, engineering, quality and market difficulties.'[21]

Fifth, although during the 1970s the Third World debt expanded very fast, the rate of growth of manufactured exports from the South was faster than the growth of debt. The developing countries' exports of manufactures increased at a much higher rate in the 1970s than in the 1960s; in the 1970s the growth rate of these exports was 12 per cent per annum (in constant 1978 prices) compared to 8.5 per cent for total world trade in manufactures. In relation to the relative performance of Asian and Latin American countries, it is interesting to observe that Brazil's rate of growth of manufactured exports (in value terms) during the 1970s was much the same as that of South Korea, while Mexico and Argentina's was significantly higher than that of India (UNIDO, 1984, Table VII.4). Overall, in relation to the record of the NICs in the 1970s, the Yugoslav economist Avramovic (see Singh 1984) rightly observed: '... the newly industrialising borrowing countries have proven that they can absorb modern technology, organize efficient production, penetrate the international market at an extraordinary speed, manage their economies in a satisfactory manner with a few exceptions ...'.[22]

All these factors taken together strongly suggest that it was the extraordinary increase in interest rates which took place after 1979 and the other exogenous shocks discussed earlier which have been directly responsible for the economic and industrial crisis in the developing countries, rather than their intrinsic supply side deficiencies in utilizing and allocating their resources.[23] It is important to stress, however, that although inefficient resource utilization in the 1970s was not in general the cause of the Third World's industrial setbacks in the 1980s, *more efficient* resource utilization will nevertheless undoubtedly be beneficial in the future. Indeed, as we shall see below, it will be a *sine qua non* for getting out of the crisis.

ECONOMIC POLICY IN THE SOUTH: THE ORTHODOX PERSPECTIVE

As a consequence of the balance of payments difficulties and acute foreign exchange constraints faced by the developing countries in the 1980s, a very large number of them have had to go to the IMF and the World Bank for balance of payments support and for adjustment assistance. These two international financial institutions[24] have imposed increasingly severe and detailed conditions with respect to the economic and industrial policy of developing countries seeking such assistance. Avramovic (1988) sums up the current situation as consisting of four layers of conditionality:

1. Demand conditionality pioneered by the IMF through its monetary approach to the balance of payments. This focuses on cutting spending, primarily that of government, currency devaluation, raising interest rates and trade liberalization. There are now also elements of supply conditionality, mainly in eliminating price controls.
2. Supply conditionality, pioneered by the World Bank, originally focused on project (or micro) formulation and implementation, and dealt with pricing of products and services to be sold by the project and its management. This was then extended to cover sectors and now, with 'structural adjustment lending', to the entire economy. The centres of attention are the investment programme system of incentives, pricing, financial liberalization and trade liberalization.
3. 'Growth' conditionality, in application during the last year or so, has focused on giving a free hand and incentives to the private sector of the economy, including 'privatization' of government-owned enterprises as much as possible, rationalization of the rest, promotion of foreign direct investment and, again, trade liberalization.
4. Cumulative total of (1), (2) and (3), called 'cross-conditionality', where lending decisions of each agency depend on the borrower having met the loan conditions of some other agency. This is now in increasing use, and it involves private as well as official lenders. The breakdown in arrangements between a borrowing country and any one of these agencies – in particular the IMF and the World Bank – can have a 'domino effect' in relation to all other agencies. The situation is still fluid: the number of instances of 'cross-conditionality' is increasing, but it is not yet clear how firmly committed to coordinated action individual lenders feel they are.

Many of these measures are highly controversial and there is a large literature on the efficacy and validity of specific parts of such programmes, including currency devaluations, rise in real interest rates, and monetary and fiscal targets.[25] However, in the context of the present chapter, this conditionality also reveals a particular approach to long-term economic policy. Central to this perspective are two elements:

1. an increase in the role of free markets and private enterprise as far as possible and a diminution in that of the state. Hence measures such as privatization, deregulation, financial liberalization, changes in taxation and other incentive systems.
2. a closer integration with the world economy. Hence the emphasis on export promotion, import liberalization, bringing domestic prices in line with the world market prices through changes in the exchange rate and promotion of foreign investment.

Denying any philosophical or ideological proclivities, the IMF and the World Bank, as well as many mainstream economists, argue that they favour such a policy programme on the basis of its empirical validity and its proven record in promoting fast and 'efficient' economic growth. Thus De La Rosiere (the former Managing Director of the IMF): 'Advocacy of these policies is not a matter of theology. It is instead grounded in the lessons of actual country experience.'[26] Similarly, Balassa et al (1986) suggest: 'The essential factor that gave impetus ... to the severity of the economic and social crisis of the 1980s was the pervasive and rapidly expanding role of the state in most of Latin America'.[27] The contrasting success of the East Asian NICs plays an essential role in the advocacy of orthodox policy prescriptions; this success is ascribed to the ability of these countries in 'getting the prices right' and to their closer integration with the world economy.

However, both the theoretical arguments and the empirical evidence bearing on these issues are far more complex. Significantly, even the East Asian experience does not in fact lend much support to IMF/World Bank views on how successful economic development can best be achieved. Sachs (1987) presents an instructive fable which is worth repeating at some length:[28]

> Let us begin with a country example. Country 'X' pegged its currency to the dollar in 1950, and kept the nominal parity absolutely fixed for more than 20 years. During the first 15 years of this period (until 1964), foreign exchange was strictly rationed by a government agency, and the currency was always overvalued. Purchasing power parity calculations using home and US consumer price indices show a 60 per cent real appreciation in the 20-year period. A Foreign Exchange and Foreign Trade Control Law of 1949 required that exporters remit all earnings to the government within ten days, making the government the only legal source of foreign exchange, a privilege jealously guarded by the bureaucrats in charge of foreign exchange rationing. No explicit rules governed the distribution of foreign exchange. Bureaucrats allocated foreign exchange to favoured sectors and clearly gave attention to particular firms that they were interested in nurturing. Government bureaucrats often retired to those firms at the end of their official careers. Rationing was so tight that private individuals were not allowed any foreign exchange for tourism abroad between 1950 and 1964.

Domestic capital markets were highly regulated and completely shut off from world capital markets. The government was the only sector with access to international borrowing and lending . Foreign direct investment was heavily circumscribed, with majority ownership by foreign firms both legally and administratively barred. During the early to mid-1950s, about a third of external funds for industrial investment originated in loans from government financial institutions, at preferential rates that varied across firms and industries. These state financial institutions remained an important source of cheap financing until the 1960s.

The country in question, as will be familiar to many, is Japan. But the description sounds like many countries in Latin America, complete with overvalued exchange rates, foreign exchange rationing, restrictions on foreign direct investment, government allocation of credit, and so on. Moreover, this policy framework was in place for much of the 'rapid growth period' in Japan (conventionally dated as 1955–73), which may arguably be the most remarkable two decades of a country's economic development in world history. I begin with this example to urge on the reader a humble and inductive state of mind regarding growth-oriented adjustment. The policies of 'outward orientation' in Japan, and in East Asia generally, have not been modelled on a free-market approach as is frequently asserted.

As for the East Asian NICs, there is a large body of evidence which shows that in countries like Taiwan and South Korea, the state has played a large and highly interventionist role. In relation to South Korea, Amsden (1990) draws attention *inter alia* to the following crucial aspects of the government's 'supply side' policies:

1.   the use of long-term credit at negative real interest rates to foster particular industries;
2.   the 'heavy' subsidization and the 'coercion' of exports;
3.   the strict control over multinational investment and foreign equity ownership of Korean industry;
4.   a highly active state technology policy.

With respect to Taiwan, Sachs (1987) points out that it is more heavily dependent on state-owned industry than probably any country in Latin America, with the possible exception of Venezuela. During 1978 to 1980, state-owned industry accounted for nearly a third (32 per cent) of domestic capital formation in Taiwan, compared with 19.6 per cent in Argentina, 22.8 per cent in Brazil and 29.4 per cent in Mexico.

State-Owned Enterprise

Turning from the general role of the state in promoting and regulating economic development to the specific case of state-owned enterprises, the IMF/World Bank proposals favouring the privatization of such industrial and commercial enterprises are not based on systematic empirical evidence.

It is often claimed by World Bank publications[29] that the public-enterprise sector in developing countries is over-extended and that its performance has been poor. However Kirkpatrick's (1986) recent survey of the subject comes to the conclusion that there is no evidence to support the view that intra-country differences in overall economic growth can be explained by differences in the size of the public sector. More significantly, Kirkpatrick's careful consideration of the evidence on productivity performance of state-owned enterprises in a number of different developing countries suggests that 'an unqualified assumption that public enterprise performance is "unsatisfactory" would be "injudicious" '.

Similarly in relation to the sub-Saharan African countries, Green (1985) notes: 'on almost any criteria ... their [the public-sector enterprises] efficiency of performance varies widely (wildly indeed) among and within countries; almost no generalizations are valid in that respect'. He points out that in Tanzania from the middle to late 1970s the large-scale parastatal manufacturing enterprises had a higher capacity utilization ratio and higher ratios of profits to output than the large private enterprises. He further reports that, in 1983, analysis of several sub-sectors of manufacturing showed substantially higher ratios of average output value to foreign exchange for public than for private enterprises.

With respect to state-owned enterprises in the East Asian NICs, Sachs (1987) concludes as follows: 'The Asian experience does suggest however that successful development might be helped as much by raising the quality of public sector management as by privatizing public enterprises or by liberalizing markets'.[30]

Import Liberalization and Export Promotion

We next consider the IMF/World Bank policy measures with respect to closer integration with the world economy. In addition to the promotion of foreign private investment, these proposals involve both import liberalization and export promotion. Import liberalization is supposed to make the domestic economy much more efficient as well as to promote exports. However, both common sense and economic theory tell us that while competition can be a spur to efficiency, it can also kill domestic industry. If domestic industry is in a weak state because of inadequate investment (as in many developing countries today on account of their acute foreign exchange constraints), precipitate import liberalization is likely to lead to deindustrialization. Moreover, in the short to medium term, such liberalization may also worsen the balance of payments, thus defeating the objectives of a stabilization programme.[31] Balassa *et al* (1986) have proposed that the Latin American economies should adopt a flat rate tariff of 10 to 20 per cent over a five-year period. Such a draconian programme of import liberalization was never adopted by Taiwan, South Korea or Japan in the course of their highly successful industrialization. Evidence suggests that in these countries import liberalization was only implemented after successful export promotion had been achieved; furthermore, it was closely tailored to the strength of domestic industry.[32]

Advocacy of export promotion for the severely foreign exchange-constrained economies of the South may appear non-controversial There are however two issues which need further reflection: firstly, the method of promoting exports; and, secondly, the alternative of efficient import substitution. The World Bank puts primary emphasis on changes in the exchange rates as the main instrument for promoting exports. However, leaving aside the question of the efficacy of a devaluation for this purpose in normal times,[33] for the developing countries in the midst of an economic crisis, such a blunt weapon has the enormous disadvantage of being likely to conflict with the requirements of stabilization of the economy. For example, stabilization may need a confidence-building measure of a stable exchange rate rather than a fall in the exchange rate which is inflationary. Export promotion in these circumstances may be better achieved by selective subsidies or the targeting of particular industries or firms by the government, as indeed was practised in the past by both Japan and South Korea. However, such non-market methods are not approved of by the international financial institutions.

Turning to the second point, when the world economy and world manufacturing trade are growing relatively slowly (see further below) and when there is increasing protectionism in the advanced countries in relation to Third World exports,[34] there is a fallacy of composition in the view that all developing countries, including important new entrants such as China, can achieve a sufficiently high rate of expansion of manufactured exports so as to be able to resume their long-term trend rates of overall economic growth.[35] In these circumstances, as Singer (1988) notes, 'efficient import substitution may be as good if not a better alternative for many developing countries'.

AN ALTERNATIVE POLICY FRAMEWORK FOR THE ECONOMIC DEVELOPMENT IN THE SOUTH IN THE 1990s

The Main Parameters

Although the appropriate long-term economic policy for any individual developing country will depend on its particular circumstances, a realistic policy framework for the developing countries in the 1990s must, in my view, be based on the following main parameters:

1. Despite the setback to the Southern economies in the 1980s, there is a continuing social imperative for fast long-term economic and industrial growth in the developing countries. Available empirical estimates indicate that the Third World countries need to expand at a long-term rate of about 6 to 7 per cent per annum if there is to be any reasonable chance of (i) providing employment to the South's burgeoning labour forces (increasing at an annual rate of about 3.5 per cent per annum in countries like Mexico and Brazil) and (ii) meeting the minimum 'basic needs of the people' for food, shelter, health and education over, say, a 20-year time span.[36] Based on the previously observed relationships between industrial and overall economic growth, these estimates in turn imply the required rate of industrial expansion in the South to be of the order of 8 to 9 per cent per annum. Thus it is socially necessary for the Third World's 'industrial revolution' of 1960 to 1980 to continue since in those years industrial growth of more or less the required order was indeed taking place (Singh 1984).

2. However, the fast growth of the South's economy and industry during 1960 to 1980 occurred in unusually propitious world economic circumstances. Up to 1973, the world economy enjoyed its 'golden years' (1950–73) of historically unprecedented growth of output, consumption, productivity and employment.[37] During this period, the volume of world trade in manufacturing expanded at a rate of about 10 per cent per annum. Between 1973 and 1980, although the developed countries' economic growth was nearly halved compared with their 1950 to 1973 trend rate, the developing countries were able, by and large, to maintain their economic and industrial momentum, mainly by their huge borrowings during the 1970s. This situation came to an end, as seen earlier, by the second oil price increase and the Volcker shock.

There are strong reasons to suggest that over the foreseeable future (say the next decade), the economies of the industrial countries and hence the world economy as a whole (as OECD countries account for nearly 80 per cent of the non-Communist world's GDP) will at best only be able to expand at its post-1973 long-term rate rather than that achieved during the Golden Age.[38] The slow growth of the world economy will have two significant implications for economic policy in the developing countries. First, world trade and world demand for manufactures will expand at a slower rate than they did in the pre-1973 period. Secondly, the developing countries are unlikely to be able to recoup the terms of trade losses they have suffered over the last decade;

even in the longer term, the relative commodity prices will continue to be weak.

3. As a consequence of these enormous changes in world economic conditions, a very large number of Third World countries, particularly in Latin America and Africa, are today faced not only with a short-term liquidity or balance of payments problem, but also with the necessity of long-term structural adjustment. Many countries are in fundamental structural disequilibrium in the sense that their economies are unable to generate sufficient exports to pay for their required imports at a rate of economic and industrial growth that will keep their per capita income constant, let alone one which will permit a steady rise in living standards. The correction of this disequilibrium requires far-reaching changes in the structure of national production, both agricultural and industrial.

A Strategic Perspective on Economic Policy in the 1990s

In the context of the above discussion, an alternative perspective on future economic strategy in the Third World suggests a simultaneous pursuit of two policies: (i) reducing the propensity to import without impairing domestic productive capabilities; (ii) enhancing the capacity to import through promotion of exports. As a consequence of the balance of payments crisis as seen above, imports were severely curtailed in the 1980s, particularly in the Latin American and sub-Saharan African economies. However, this import compression has led to greatly reduced domestic production. What is required for the correction of the disequilibrium is a phased reduction over time in the *import elasticity* of production – a process which would represent a major structural change in the development and functioning of these economies. Given the size of the structural disequilibrium in many of the developing countries, this efficient import substitution is at least as necessary as export promotion for future economic development.

More significantly, it has to be appreciated that in the medium to long term, if the developing countries are to reach their socially necessary rates of growth in a slow-growing world economy, they will have to rely much more on domestic rather than world demand, on their own internal technological dynamism and on economic and technical cooperation amongst themselves. This does not mean that exports should be neglected; quite the contrary, in foreign exchange-constrained economies they should be vigorously pursued through appropriate market (currency changes) or non-market (direct state assistance to particular firms or industries) methods depending on the circumstances of each particular country. Moreover, an extension of migrants' remittances can also make a significant contribution to a country's foreign exchange earnings. Nevertheless, as argued in Singh (1984), the essential point is that with slow world economic growth, if the developing countries are to resume their golden years' growth path – their industrial revolution – the main dynamic will have to come increasingly from internal factors rather than from the external economy.

Turning to the strategic question of how 'open' or how closely integrated a developing country's economy should be with the world economy, the answer cannot simply be in terms of free trade and liberalization. Even modern neoclassical theory rejects this view: in a world of imperfect competition, of learning by doing and of static and dynamic economies of scale – that is, in the real world – the optimum level of trade for all countries is not free trade.[39] As argued in Chakravarty and Singh (1988), 'openness' is a multi-dimensional concept; apart from trade, a country can be 'open' or not so open with respect to financial and capital markets, in relation to technology, in science, culture, education, and inward and outward migration. Moreover, a country can choose to be open in some directions, say trade, but not so open in others, such as foreign direct investment or financial markets. Chakravarty and Singh's analysis suggests that there is no unique optimum form or degree of openness which holds true for all countries at all times. A number of factors affect the desirable nature of openness: the world configuration, the timing, the sequence, the past history of the economy and its stage of development. There may be serious irreversible losses if the wrong kind of openness is attempted or the timing and sequence are incorrect. The significance of the world configuration in this context cannot be exaggerated.

Policy Lessons from Past Economic Development

Apart from the above general perspective on the medium- and long-term economic development in the 1990s, the developing countries must also learn from the successes and failures of their own economic history over the last three decades as well as from that of countries like Japan. Briefly, the following are some of the lessons which appear to be particularly relevant for the future.

Efficiency of public enterprises
Although it was noted earlier that privatization is neither a necessary nor a sufficient condition for improved performance, the efficiency of the state-owned industrial and commercial enterprises in many developing countries needs to be greatly enhanced if these countries are to achieve fast economic growth. Aylen (1987) provides an interesting comparison (see Table 4.4 below) between two different models of public enterprises in developing countries, both producing steel. One is the Pohange Steel Company (POSCO) in South Korea and the other is the Steel Authority of India (SAIL).

Table 4.4 *Public enterprises in developing economies: organizational models*

Market model	Bureaucratic model
Financial autonomy with emphasis on profitability.	Finance overlap with national budget. Losses accepted for social reasons.
Clear commercial and social objectives.	Confusion about objectives and political interference in decisions.
Operating independence.	Close scrutiny of input decisions (employment, investment) and attention to politically sensitive outputs (prices). Lack of concern with overall enterprise efficiency.
Potential competition from domestic rivals and imports.	Tariff barriers and import licensing to limit competition. Legal restrictions prevent market entry by potential domestic competitors.

Source: Aylen (1987).

POSCO represents the market model of organization while SAIL typifies the bureaucratic model. The contrast between the economic performance of the two companies could not be greater. POSCO is the most efficient steel producer in the world; its output of 467 tons of crude steel per man in 1986 compared with an average of 327 tons for Japan's five biggest steel producers. POSCO's efficiency advantage is passed on to its Korean customers. It charges its domestic steel consumers only $320 per ton; according to POSCO, American and Japanese car makers pay $540 and $430 respectively.[40] SAIL, by comparison, is grossly inefficient, with low productivity and high costs. Aylen suggests that 'a significant part of the overmanning at SAIL is due to a superstructure of administrators absent at POSCO'. Although cultural and other factors may explain some of the performance differences between POSCO and SAIL, the influence of organizational factors cannot be exaggerated.[41] Experience suggests that efficiency of public sector enterprises requires *inter alia* managerial autonomy, setting of clear economic targets, transparency of accountancy and, where possible, private sector competition.

Role of industry
Even in the industrially most underdeveloped Third World economies such as those of sub-Saharan Africa, in the medium to long term industry will have to play a crucial role in correcting the structural disequilibrium noted

above. In this connection, the thwarted industrialization of sub-Saharan African countries during the last decade has important lessons for the future. [42] Of course after their independence in the 1950s and early 1960s, these countries started at a much lower initial level of industrial and skill development compared with Asian and Latin American countries. The African governments were certainly right in their aim during the past two decades of attempting to change the structure of these economies by building up industry. However, although possibly appropriate for the Golden Age, the industries they established have turned out to be unsuitable for the new world economic conditions. The African economies diversified by moving from the production of mineral or agricultural commodities to the production of some manufactures. This reduced imports of consumer goods, but overall dependence on manufactured imports increased for two reasons: (i) the dependence on intermediate industrial imports did not decrease in most countries and, more importantly, (ii) capital goods imports increased both as a consequence of the industrialization process itself and of infrastructural development. As long as the world economy was expanding fast, as long as foreign aid and other capital inflows were forthcoming and, equally importantly, as long as the agricultural sector was functioning adequately, this pace of industrial and economic development was sustainable. However, once all these conditions changed simultaneously in the middle to late 1970s, the crisis was inevitable.

There were serious shortcomings in the model of economic development followed in sub-Saharan Africa during the Golden Age which were pointed out by observers at the time and which have become even more glaring in retrospect. In relation to industrial development, the most important of these were the lack of inter-sectoral linkages and, in particular, appropriate linkages with agriculture. As Gulahti and Sekhar (1981) note, African agriculture hardly uses any tools or implements manufactured locally by modern African industry. The main reason for this is that by and large African agriculture employs traditional technology which does not use modern tools; at the other extreme, there are heavily mechanized pockets which use imported tractors and other heavy agricultural machinery. A more gradual and phased mechanization of agriculture as a whole would not only help improve agricultural productivity but also aid sustainable industrial development. The local production of simpler modern agricultural tools and implements would promote small-scale industrial development which in turn would increase industrial skills and employment.

Foreign aid and private foreign capital have played a leading role in establishing industry in sub-Saharan African countries during the last two decades. Unfortunately, however, African governments have tended to accept from the donors any industrial projects which the latter were willing to provide regardless of their linkages with other industries or their suitability for the current state of the country's industrial development. In choosing industrial investment projects African countries must in future pay close and serious attention to the inter-industry and the agriculture-industry linkages and to the viability of such projects in an uncertain world economic environment.

External or internal liberalization
Turning to the experience of 'large' semi-industrial countries, there is reason to believe that at the present world conjuncture, external liberalization is for many far from being the best policy; in fact, it may be harming their economic development. Nevertheless there may be gains from internal liberalization such as the promotion of vigorous internal competition. Large countries have the advantage of being able to substitute 'domestic competition' for 'external competition' without incurring the large penalties which the latter may impose on a foreign exchange-constrained economy. In a recent paper on India's new economic strategy, Singh and Ghosh (1988) have argued that the external liberalization policy which the Indian government has embarked on in recent years with the encouragement of the World Bank carries with it a serious danger of leading to an unsustainable debt burden, economic failure and low growth of output and employment. Instead of further import liberalization and a greater integration with the world economy, Singh and Ghosh propose an alternative policy of more internal competition, greater internal technological development and a reduction in the propensity to import capital goods.

Cooperation among small countries
There are some important lessons for small countries from the experience of the last quarter century. Small countries must necessarily rely on trade and specialization in order to achieve economic development, a fact which has led to a number of schemes for establishing common markets of contiguous countries. However, these integration schemes have not been conspicuously successful to date, the main reason being the large differences in the level of development of the various countries. In a common market with internal free trade, the stronger regions or countries have a tendency to develop even further without commensurate advance in the less developed member countries (Kaldor 1978). Nevertheless, to promote industrialization, smaller developing countries must trade more with each other in a planned – rather than free trade – environment. Considering the widely varying conditions of economic and industrial development in small countries, what is needed for integration schemes to be successful is not so much the creation of a common market but the coordination of trading, industrial and indeed macroeconomic policies of the participating countries. As is shown by the

history of the European Economic Community – from its initial beginnings in the early 1950s of six countries participating in the production only of steel and coal to its present state of wide-ranging economic integration among 12 countries – such economic cooperation can only occur with political will and over time. In view of the very large possible gains from economic and technical cooperation, the small developing countries should persist with their endeavours in this direction despite all the difficulties they have experienced in the past.

SUMMARY AND CONCLUSION

This chapter has argued that the 'actual' crisis of economic development in the Third World during the last decade has been caused overwhelmingly by world market forces over which the developing countries had no control. The superior performance of the Asian countries in the 1980s relative to those in Latin America was not due to their greater openness, but because they were less subject to interest rate, demand and capital supply shocks.

It has also been suggested here that the abrupt interruption in the 1980s of the 'industrial revolution', which had been taking place in the countries of the South during the previous two decades, cannot be explained in terms of microeconomic or supply-side inefficiencies or an *ex ante* misallocation of resources. Nevertheless, the chapter argues that although inefficient resource utilization was not the cause of the crisis, more efficient allocation and employment of resources will be necessary for the Southern economies to achieve recovery.

The chapter points to serious flaws in the economic policy proposals of the international financial institutions – privatization, deregulation, liberalization and closer integration with the world economy. The World Bank, the IMF and many mainstream economists often appeal to the economic successes of the East Asian NICs to support their policy programme. The chapter suggests that a proper reading of the Japanese and East Asian experience lends scant support to the extensive liberalization policies currently being recommended by the Bretton Woods institutions.

An alternative perspective on economic strategy for the developing countries is set out for the 1990s. This is predicated on the following postulates: (i) there is a compelling social imperative for the Southern economies to expand at a long-run rate of 6 per cent or more per annum – the kind of rate actually achieved from 1960–80; and (ii) the world economy during the next decade will grow at its slow post-1973 trend rate rather than that which obtained during the Golden Years 1950–73. There is therefore a daunting agenda before the economic policy-makers, managers and workers in the

Third World. The chapter has outlined some of the essential elements of this agenda.

NOTES

1. General Assembly Resolution 35–36 of 5 December 1980, para 20.
2. See further Singh (1989).
3. Table 4.2, for which the source is the World Bank, provides information on a somewhat different aggregation of developing countries than Table 4.1. However this does not affect the substantive point made in the text.
4. For the views of the international financial institutions, see for example the World Bank's *World Development Reports* for 1987 and 1988, and some recent issues of the IMF's *World Economic Outlook*. See also De La Rosiere (1986). For examples of more academic and rigorous analyses within this approach, see Lindbeck (1984, 1986).
5. For reasons of space, we shall concentrate here on only the first two questions. For an analysis of the relative performance of agriculture and industry, see Singh and Tabatabai (1990).
6. Again for reasons of space, the question of the poor performance of the sub-Saharan African countries will not be discussed here. This issue is examined at length in Singh (1987, 1990).
7. For an analysis of the process of competitive deflation and of the reasons for the change in US policy, see Glyn, Hughes, Lipietz and Singh (1988).
8. See IMF (1986) supplementary note 3 on Non Fuel Primary Commodity Prices.
9. Quoted in Singh (1984).
10. The UN estimates refer to the net flow of foreign financial resources available for imports of goods and services (i.e. after payment of interest on foreign capital outstanding). The flows include both private and public capital flow, as well as direct investment and official grants.
11. The source of these figures is Cornia, Jolly and Stewart (1987). They refer to the net transfer of funds which are calculated as current account balance less interest payments.
12. The only exception to this was a group of Asian countries which were relatively little affected by the balance of payments crisis and hence not subject to import compression. See further below.
13. This is the familiar distinction between a 'cyclical' and a 'structural' budget deficit which is often made with respect to deficits in the US and other advanced countries. Unfortunately such distinctions are often ignored in relation to developing countries.
14. For estimates of the size of the shocks experienced by particular developing countries and the magnitude of the economic disruption which they suffered as a consequence, see Singh (1990). See also World Bank (1985).
15. Deflated by the prices of manufactured products exported by advanced economies.
16. As mentioned earlier, for reasons of space, the question of differential economic performance of sub-Saharan African countries will not be discussed here. For analysis of that issue, see Singh (1990 and 1987).
17. The Korean economy is certainly not open in the sense of having free trade. Despite some recent import liberalization measures, it has traditionally implemented rigorous selective import controls. See Singh (1985).
18. There is a complex relationship between 'openness' and the vulnerability of an economy to external shocks. For a further analysis, see Hughes and Singh (1988).
19. Lindbeck (1986), p. 3.
20. The source of these data is UNIDO (1984), Table III.10, last row, p. 75.
21. Quoted in Fishlow (1987). The reasons why South Korea did not subsequently succumb to the debt crisis and Brazil and Mexico did, have been discussed above.
22. Quoted in Singh (1984).

23. The question of possible errors in macroeconomic policy management (such as the role of the exchange rate, the issue of capital flight) has not been discussed here. This is a large controversial subject in its own right which will take us too far afield in relation to the central discussion of this chapter. For an analysis of these issues see, among others, Fishlow (1987), Hughes and Singh (1988), Singh (1986a), Singh (1988) and Taylor (1988). In these contributions the orthodox view that inappropriate exchange rate management and related macroeconomic policy errors in the developing countries played a major role in the economic crisis of the 1980s is confronted and seriously challenged. Instead these authors point to the extraordinary size of the adjustments required in many of these nations as a consequence of the external shocks – far greater than anything suffered by the developed countries – and to the complexities of the political economy of macroeconomic management in the affected countries.

24. In principle, the IMF is supposed to deal with short-term adjustment problems and the World Bank with long-term questions of economic development. In practice, because of cross-conditionality, because of the IMF's own structural adjustment loans and the greater cooperation between the two institutions, the distinction has been much blurred. See further, Helleiner (1988).

25. See among others Singh (1986b), Avramovic (1988), Taylor (1988) as well as The WIDER Studies on economic adjustment for 20 developing countries referred to in Taylor's book.

26. De La Rosiere (1986), p. 308. For an expression of similar views by the current managing director of the IMF, see IMF *Survey*, 10 December 1990.

27. Balassa *et al* (1986), p. 124. Quoted in Fishlow (1987).

28. Sachs (1987), pp. 295–96. As will be clear from the above discussion, I have found a great deal to disagree with in the analysis of one of Professor Sachs's earlier papers (1985). However, I am very much in agreement with the basic argument of Sachs (1987).

29. See the *World Development Reports* for 1983, 1987 and 1988. See also the *Berg Report on Sub-Saharan Africa*, World Bank (1981).

30. Sachs (1987), p. 294. Even for the UK, where Mrs Thatcher's privatization programme over the past ten years has won worldwide attention, Bishop and Kay (1988) found that on a number of different indicators, the performance of privatized enterprises during the 1980s had been no better than that of companies still under public ownership. They conclude that privatization was neither necessary nor sufficient for improvement in enterprise performance. Rather, Bishop and Kay suggest that the promotion of competition is a greater spur to enterprise efficiency than the transfer of ownership. On this issue, see also Chang and Singh (1991).

31. See also Sachs (1987).

32. See further Sachs (1987) and Lin (1985).

33. On these issues see Kaldor (1978), Fishlow (1987) and Hughes and Singh (1988).

34. See Chapter 2 of *World Development Report, 1987* on this point.

35. See Cline (1982 and 1985); Ranis (1985); Singh (1984, 1989b, 1990b).

36. For a fuller discussion of these estimates, the underlying economic analysis and the empirical methodology, see Singh (1984, 1990).

37. See Maddison (1982).

38. For a fuller discussion, see Glyn, Hughes, Lipietz and Singh (1990).

39. See, for example, Krugman (1987).

40. The source of these data on POSCO is the *Economist*, 14 May 1988.

41. The Indian government is conscious of these problems and in recent years has been taking steps to improve the efficiency of its public sector enterprises. See Isher Ahluwalia (1987).

42. The analysis of the following paragraphs is based on Singh (1987).

REFERENCES

Ahluwalia, I.J. (1987), 'The Role of Policy in Industrial Development', paper presented at the Orstom Conference on 'Economics Industrielles et Stratégies d'Industrialisation dans Le Tiers Monde', Paris.

Amsden, A.H. (1989), *Asia's Next Giant*, New York: Oxford University Press.

Avramovic, D. (1988), 'Conditionality: Facts, Theory and Policy – Contribution to the Reconstruction of the International Financial System', Helsinki: World Institute of Development Economic Research (Wider).

Aylen, J. (1987), 'Privatization in Developing Countries', *Lloyds Bank Review*, January.

Balassa, B. (1984), 'Adjustment Policies in Developing Countries: A Reassessment', *World Development*, **12**(9), September, 955–72.

Balassa, B. *et al* (1986), *Toward Renewed Economic Growth in Latin America*, Washington DC: Institute for International Economics.

Baran, P.A. (1957), *The Political Economy of Growth*, New York: Monthly Review Press.

Bienefeld, M. (1982), 'Evaluating Tanzania's Industrial Development' in Fransman (1982).

Bishop M. and Kay, J. (1988), 'The Impact of Privatization on the Performance of the U.K Public Sector', paper presented at the 15th Annual Conference of the European Association for Research in Industrial Economics (EARIE), Budapest, September.

Brailovsky, V. (1981), 'Industrialisation and Oil in Mexico: A Long-Term Perspective' in T. Barker and V. Brailovsky (eds), *Oil or Industry*? London: Academic Press.

Brailovsky, V. and Barker, T. (1983), 'La politíca económica entre 1976 y 1982 y el plan national de desarrolo industrial', paper presented at the Seminar on Mexican Economy al El Colegio de Mexico, 8–10 August.

Chakravarty, S. and Singh, A. (1988), 'The Desirable Forms of Economic Openness in the South', Helsinki: Wider.

Chang, H.J. and Singh, A. (1991), 'Public Enterprises in Developing Countries and Economic Efficiency', mimeo, February, University of Cambridge.

Cline, W.R. (1982), 'Can the East Asian Model of Development Be Generalized?', *World Development*, No 10, February.

Cline, W.R. (1984), *International Debt: Systemic Risk and Policy Response*, Washington DC: Institute for International Economics.

Cline, W.R. (1985), 'Reply', *World Development*, **13**(4), April, 547–8.

Cornia, G., Jolly, R. and Stewart, F. (eds) (1987), *Adjustment with a Human Face*, Oxford: Clarendon Press.

De La Rosiere, J. (1986), 'The Debt Situation', *Labour and Society*, September.

Fishlow A. (1987), 'Some Reflections on Comparative Latin American Economic Performance and Policy', Berkeley: University of California, Working Paper 8754.

Fransman, M. (ed.), (1982), *Industry and Accumulation in Africa*, London: Heinemann.

Fransman, M. (ed.), (1986), *Machinery and Economic Development*, London: Macmillan.

Glyn, A., Hughes, A., Lipietz, A. and Singh, A. (1990), 'The Rise and Fall of the Golden Age', in Marglin and Schor (1990).

Glyn, A. and Rowthorn, R. (1990), 'The Diversity of Unemployment Experience', in Marglin and Schor (1990).

Green, R.H. (1985), 'Malaise to Recovery: An Overview', *Journal of Development Planning*, No 15.

Guhlati R. and Sekhar, K. (1981), 'Industrial Strategy for Late Starters: The Experience of Kenya, Tanzania, and Zambia', Washington DC: World Bank Staff Working Paper No 457.

Helleiner, G.K. (1988), 'Growth Orientated Adjustment Lending: A Critical Assessment of IMF/World Bank Approaches', Geneva: South Commission, Discussion Paper.

Hughes, A. and Singh, A. (1988), 'The World Economic Slowdown and the Asian and Latin American Economies: A Comparative Analysis of Economic Structure, Policy and Performance', Helsinki: Wider.

ILO (1987), *World Recession and Global Interdependence*, Geneva.

IMF (1985), *World Economic Outlook*, Washington DC.

IMF (1986), *World Economic Outlook*, Washington DC.

JASPA/ILO (1982), *Tanzania: Basic Needs in Danger*, Addis Ababa.

Kaldor, N. (1978), *Further Essays on Applied Economics*, London, Duckworth.

Khan, M.S. and Knight, M.D. (1988), 'Import Compression and Export Performance in Developing Countries', *Review of Economics and Statistics*, May.

Kirkpatrick, C.H. (1986), 'The World Bank's Views on State Owned Enterprises in Less Developed Countries: A Critical Comment', *International Review of Economics and Business*, June.

Krugman, P. (1987), 'Is Free Trade Passé?' *Journal of Economic Perspectives*, **1**(2), Fall.

Lewis, W.A. (1980), 'The Slowing Down of the Engine of Growth', *American Economic Review*, September.

Lin, C. (1985), 'Latin America and East Asia: A Comparative Development Perspective', unpublished, Washington: International Monetary Fund.

Lindbeck, A. (1984), 'The International Economic Environment and Industrialization Possibilities in Developing Countries', *Industry and Development*, No 12.

Lindbeck, A. (1986), 'Public Finance of Market Orientated Developing Countries', Stockholm University Institute for International Economic Studies Working Paper 348.

Maddison, A. (1982), *Phases of Capitalist Development*, Oxford.

Maddison, A. (1985), *Two Crises: Latin America and Asia 1929–38 and 1973–83*, Paris: OECD.

Marglin, S. and Schor, J. (ed.) (1990), *The Golden Age of Capitalism: Lessons for the 1990s*, Oxford University Press.

Marquez, J. and McNeilly, C. (1988), 'Income and Price Elasticities for Exports of Developing Countries', *Review of Economics and Statistics*.

Park, Y.C. (1986), 'Foreign Debt, Balance of Payments and Growth Prospects: The Case of the Republic of Korea, 1965–1988', *World Development*, August, **14**(8).

Raj, K.N. (1984), 'Economic Growth in India 1952–53 and 1982–83', *Economic and Political Weekly*, **19**(41), October.

Ranis, G. (1985), 'Can the East Asia Model of Development Be Generalized? A Comment', *World Development*, **13**(4), April, 543–5.

Reisen, H. (1985), *Key Prices for Adjustment Towards Less External Indebtedness*, OECD, Development Centre.

Ros, J. (1986), 'Mexico's Stabilization and Adjustment Policies (1982–85)', *Labour and Society*, September.

Sachs, J.D. (1985), 'External Debt and Macroeconomic Performance in Latin America and East Asia' in *Brooking Papers in Economic Activity*, 2.

Sachs, J.D. (1987), 'Trade and Exchange Rate Policies in Growth Oriented Adjustment Programme' in V. Corbo, M. Goldstein and M. Khan (eds), *Growth Oriented Adjustment Programme*, Washington DC: World Bank.

Singer, H.W. (1988), 'Industrialization and World Trade: Ten Years After the Brandt Report', paper prepared for the International Symposium 'The Crisis of the Global System: The World Ten Years After the Brandt Report – Crisis Management for the 90s'.

Singh, A. (1979), 'The Basic Needs Approach to Development versus the New International Economic Order', *World Development*, 7(6), June, 585–606.

Singh, A. (1984), 'The Interrupted Industrial Revolution of the Third World; Prospects and Policies for Resumption', *Industry and Development*, June.

Singh, A. (1985), *The World Economy and the Comparative Economic Performance of Large Semi-Industrial Countries*, Bangkok: ARTEP/ILO.

Singh, A. (1986a), 'The Great Continental Divide: Asian and Latin American Countries in the World Economic Crisis', *Labour and Society*, September.

Singh, A. (1986b), Tanzania and the IMF: the Analysis of Alternative Adjustment Programmes' in *Development and Change*, 17(3), July, 425–54.

Singh, A. (1986c), 'The World Economic Crisis, Stabilisation and Structural Adjustment' *Labour and Society*, 2(3).

Singh, A. (1986d), 'Crisis and Recovery in the Mexican Economy: The Role of the Capital Goods Sector', in M. Fransman (ed.), *Machinery and Economic Development*, London: Macmillan.

Singh, A. (1987), 'Exogenous Shocks and De-Industrialisation in Africa: Prospects and Strategies for Sustained Industrial Development', in RISNOC, *Africa's Economic Crisis*, New Delhi.

Singh, A. (1988), 'Employment and Output in a Semi-Industrial Economy: Modelling Alternative Economic Policy Options in Mexico' in M. Hopkins (ed.), *Employment Forecasting*, London: Pinter Publishers.

Singh, A. (1989a), 'Urbanisation, Poverty and Employment: The Large Metropolis in the Third World', Geneva: ILO Working Paper.

Singh, A. (1989b), 'Third World Competition and Deindustrialization in Advanced Countries', *Cambridge Journal of Economics*, 13(1), March, 103–20.

Singh, A. (1990a), 'The State of Industry in the Third World in the 1980s: Analytical and Policy Issues', The Helen Kellogg Institute for International Studies, Working Paper 137, University of Notre Dame.

Singh, A. (1990b), 'Southern Competition, Labour Standards and Industrial Development in the North and the South', in *Labour Standards and Development in a Global Economy*, Washington DC: US Department of Labor.

Singh, A. and Ghosh, J. (1988), 'Import Liberalization and the New Industrial Strategy: An Analysis of their Impact on Output and Employment in the Indian Economy', *Asian Employment Programme Working Papers*, New Delhi: ILO.

Singh, A. and Tabatabai, H. (1990), 'Facing the Crisis: Third World Agriculture in the 1980s', *International Labour Review*, September.

Taylor, L. (1983), 'The Crisis and Thereafter: Macro Economic Policy Problems in Mexico'. Paper prepared for a conference on Economic Problems of Common Concern to Mexico and the United States, University of California at Santa Cruz, November.

Taylor, L. (1988), *Varieties of Stabilization Experience*, Oxford: Clarendon Press.

UN (1986), *World Economic Survey*, New York.

UN (1990), *World Economic Survey*, New York.

UNCTAD (1986), *Trade and Development Report*, Geneva.

UNIDO (1979), *World Industry since 1960: Progress and Prospects*, New York.

UNIDO (1984), *Industry in a Changing World*, New York.

UNIDO (1985), 'Industrial and External Debt in Africa: A Preliminary Analysis', UNIDO/IS 536, Vienna, June.

UNIDO (1988), *The Handbook of International Statistics*, Vienna.

Wheeler, D. (1984), 'Sources of Stagnation in Sub-Saharan Africa', *World Development*, **12**(1), January, 1–24.

Williamson, J. (1985), 'Comment on Sachs (1985)' in *Brooking Papers on Economic Activity*, 2.

World Bank (1981), *Accelerated Development in Sub-Saharan Africa: An Agenda for Action* (The Berg Report), Washington DC.

World Bank (1982), *World Debt Tables*, Washington DC.

World Bank (1983), *World Development Report*, Washington DC.

World Bank (1984), *World Development Report*, Washington DC.

World Bank (1985), *World Development Report*, Washington DC.

World Bank (1986), *World Development Report*, Washington DC.

World Bank (1987), *World Development Report*, Washington DC.

World Bank (1988), *World Development Report*, Washington DC.

5. Grassroots Development in the 1990s: Resolving the Development Conundrum

Kenneth P. Jameson*

INTRODUCTION

The success of the Soviet Union in becoming a world power in less than three decades, the persistent sluggishness of the Eastern European economies during the twentieth century, the first glimmerings of decolonization in India and then its spread to every continent – these changes combined with the success of the Marshall Plan in Western Europe to set economic development at the top of the international policy agenda by the late 1940s. Harry Truman's inaugural address in January 1949 can be used to represent the understanding of development at the time, while also illustrating the contextual importance of the Cold War:

> Fourth, we must embark on a bold new program for making the benefits of our scientific advances and industrial progress available for the improvement and growth of underdeveloped areas.
> More than half the people of the world are living in conditions approaching misery. Their food is inadequate. They are victims of disease. Their economic life is primitive and stagnant. Their poverty is a handicap and a threat both to them and to more prosperous areas.
> For the first time in history, humanity possesses the knowledge and skill to relieve the suffering of these people. ... Our aim should be to help the free peoples of the world, through their own efforts, to produce more food, more clothing, more materials for housing, and more mechanical power to lighten their burdens. ...The old imperialism – exploitation for foreign profit – has no place in our plans. What we envisage is a program of development based on the concepts of democratic fair-dealing (Truman, 1949, pp. 114–115).

A retrospective on development in the 40 odd years since Truman's address would stagger under the weight of the continuing stream of social

* My thanks to Solomon Namala for his assistance and to Michael Saperstein and Nilufer Cagatay for their comments.

change, of the political and social events which development and
decolonization unleashed and, one hopes, of the amount that has been learned
about the development process and the economics of development. Adding
to this weight are the many recent studies which have surveyed these four
decades (Morawetz 1975, Hirschman 1982, Sen 1983, Lal 1983, Meier and
Seers 1984, Helleiner 1989, Meier 1987 and 1989).

Nonetheless a new student of development would have difficulty assessing
the development experience. There is some consensus that improvements in
some measures of human development have occurred: life expectancy, infant
mortality and access to education and potable water have improved. However
even these accomplishments have begun to erode during the 'lost decade', the
1980s, which saw a deterioration of development performance in Latin America,
Africa and many other areas of the world. There is also consensus that some
developing countries, primarily in East Asia, have performed well on almost
all indicators, though it is doubtful that those successes can be replicated
elsewhere (Cline 1982, Hamilton 1987). Development economists can also
claim that policy analysis has improved measurably since the rather naive
pronouncements of Harry Truman – but policy-making continues to lag and
has not improved its success rate over the 40 years (Meier 1987, p. 11).

Beyond these minimal areas of agreement, our development neophyte
would find few firm conclusions to cling to. Indeed a set of readings could
be found which would give diametrically opposed perspectives, presenting
the entire question of development as a conundrum. On the one hand are
current macroeconomic and country studies which point to continuing, re-
curring or even growing problems; on the other are analyses of grassroots
development projects at a local or perhaps regional level which show vibrant
activity and progress in dealing with the felt needs of populations.[1]

Studies of national development failure abound (for instance, Lal 1983).
One of the most influential annual development publications, the World
Bank's *World Development Report*, spends most of its pages cataloguing the
continuing and major problems in the development process; of course it then
holds out the possibility that action by international agencies can successfully confront these problems. For example the 1989 version documented
the financial turmoil which has beset most developing countries during the
1980s, and followed with a strident plea for more financial liberalization,
exactly the policies implemented during the period of turmoil (IBRD, 1989)!
Gerald Helleiner (1989) has termed such analysis 'conventional foolishness'. From this exposure our reader would certainly conclude that development since the 1950s had failed in most countries and that retrogression was
in store for the 1990s.

The second set of readings – on 'grassroots development' – would provide a very different perspective. For example, Albert O. Hirschman visited

projects in six Latin American countries and found them both intriguing and impressive:

> The wide distance separating the actual conditions of life of countless Latin Americans from what is increasingly felt as the conditions to which they have a *right* is the source of enormous tensions in that continent; at the same time, it is the mainspring of the manifold local efforts at overcoming that distance – efforts I have found inspiring to visit and absorbing to record (1984, p. 101).

Another observer of grassroots efforts, Denis Goulet, has found in them wellsprings of human development. For example, in studying the Buddhist based Sarvodaya movement in Sri Lanka (1981), he found new energies unleashed by this grassroots effort which held the promise, or at least the possibility, of moving development in a more humane direction.

There are also many specific examples of institutional innovations which have aided grassroots development endeavours. One of the most successful is the Grameen Bank of Bangladesh which has discovered mechanisms to generate and collect resources and to distribute them efficiently. The result has been to empower the poor and improve their economic well-being (Fugelsand and Chandler 1986). Numerous other efforts replicate this success.

Finally, there are many surveys of grassroots development efforts which document their contributions to the peoples of developing countries (Gran 1983, Rahman 1984, Wasserstrom 1985, Yudelman 1987, Annis and Hakim 1988). In general the claims of these studies are quite careful and are limited to the cases examined. As Annis and Hakim write: 'Yet [grassroots development] does work, sometimes. It has made a difference, for some people and some communities. It does start larger processes in motion, if not inexorably. This is a book about small victories' (1988, p. 3). The consistently positive results of grassroots development and the optimism about the development process viewed from the grassroots would certainly give our neophyte a radically different perception of development and its possibilities.

These diametrically opposed expositions of the development experience make development a conundrum, a puzzle. Surely the dynamism and success at the grassroots level should be reflected in the aggregate; there is no obvious reason for the two domains to exhibit such inconsistent performance. The existence of the puzzle raises two questions. How can we explain that development at the aggregate level has lost momentum, while at the same time evidence grows that successful grassroots development efforts continue and increase in number?[2] Secondly, and more importantly, is there any likelihood that this conundrum will be resolved in coming years, that macro and grassroots tendencies and processes will become more consistent?

The first question was addressed in the narrower realm of rural credit by Dale Adams (1988). He noted the apparent success of small-scale credit projects in developing countries, despite the apparent 'floundering' of the larger rural financial markets. His explanation for the puzzle was to argue that 'many credit project evaluations are misleading, address questions that realistically cannot be answered, and are emphasizing the wrong issues' (p. 356). He suggested that the focus of analysis shift towards financial intermediaries and the broader financial market where it would be found that preferential credit programmes overloaded financial intermediaries, lowered their functional effectiveness and resulted in their 'floundering' (pp. 365–66).

My explanation for the contrast between grassroots and macro development performance is quite different from Adams'. The second section below develops an historical argument that the process of development since the 1940s has worked systematically against the interests and livelihood of the grassroots, utilizing unequal political and economic power to siphon away the benefits of development. The grassroots were sacrificed to the ruling elite in the pursuit of better macroeconomic performance. The only notable exceptions were in public works and in education, which explains the important improvements that have been made in these areas. Development is an 'unbalanced' process (Hirschman 1958), and the unbalanced growth of the first decades was costly to the grassroots. The unbalance of the 1970s and 1980s – unbalanced decline – turned the grassroots into a sector of refuge for those pushed out of the formal economy, though it also provided room for more grassroots activity.

The second problem is whether the coming decades of development will bring a resolution of the conundrum. As a preliminary, the third section examines three competing – but optimistic – conceptions of grassroots development. The first draws upon the work of Albert Hirschman (1984) which focuses on the innovative mechanisms of cooperation that grassroots efforts engender. Hernando de Soto (1986) sees the grassroots as a fountain of potential entrepreneurial energy which must simply be freed from government constraints. And finally the Peruvian guerrilla movement, Sendero Luminoso, has another and chilling definition of grassroots development which must be taken into account.

The fourth section examines national and international changes which suggest that the divergence observed in the past will be reduced in coming decades. The resolution scenario originates in changes in the international economy and in the power of the nation-state. These should increase the role and importance of grassroots efforts, resulting in greater correspondence between the two development levels. The final section of the chapter investigates steps that could strengthen the correspondence of grassroots and macro performances. The basis that is being laid at the grassroots level could provide the launching pad for future development efforts; the knowledge, skills and techniques that are created there could create a social infrastructure and an impetus to development with positive macroeconomic effects.

For most developing countries, the 1980s were lost years in which macroeconomic instability played an important role; this level of instability is unlikely to change dramatically in the 1990s. However, this chapter's analysis suggests that continued grassroots development in the 1990s can provide a launching pad for a new development impulse, for a human development process.

The argument starts with an historical treatment, showing how the imbalances of development have been detrimental to the grassroots of developing countries.

AN HISTORICAL PERSPECTIVE ON DEVELOPMENT

Harry Truman's 1949 address signalled an awareness of the challenge of development, of the tremendous disparities in standards of living across the world, while proferring a simple solution to the problem. He wholeheartedly accepted the need for modernization and, implicitly, for social change. The address also incorporated a naive belief in the inevitability of progress, a constant sub-theme in treatments of development (Wilber and Jameson 1979). Most important from a grassroots perspective was his effort to frame development in terms of the Cold War – of a battle for the hearts and minds of humanity, a battle between US-style democracy and 'that false philosophy [which] is communism' (Truman 1949, p. 113). This battle was to be joined country by country. Thus countries became the focus of development as well as of the international struggle. In retrospect this formulation engendered three characteristics of the development experience evident since the 1950s.

The first was a dramatic change in the political structure of the world economy, also reflected in the domestic political structures of developing countries. Decolonization was the most tangible change, India leading the way, followed by the rest of Asia and the Middle East, then Africa and the Caribbean. In many cases these newly independent countries were administrative fictions created by colonial powers; nonetheless, they quickly became political and economic realities with a mandate to create a nation, even if that meant submerging longstanding ethnic or regional differences. In this they were to follow the earlier pattern of the US and the USSR.

Secondly, in virtually all cases, including even Latin America (notwithstanding its more distant colonial history), new elites were charged with governing the countries and with forcing through their modernization. Kalecki (1976) described such governments as 'intermediate regimes' dominated by the 'lower middle class', a new elite formed in opposition to the traditional elites and to foreign owners, but with little base in the 'lower class', the groups we have categorized as the grassroots. They and the governmental structures they took charge of were well-suited to the macroeconomic initiatives believed to be central to development, particularly the increase in capital formation as a component of an industrial development strategy (Sen 1983).[3]

The third characteristic grew out of the second: a disregard for or even an active antagonism towards the grassroots, the poor, the powerless, the rural, to society's marginals. The attitude was captured best by the 'social dualism' school of developmentalists who felt that the grassroots was a drag on development and that traditional society would not contribute to the development process, continuing to exist as a separate and stagnant element in the developing nation-state. As Boeke put it:

> one of the two prevailing social systems, as a matter of fact always the most advanced, will have been *imported from abroad* and have gained its existence in the new environment without being able to oust or assimilate the divergent social system that has grown up there ... (1953, p. 4).

These three characteristics established a starting point for the development process and charted its course. The issues and problems of development today have their roots in this earlier period. Most importantly for purposes of this chapter was the acceptance or even encouragement of a pattern of differential development at the macro and at the grassroots level, a pattern we see manifest in the conundrum of development noted above. The divergence between the macro and the grassroots had different characteristics in two sub-periods of the last 40 years.

Unbalanced Growth: 1950–70

During this first period of development, countries exhibited excellent performance at the macro level, while at the grassroots there was either little change or in many cases a deterioration in the level of living. Economic performance reflected political power relations.

The evidence for this period is more extensive at the macro level and paints a consistently positive picture. Morawetz (1975) carried out the most extensive study of economic performance during this period. The growth rate of GNP per capita in developing countries between 1950 and 1975 was 'faster than either the developing countries ... or the developed nations ... had grown in any comparable period before 1950 and exceeded both official goals and private expectations' (p. 12). Open unemployment was more difficult to calibrate, but he concluded that 'in most countries for which partial, unsatisfactory evidence is available, the situation at least may not have worsened' (p. 36). He was also cautiously optimistic about the effect of these changes on the countries' income distributions, stating that in 'quite a large number of countries the share of the poorest people in GNP seems to have either increased or at least remained fairly constant over time' (p. 40). In areas of basic human needs, Morawetz found that 'between 1961–65 and 1974, per capita calorie availability seems to have increased in 47 of 57 FAO countries, and it no doubt increased in China as well' (p. 45); also in the past couple of decades 'the developing countries have registered increases in life expectancy that took a century to achieve in the industrialized countries.' (p. 48). On housing 'the time series data that are available on housing indicate that in a number of countries the average number of persons per room declined between 1960 and 1970, and that some progress was also made in bringing piped water and electricity to dwellings' (p. 51). And, finally, 'the crude indexes of school attendance and literacy 'demonstrate indisputably that there have been significant increases in the quantity of education in developing countries during the past couple of decades' (p. 52)

Morawetz offered more qualifications than the quotes indicate, differentiating three categories of countries according to their growth rates and domestic economic policies; nonetheless his overall conclusion was that the accomplishments of the 25 years of development after 1950 were 'impressive' (p. 68).

Sen (1983) noted that development economics had concentrated on four steps to accelerate development: industrialization, rapid capital accumulation, mobilization of underemployed manpower, and planning by an economically active state. This understanding combined with the new intermediate regimes of the 1950s and 1960s to generate impressive macro development performances.

These regimes did not depend on grassroots support and therefore generally placed much less importance on the welfare of the citizenry at the grassroots level, especially since macroeconomic performance was quite good. And the grassroots and poor were not organized politically to influence policy. Observers of development first pointed out that the excellent macro performance was often not reflected at the grassroots level; this became the basis for calls for 'growth with equity' policies towards development (Weaver and Jameson 1981). At the extreme there were many cases of the poor and the powerless being harmed by development. In the words of Peter Berger (1974), they were victims of modernizing processes and they suffered on a 'pyramid of sacrifice'; for Davis (1977) they were 'victims of the miracle'. Traditional life patterns at the grassroots, most particularly in rural areas, were severely disrupted. The clearest examples were the large irrigation and hydroelectric projects which displaced thousands of rural dwellers. Denis Goulet (1989, Chapter 5) provided a case study of the many detrimental effects of dam-building in Brazil and also noted that the proposed Yangtze River dam in China would displace between 300,000 and 1,000,000 people. Recent estimates indicate that between 1979 and 1985 some 600,000 persons were displaced by World Bank-funded projects (Cernea 1988)!

While major developmental efforts were often costly to the poor, even smaller elements of the modernization effort had similar effects: the extension of the road network allowed easier access to major cities and encouraged migration flows from the countryside during these years; the extension of modern cultivation techniques with their requirements for inputs such as fertilizer forced more direct links with the modern economy, often placing grassroots producers in vulnerable positions; even efforts to expand the educational and health systems put cultural and demographic pressures on low-income or 'steady state' areas.

Successful macroeconomic performance was often in direct contrast to the grassroots experience. James Scott's (1976) treatment of peasant revolts in Southeast Asia explained how disruptions in rural systems could generate reactions and outright revolt. This was a political sub-theme of the 1950s and 1960s when regimes which had popular support, such as Mossadegh in Iran and Arbenz in Guatemala, were overthrown in the interest of the urban modernizing elites and in service to the Cold War. Even simple development projects, such as introducing new nets and motors into fishing villages, were often disruptive and sparked violent opposition (Emmerson 1977). Griffin and Ghose (1979) found not only increasing income inequality in rural Asia, but also some indication of increased absolute impoverishment in rural areas.

The result was described by de Janvry, Sadoulet and Young (1988) who surveyed land and labour in Latin America since the 1950s and concluded that the peasant sector had become 'a large refuge sector that symptomizes the developmental failures of the rest of the economy' (p. 396). The other side of peasant-sector stagnation and disruption was the centralization of population in the slums of a few major cities, a macrocephalic pattern of development with very mixed implications (Brown 1987). In projections of city size to 2025, nine of the ten largest world cities will be in developing countries.

Albert Hirschman is one of the most insightful observers of development; he long ago concluded (1958) that a viable development process must rely on 'unbalanced growth', imbalances which provide incentives towards problem-solving and which encourage creative efforts towards improvements. From a grassroots perspective, unbalanced growth stimuli abounded; however the imbalance often resulted in a drain of resources from the grassroots when younger and more educated members of communities migrated, when the savings of the grassroots were siphoned away into the modern sector, or when traditional forms of production were displaced by newly-introduced goods. The first decades of development were indeed decades of unbalanced growth: the macro economy experienced the growth side of the equation; the grassroots suffered the negative effects of the imbalance.

Unbalanced Decline: 1970–90

After the 1960s development took a different turn. The 1970s experienced unbalanced decline which accelerated during the 1980s. Some countries continued their growth process, most notably the smaller East Asian countries of Korea, Taiwan, Singapore, Hong Kong and the Asian giant, China. It is significant that the imbalance between grassroots and macro performance has historically been much less stark in these countries (Weaver and Jameson 1981). Most other countries experienced macroeconomic decline: high and rising inflation, stagnant or even negative growth in per capita income and severe balance of payments pressures. Latin America was heavily affected; per capita GDP fell from $2512 in 1980 to $2336 in 1988 (IDB 1989). GNP per capita fell even more rapidly in many African countries (IBRD 1990).

This was a period of unprecedented structural economic change, often under the pressure of structural adjustment loans from the World Bank or the IMF. The pattern of development which had begun in the early post-war years was attacked; the structures which had grown up over that time period were weakened and in some cases dismantled, always with the goal of accelerating growth and development in the long run. For example, a World Bank study of Ghana stated:

> While the stabilization program would, with adequate external assistance, provide some relief from the present crisis situation, it has been conceived as a first step in a longer run recovery program aimed over time at returning the economy to a more satisfactory growth path (IBRD 1984).

There were very few cases in which this promise of revived macroeconomic growth and development actually materialized. These became years of macroeconomic decline.

At the grassroots level, the period has been much more complex. On the one hand the micro level served as a shock absorber or 'refuge sector'. There is some evidence of a net movement back to the countryside or at least to smaller cities; and city dwellers have drawn more actively on their links with traditional communities and on their rights to land or produce from land in order to aid their economic situation in the cities (Isbell 1978, Prudencio 1986). There is strong evidence of rapid growth in the informal sector in many countries, when the modern sector contracted and forced more people to rely on less formal undertakings.[4] But evidence is growing that some of the main indicators of successful development – improvements in education, health and life expectancy – are beginning to be reversed (Sell and Kunitz 1986). In all too many cases the concern of the grassroots level, of the urban and rural poor, has become the search for mechanisms for survival since deteriorating macro performance has closed possibilities for improvement and threatened the very base of their livelihood. The case studies of responses to this threat are numerous and sobering, and they stand as a tribute to the resourcefulness and courage of the individuals involved (see Agarwal 1987, Beck 1989, Lapierre 1985, Redclift 1988).

Thus development since the 1960s has again been unbalanced: unbalanced decline, unbalanced underdevelopment.

There is one clear exception to this pattern which generates the puzzle this paper examines. Evidence on grassroots development projects continues to indicate that they are often successful in improving the lives of their participants. Of course they have often suffered from the general problems of developing countries, including the macroeconomic decline. However, evidence of continued success, even in the face of macroeconomic disruption and micro pressures, appears regularly in the case studies of continuing projects. The studies noted above provide confirming evidence.

These 40 years provide an historical context for observing grassroots development today and for assessing its potential role during the next decades. Development's initial macro success, accompanied by grassroots imbalance and decline, followed more recently by most countries' imbalance and decline at both micro and macro level, make the continued success of grassroots efforts a puzzle.

The remainder of the paper suggests that continued grassroots dynamism is likely to resolve the conundrum and potentially to provide the basis for a new era of 'development'. In making the argument we first examine three separate understandings of the 'grassroots', its activity, and its likely evolution over time. Any resolution of the conundrum in coming decades will depend upon the evolution of the world and of national economies and polities; the likely direction of such changes and their effect on the grassroots is the concern of the section on national societies. These threads are then combined to claim that the resolution of the conundrum will be through the extension of the dynamism of the grassroots to the entire economy. This will take place in the context of a new national political structure that will ensure a greater consistency of macro and grassroots performance, and in an international context moving in a different direction, more supportive of consistent macro and grassroots performance.

COMPETING CONCEPTIONS OF GRASSROOTS DEVELOPMENT

The conceptualization of the grassroots and its dynamic has evolved considerably since the late 1940s. Harry Truman (1949) treated it as having an 'economic life [that] is primitive and stagnant', reflecting the social dualism or marginalization understanding of the grassroots. By the 1970s there was a much greater appreciation of its internal dynamics, mainly from extensive work on 'the informal sector' led by the International Labor Office (ILO 1972). The concept of the informal sector still embodied a dualistic orientation. Its inadequacies stimulated detailed studies of the interactions of the informal and formal sectors, for example the 12 studies in the volume edited by Bromley (1978).

Since then research on grassroots development has become balkanized into a welter of subtopics: the role of PVOs (private voluntary organizations), the role of NGOs (non-governmental organizations), women in development, private enterprise development, micro-enterprises and development, the underground economy – and the list could go on. All of these literatures are interesting and important, though they often represent a return to a dualistic approach incapable of resolving the central puzzle of this chapter. Three other efforts to understand the grassroots and its dynamic are more useful, suggesting fruitful insights into resolving the conundrum presented by continued successful grassroots development projects in the face of macroeconomic disarray.

The first view of the grassroots – its history and developmental role – is provided in the work of Albert Hirschman. His early writing (1958) on development contrasted the 'group-focused' with the 'ego-focused' image of change: the former was represented by the traditional village which prevented any individual from progressing, the latter by our image of the lonely entrepreneur in capitalist development. He claimed that successful development and innovation corresponded to neither of these images; that it always had a cooperative element. The entrepreneur might indeed be the creative innovator; however, the effort would come to naught without 'the ability to engineer agreement among all interested parties ... the ability ... to enlist cooperation of official agencies ... the ability to bring and hold together an able staff ...' (1958, p. 17). For Hirschman the key to development was the collective effort and the linkages forged among all of the elements of social and political change. Even market-based activity was essentially collective because of its many linkages; the market-versus-planning division was not helpful. Difficulties in fostering cooperation and in making productive linkages throughout the entire economy, combined with a flawed institutional structure, could generally account for development failures. The discrepancy between macro performance and grassroots activity would be an outgrowth of just such a situation.

When he turned in the 1980s to specific studies of grassroots efforts, Hirschman again found the collective or cooperative element central to the successes he observed and documented in a book entitled *Getting Ahead Collectively* (1984). He also found an historical legacy that may play a role in resolving the development puzzle. Not only were the successful projects based on innovative modes of cooperation, but they were also often led by or incorporated persons with a long history of involvement in grassroots efforts. The projects succeeded in the traditional development task of combining underutilized resources to increase production and economic activity. Their history was sometimes marked by failures along the way and often by repression of earlier efforts; this history had only tempered and solidified the commitment of the participants and provided them with the experience and knowledge that facilitated later success. Hirschman termed this the 'principle of conservation and mutation of social energy' (1984, pp. 42–43). He implied that the bases of development have been continually established at the grassroots, despite the inconsistent performance at the aggregate level. The experience and mechanisms of cooperation have been put in place and continue to recur and succeed when conditions allow. This may well provide a mechanism whereby the puzzle of development can be resolved in coming years.

The second perspective on grassroots development originated in Peru at the Institute of Liberty and Democracy founded by Hernando de Soto (1986). Its members were even more optimistic about the developmental role of the informal sector than Hirschman, though their perspective differed fundamentally. The sector for them was a sea of entrepreneurial energy ready to be tapped for development, but blocked by the dampening role of governmental rules and bureaucratic procedures. Members of the informal sector were those who pursued legal ends but did not meet all the legal requirements for their activities. De Soto developed measures of the size of the sector, noted earlier (footnote 4), and then undertook case studies of governmental constraints on economic activity in Peru. For example, the studies found that the process of adjudicating a piece of undeveloped desert land would take on average seven years; as a result Peruvian informal-sector members resorted to land invasions.

De Soto concluded that the removal of government control would release wells of energy and entrepreneurial ability which would result in major strides towards development. This is the 'other path' to development, one with obvious appeal in a time of limited government resources and abilities and which resonates with the critiques of *dirgiste* development (Lal 1983). It clearly spoke to the same frustrations that spawned the Reagan-Thatcher programmes of the 1980s to reduce the role of government. De Soto (1988) counted 70,000 sales of his book as well as over 800 articles published about it. This popularity has been translated into a public policy programme in Peru which has been successful in modifying a number of government regulations; it also played an important role in the 1990 victory of the enigmatic Alberto Fujimori in the race for president of Peru. In his euphoric moments, de Soto (1988) saw this programme not only as a counter to Marxism and the left's popular appeal, but also a solution to the problems of underdevelopment, ranging from slow growth to international debt. Even a less euphoric understanding would see it as one possible mechanism to solve the puzzle of development which is our concern.

It is no accident that de Soto's work emanated from Peru. Most evidence suggests that the informal sector in Peru is the largest in Latin America (Feige 1990, p. 999). In addition Peru is extreme in its degree of inequality; Ahluwalia and Chenery (1974, p. 42) found that income in Peru was the most unequally distributed of the 13 countries they studied. The origins of this reality were in the overthrow of the Inca empire by the Spaniards, which created a two-tier society, Spanish at the top and Indian below. This was later reinforced by the hacienda system and then by the development of a modern industrialized state. Even the modernizing leftist military government of General Juan Velasco Alvarado (1968–75) was unable to change the situation. The large Indian population was always kept to the margin, often tied to the haciendas. When that system weakened, peasants began to move to the cities and into the informal sector. So Peru may best represent those countries whose macroeconomic successes were translated only marginally into improvements in life at the grassroots level. These conditions spawned the third approach to 'grassroots development' – Sendero Luminoso.

Sendero Luminoso, or the Shining Path, is a guerrilla movement which had its origins in the rural areas of Peru starting in the mid-1960s (Degregori 1987). By 1979 Sendero was strong enough to launch a series of offensive activities in mountainous areas; at present it is able to operate in virtually every area of the country, with guerrilla activities during the 1980s resulting in as many as 15,000 deaths (McCormick 1990). Sendero's ideological origins were in Mao's concept of the peasant-based revolution and in Peru's own Jose Carlos Mariategui. Its initial recruits were rural highland students who then took the message to rural villages and laid the base for future actions.[5] The long-run vision saw a peasant support base from which an eventual civil war could be launched, leading to the siege of the cities and the final collapse of state power (McCormick, 1990, p. 15).

So in a very real sense the goal of Sendero has been to resolve the conundrum of development by using a vanguard action to allow the 'grass-roots' to take over society. As McCormick put it:

It is not clear to what degree Sendero has been able to enjoy the willing support of the peasantry and to what degree it has been required to solicit local aid through force or the threat of sanctions. Even where the group has extracted support at the point of a gun, however, it has generally been able to depend on the peasantry's hostility toward the government and their fear of reprisals to keep the local population in check. After generations of exploitation and neglect, the Indian finds it difficult to see the central government as his savior, regardless of what abuses he may have suffered at the hands of the Shining Path (1990, pp. 20–21).

Sendero's path to grassroots development is radically different. It does not unite and organize, nor does it free up indigenous energies through micro-enterprises. It is based on a new vanguard, a political and ideological elite which is in touch with the resentments of the grassroots; it presupposes a complete reeducation of the masses as a step towards a total overthrow of the existing system. When the people – the grassroots – take power, there will be no puzzling difference between the performance of the economy at the macro level and the life experience of those at the grassroots. Revolution answers the puzzle of development quite clearly: only by a complete purging of the system from top to bottom can the lack of development at every level be changed.

These three perspectives on the grassroots are quite different, though they have one similarity. All are quite optimistic about the dynamics of the grassroots; all suggest that energizing the grassroots may indeed enable the development puzzle to be resolved.

The effectiveness of future development will be influenced by the context in which grassroots efforts take place. The necessary starting point, therefore, is an analysis of the changes in the world system and in national societies which are likely to condition grassroots efforts in coming decades. It is clear that the resolution of the development puzzle will not come from better or more successful policy at the macro level. A dominant theme of the 1980s, this has had minimal success. Grassroots advances have occurred despite the failure of World Bank- and IMF-mandated macro policies. The resolution must come from a vibrant and active grassroots movement; this is far from assured. The final section examines possible directions for grassroots activities that can increase their chances of success. Which of the three competing visions of grassroots development may finally dominate is unclear, though solutions are likely to vary from country to country. What is clear is that the only possible resolution will come in response to activity at the grassroots level.

THE WORLD SYSTEM AND NATIONAL SOCIETIES IN THE 1990s

The puzzle of development is a direct outcome both of the definition of development represented by Harry Truman's address and of the establishment of intermediate regimes in developing countries. Countries with a strong political and cultural identity and therefore with regimes that were not 'intermediate' in Kalecki's sense (for example Korea, Taiwan and China) were more able to chart a course that diminished the gap between micro and macro levels. However, those exceptions show the power of the more general process and of the world system, emphasizing the importance of world trends to future patterns of development. Of necessity any view of these tendencies must be conjectural, though there is enough clarity to the trends to make speculation anything but idle.

There are six discernible trends that will affect the influence that grassroots efforts finally exert on development and on the possibility of unifying the two realms of development.

The first is *the likely establishment of a new international regime* in virtually all aspects of economic and political relations. The Soviet Union and the United States, the hegemonic powers, have organized the world economy since the Second World War. Their leadership has been challenged during the 1980s, especially in the case of the USSR; the period the world system is now entering has been called 'after hegemony' (Keohane 1984).[6] While they will remain first among equals, neither country will be able to enforce its will on the international system because of the greater equality of power among nations. The war on Iraq and the reassertion of Soviet power in the Baltic are reactive efforts which simply reaffirm this reality. The initial phases of the effort to resolve the Middle Eastern crisis over the invasion of Kuwait provide indications that new forms of cooperation may be found that could be beneficial to development. The Cold War does indeed appear to have ended 40 years after Truman's address; it will no longer be a key to defining the stakes in developing countries.

This new era will have differential results for the direction of development. Countries which had been in the Western sphere are likely to put greater emphasis on internal equity, for there will be less external support for illegitimate regimes which oppress their people. In the newly independent socialist countries, the opposite may be the case: inequalities which had been suppressed may grow and thus the grassroots may be hampered as resources are concentrated, much in the fashion of the early years of Western development. One possible counterforce is the experience of mobilization in those countries and the success of grassroots political rebellions that precipitated the overthrow of their governments (Gunder Frank 1990). The relevant effect in both sets of countries will be to provide the grassroots much more space for action and much more control over the direction of its own fate, with greater influence on the domestic national economy.

Though the outlines of the reorganization of the world economy are as yet unclear, one certainty is *the emergence and growth of regional blocs*, with Japan and China dominating an Asian bloc, Europe and especially Germany dominating Eastern Europe and much of Africa, and the United States dominating Latin America and the Caribbean.[7] All will try to exert influence in the Middle East, but international cooperation may be the only effective mechanism to do so. Regional blocs will provide more scope for grassroots groups whose appeal can be more understandable on a regional basis than on a wider international scale. In addition competition between bloc leaders will force greater identification with the performance of the entire bloc and will thus encourage a more supportive stance by the bloc leader towards grassroots efforts.

Another trend will be *the continued weakening of the central government and of the state in developing countries*, hastened by the emergence of grassroots movements and parties in opposition to the dominant political powers. The World Bank's *World Development Report, 1990* (IBRD 1990) documented the fiscal crisis of developing country governments and their inability to confront poverty directly – in no small part a result of the very structural adjustment policies pushed by the Bank and the IMF. Peru is an extreme example in which the state has virtually stopped functioning; but there are strong similarities in most Latin American countries. In Africa tribal challenges to central governments have grown, resulting in civil war in Liberia, Somalia and Chad, in addition to viable challenges to long-term rulers in Malawi, Zambia and Ivory Coast. Tribalism has thus outlasted the arbitrary national boundaries established with the demise of colonialism. In Asia the stable pattern of submission to central government has been broken by riots and strikes in Korea, student challenges to the central government in China, and continued insurrection and coup threats in the Philippines. Ethnic Taiwanese have moved to a dominant position in Taiwan, though only after very tense political manoeuvring. General Ershad was overthrown by popular mobilization in Bangladesh; the Nehru dynasty in India cannot govern, and the populist Bhuttos in Pakistan must be reckoned with. Finally, the war against Iraq is likely to further mobilize popular challenges to Middle Eastern governments and to national boundaries imposed by colonial powers.

For the most part the central governments and intermediate regimes which have dominated national development during the entire post-war period are currently having a much more difficult time, with challenges arising from various directions. These intermediate regimes established the pattern of development and the contrast of macro and grassroots performance. Their replacement is not clear and will vary from country to country.

The Eastern European mobilization indicates that a politicized grassroots should become the dominant force in those countries, unless ethnic and regional rivalries threaten the nations' very existence. Grassroots movements in Latin America show similar political power, for example the remarkable showing of the Brazilian Workers' Party presidential candidate, Lula. In Peru's 1990 presidential election, the candidate of the ruling elite, renowned novelist Mario Vargas Llosa, was upset by the unknown Alberto Fujimori, who was able to mobilize grassroots support.

> The electoral majority was not led by those who control the media ... [but] fliers, radio messages, religious group sermons and the simple method of direct oral communication. ... [T]he emerging social movement in Peru is structurally informal, marginal, or 'chicha' as sociologists call this process of cultural, social, economic and political mixing which is occurring (Malaga 1990).

This effort was very much in the mode espoused by de Soto and his Institute, though the limits of such a programme-free electoral mobilization were soon seen when Fujimori adopted a stringent stabilization programme and removed price controls, directly contradicting his electoral promises. Poland's presidential election had many similarities; the unknown Stanislaw Tyminski, who promised to make Poles rich, upset the actual premier, Tadeusz Mazowiecki, though the grassroots political organization of Solidarity soundly defeated him in the final round.

There are many tribal and ethnic challenges to existing regimes throughout the world, challenges that were suppressed or restrained in the interests of the nation-states created after World War II. In their least desirable form they are often directed against other groups within a society, as described below:

> The frustration and despair generated by a development that no longer holds forth a credible promise of a brighter future is driving growing numbers of the poor and marginalized to embrace the security of narrow and exclusive religious dogmas and ethnic causes that encourage social cleavages and communal violence (Korten 1990, p. 1).

However, in many cases there is a strong and authentic grassroots base to the movements and the possibility that such bases will be more sensitive to resolving the tensions between grassroots and macro performance (Wiarda 1983). Grassroots movements will certainly have a greater importance in the entire political and economic structure of societies, and there will be greater scope and opportunity for grassroots development initiatives. The current momentum that democratization movements have gained, following the discrediting of military governments in many countries, can also encourage the positive elements of grassroots efforts. To the extent that democracy or at least a more open system is implemented, the space that the grassroots needs to flourish will be expanded; the challenge will be to encourage new forms of cooperation across grassroots movements.

The continued denationalization of elites of developing countries will also affect the direction of grassroots development efforts. Changes in the international financial system have facilitated capital flight and transfer of assets abroad, and as a result have lessened the identity of elites with their national economies. The estimates of capital flight from Latin American countries are staggering, often roughly comparable to the debt they owe. For example, between 1981 and 1987 dollar deposits by Latin Americans in the international banking system increased by $67 billion (Jameson 1990, p. 523). The operation of international institutions such as the World Bank, the IMF, the UN, and the regional public banks has created a new technocratic elite of economists, engineers and financial analysts with loose ties to their nations. The multinational corporations have significantly denationalized to the point that their chief operations officers are quite likely to be non-nationals. The result is a new international elite oriented to the international economy and whose income and wealth may depend much more on the international economy than on the performance of any national economy. The quality of life of the new elite is certainly better in the developed than in their own developing countries. For our purposes this trend suggests that elite opposition to grassroots demands and initiatives may lessen in particular countries, once again offering more space to the grassroots.

The ongoing restructuring of international economic activity will have a similar effect. Structural adjustment loans combined with trade liberalization will result in measurable deindustrialization of many developing countries. Steel plants, cement factories, small appliance manufacturers, automobile assembly plants – all can generally be categorized as 'inefficient' based on the market calculus. Other economic activity which had created a labour elite will also be dismantled. For example the tin miners in Bolivia dominated the politics of the country from 1952 until 1986 when the collapse of the market and the dismantling of the state mining industry put three-fourths of them out of work. These 'modern' industries will be replaced by informal activity or labour-intensive industries, often in the form of assembly plants that have become common in duty-free zones of many countries. This is one contributor to the apparent 'global feminization' of the world labour force (Standing 1989).

The result will be two-fold. First the share of the informal sector in the economically active labour force will increase. Secondly, the differentiation among workers will diminish as the labour elite, whose interests were often more closely aligned with the industrial elite than with the grassroots, becomes smaller and weaker. Both will increase the strength of the grassroots.

Finally it is likely that *uneven macro performance across countries will continue*, with growth in some and decline in others. This will now be the case in a larger sphere, for the East European countries have entered the Western system and will become part of the same trends. Their stability had been assured by the CMEA (Council on Mutual Economic Assistance), though resultant stagnation has brought its demise. In coming years they will exhibit the same divergent patterns that have appeared in other countries of the world.

One of the unknowns in the future is whether there will be more or less stability in the international economy. The demise of the socialist bloc suggests that there will be less; if it did nothing else, the CMEA was successful in stabilizing those economies, albeit at low rates of growth. Their insertion into the world economy may thus contribute to aggregate instability. One countervailing influence is that the adventure of free market economics has been less than successful on a world scale. The unmanaged financial flows of the 1970s gave rise to the uncontrollable deterioration of many economies in the 1980s. Exchange rate fluctuations allowed wildly erratic balance of payments performances and led to supranational efforts to stabilize exchange rates, such as the European Monetary System. It is likely that the operation of the international economy will be much more consciously controlled in the 1990s and beyond, and that unabashed free market liberalization will be greatly tempered by regional efforts at stability and economic control (Jameson 1990, Bergsten 1990). Since the grassroots is often used as the shock absorber and must adjust to international instability, greater stability would be beneficial to a longer-run and sustained grassroots development effort.

When all of these trends are summed, it appears that national and international conditions will prompt grassroots initiatives to move to the centre stage of development in coming decades. The basis has been laid; the alternatives that generated the distortions of development have been discredited; while the trends seem likely to be quite permissive to grassroots approaches. The result may be that the notable discrepancy between macroeconomic performance and the grassroots experience of large parts of humanity will lessen and perhaps even disappear. Thus the development puzzle which motivated the concerns of this chapter may indeed be solved.

This likelihood is not suggested with any euphoric expectations of a resurgence of progress towards some brighter future. Grassroots efforts may often be reactive and antagonistic to other societal groups who differ by region or ethnicity. Their energy and level of technical skill may often be sufficient to allow only a minimal contribution to development. Devolution of responsibility to smaller groupings may indeed result in a proliferation of 'tragedies of the commons'. It is clear that the future pattern will be different, however, and that there are certain areas in which greater grassroots activity and responsibility are likely to result in better results than those obtained before.

The challenge of development in coming decades is to accept the centrality of the grassroots and the demise of the intermediate regimes, while finding mechanisms to amplify its beneficial effects and to diminish those detrimental elements. Then the unification of macro and grassroots experience can occur in a positive and truly developmental context. The next section examines the directions which might be followed and the steps that might be taken in this regard. It ends by considering the three patterns of grassroots development and where each is likely to hold sway.

POSITIVE STEPS TOWARD RESOLVING THE CONUNDRUM

If the 1990s do indeed become the 'decade of the grassroots', there are a number of elements of development that will be profoundly altered: the meaning of development, the developmental processes, and relevant economic dimensions of development. In short, the conception of development that we traced back to the fourth point in Harry Truman's address will be largely unrecognizable in terms of the new realities detailed above. Six changes will be of most significance.

One essential starting point will be *a refinement and reformulation of our understanding of 'development'*. How development is defined affects not only the perception of ongoing processes, but also determines the policies undertaken in the name of development. The view that growth of GDP per capita is not synonymous with development is not new, having been at the centre of the debate over 'growth with equity' during the 1970s (Weaver and Jameson 1981). And the central lesson to be learned from the failed and distorted development of Eastern Europe and the Soviet Union is that the costs of placing accumulation and industrialization above the welfare of people are literally unbearable; that a strategy which focuses solely on growth is doomed to fail, leaving a heritage of environmental degradation and the suppression of human vitality.

Reflection on the dominant thrust of development thinking during the 1980s indicates that this lesson is not otiose; for the main, and often the only, concern of development policy and programming was the issue of resource allocation. Improvements in efficiency, and therefore in economic growth, was the goal of the structural adjustment efforts as well as of the trade, price and financial liberalizations that constituted development policy during the 1980s. Questions of efficiency, or of inefficiency, are certainly important to economic performance; however, their dominance reduced development to its growth dimension. This was a double error. The desperate macroeconomic failures of the 1980s were in good measure generated by the effort to reallocate resources and to close down inefficient activities. Perhaps there was some aggregate welfare improvement in the world economy – scant solace to those who saw their level of living deteriorate and their way of life disrupted. Secondly, it distracted attention from the grassroots or micro level, contributing once again to the unfortunate division of macro and grassroots development processes.

During the 1990s the meaning of development must be returned to its traditional focus: concern with the underutilized resources of poor countries and with their mobilization, rather than with policies of resource reallocation under an implicit assumption of full employment. The problem is human welfare, not optimal resource allocation.

The refinement of the problematic of development should follow the outlines suggested by Amartya K. Sen (1989). The focus must be on the welfare of individuals in a society and must be seen in terms of the expansion of their 'capabilities' for functioning and of their freedom to achieve combinations of functionings. Sen's proposals at once narrow the focus of development to the people involved, to the grassroots which are the concern of this chapter, while at the same time expanding development's meaning beyond the simple attainment of some physical measures of well-being. In part the puzzle of development may be a matter of definition, and adoption of Sen's approach can solve this element of the puzzle.[8]

With this rethinking as a point of departure, there are a number of specific processes which can ensure that development is defined by the dynamics of the grassroots rather than the trends of the macroeconomy.

One is *a conscious programme of 'scaling-up' grassroots development to the macro level* (Annis 1988) In his study of Latin America, Annis found a whole web of grassroots organizations linked to each other and to the state which were quite responsive to macro policies. Annis suggested a variety of ways in which grassroots organizations could expand their activities: by using internally or externally generated resources to provide services that are otherwise not provided; by pressuring the state to provide these services; or by co-producing such services with the state (p. 213). Given the weakening of the state noted above, these activities will be more successful during the 1990s and could result in scaling-up the type of activity and the nature of interaction that characterizes grassroots organizations. Such a scaling-up process could greatly reduce the division of the micro and the macro in developing countries. It would involve organizational structures of the social nature suggested by Albert Hirschman, but at a level higher than the village or even the region. It would draw upon the 'conservation and mutation of social energy', but would expand them in a much more permissive atmosphere. It would have the potential for dealing with the externalities that grassroots activity can generate and for incorporating them into a much more coherent development process. A key issue will be the expansion of the political base and of political organizations, for a coherent political programme -- such as that of the Workers' Party (PT) in Brazil – will be an essential component of the scaling-up.

A second process can be termed 'aggregation'. Annis and Hakim (1988), de Soto (1986), Feige (1990) and other observers have noted the rapid increase in grassroots activity. Encouraging and supporting such efforts lies at the base of de Soto's 'other path' to development. As central governments weaken and their traditional external support on Cold War grounds also shifts, further grassroots activity is likely to occur; put less positively, the informal sector is likely to expand further, and the reduction in formal sector activity will amplify this effect. Thus a natural process may be underway during the 1990s which would diminish the distinction between the macro and the grassroots, and would make the dynamism of development heavily dependent on the motor of the grassroots.

Such an aggregation effect may have benefits for participation and capability creation, but might also negatively affect the 'achievement of functionings' (Sen 1989, p. 51), lowering longevity and raising morbidity. As Annis (1988, p. 209) put it: '"small-scale" can mean merely "insignificant" ... "low cost" can mean "underfinanced" or "poor quality" ... "innovative" can mean simply "temporary" or "unsustainable"'. In addition, it is clear that this uncoordinated and individualistic behaviour could generate many negative externalities which would not be internalized by the weakened state.

De Soto does not foresee these as problems and feels that the unlocked energies of the informal sector will bring about a broad-based development. The Fujimori experience currently underway in Peru should be a bit sobering to these expectations; nonetheless, there is ample evidence of un- and under-utilized human and physical resources in developing countries, and policies to remove limits on their mobilization would certainly be beneficial in general. The question is whether they would aggregate quite as easily as de Soto believes. One determinant will be their success in the political realm; cooptation by populist leaders will always be a danger.

Either or both of these approaches would be able to benefit from two contemporary realities.

The first has to do with *a change in the relative effectiveness of different incentives in contemporary societies*. Intermediate regimes gave the lower middle classes ample incentive to operate in their own interest and in that of the nation-state. But as the limits of the nation-state have been reached, these incentives have been attenuated, and we have seen the denationalization of the existing elite. Denis Goulet (1989) has made a strong case that the entire incentive structure in 'alternative development strategy' undertakings generally differs from that in the macro economy and is currently much more effective in motivating human action. A more effective set of incentives is one reason for grassroots success, and participation at the grassroots level provides a fertile context for freeing up the creative energies of a population. Goulet suggests that authentic development will occur when the relation of the 'larger' and 'lesser' spheres is renegotiated, the incentive structure being a leverage point for the renegotiation (pp. 8–9). Our analysis indicates that this relation is in the process of redefinition as central government power wanes. The 'micro-macro linkage' desired by Goulet may occur as this process unfolds and grassroots dynamism scales up or aggregates towards the macro level .

A second favourable factor is *the change in production technology* which is occurring in the world and which may indeed shift technological dynamism towards the grassroots, towards small-scale and flexible production. Piore and Sabel's (1984) work in Italy has documented a new form of technological development – 'flexible specialization' – which they contrast with mass production. It is characterized by the production of specialized products with general resources such as skilled labour and universal programmable machines. Sabel (1986) has suggested that this change could be the basis for a new strategy and direction of industrial development. There are enough examples of such processes beginning at the grassroots level – Bologna (Italy) and Mondragon (Spain) – that the possibility of its extension in developing countries is significant. The prerequisite seems to be the establishment of a groundwork of 'social and political energy' and a strong political organization to encourage and integrate such efforts, the kinds of base that Hirschman found in his study of grassroots projects. Thus changes in technology again suggest that grassroots efforts may be able to scale-up to dominate the macro economy, given careful technical development in the context of strong political organization.

The redefinition of development, the scaling-up and aggregation processes, and the new incentive and technical realities may finally be fused together into a new development dynamism in the coming decades by the support they receive from the international network of organizations that has grown up in response to the conundrum of development and in conjunction with the grassroots efforts that have been undertaken.

The growth, maturity and experience of NGOs (Non-Governmental Organizations), PVOs (Private Voluntary Organizations) and GGOs (Grassroots Governmental Organizations)[9] can provide the crucial technical, informational and resource base for the growth of grassroots efforts. They can be part of a process of enlarging and empowering civil society in response to the weakening of central governments. Korten (1990) links this effort to a reorientation of the international resources that are provided for development activities:

> A new concept is developing within the international community of a model of international cooperation based on *mutual empowerment* in which people work together and through their governments within and across national borders to empower themselves and their institutions to make better use of available resources to meet their self-defined needs within a finite world (p. 13).

So the international, national and local networking of grassroots organizations can again encourage and support the dynamism of the grassroots movements as their importance and success increases in coming years. VanSant (1989) has pointed out the dangers to all involved in such efforts; however, the possibilities for success are great.

The final question which must be addressed is which of the three models of grassroots development will eventually prevail. This will vary from country to country; there are currently very few insurrections of the Sendero Luminoso variety, though smaller insurgencies exist in every continent and in countries from Sri Lanka to Zaire which may indeed take control of power and are quite likely to wish to obliterate all traces of former regimes. The Sendero path will be taken in countries which make no progress in dealing with the failures of development and the inequalities and injustices that have grown over time.

The Hirschman model will be most feasible in circumstances where there has been a long history of grassroots organization and mobilization, or when there are already coherent bases for identification (such as an ethnic identity) ranged against the wider society. For example, the ethnic independence movements in Yugoslavia and the rest of Central Europe are likely to provide a new development impetus for populations freed from the constraint of adapting to the needs of a national state.

Hernando de Soto's 'other path' is most likely to be attempted in situations of central government collapse and when no alternative movement, vision or organization has been created. It would tend to lead to populist regimes whose success record is, at best, mixed.

CONCLUSION

The 1990s and beyond are likely to be the time of grassroots development, where pressure from below will force a greater consistency of micro and macro processes. There is no justification at present for development euphoria such as existed in the 1950s. On the other hand there is no reason for the sense of despondency that the experience of development – or underdevelopment – in the 1980s would suggest. Forty years of development have provided a basis of knowledge, experience, techniques and of human social energy. The task is now to harness this in a positive fashion and to undertake a new push forward for human development, a push beyond the intermediate regimes and Cold War context which have dominated development until recent years.

NOTES

1. There is an unavoidable imprecision in the term 'grassroots' which is used interchangeably with 'micro', 'local', 'poor' and 'popular'. In their most general form these terms refer to the development experience of poor people and their efforts to organize to improve their welfare. For the most part these are efforts independent of central governments, though often supported by extra-national funding. In some cases they can include efforts to oppose and even overth: : · ntral governments, as in the case of Sendero Luminoso, discussed below.
2. One possibility which cannot be discounted is that the macro and grassroots patterns are incorrectly represented by the literature chosen. I disagree with this view while admitting that the claims are not indisputable.
3. There were some obvious exceptions to this pattern, most notably China whose revolution was firmly based in the lower classes and whose development direction differed dramatically as a result. Bolivia's 1952 revolution seemed to move it in the same direction, but international pressures and domestic politics soon moved it back towards the intermediate regime type.
4. The size and growth of the informal sector are a matter of some controversy simply because they are so hard to measure. Feige (1990) has summarized the evidence that places between 25 and 60 per cent of the economically active urban population of Latin American countries in the informal sector; this was in the course of proposing his 'new institutional economics' approach to the measurement problem. De Soto's (1986) estimates for Peru suggested that the informal sector accounted for 61 per cent of the hours worked and that its share of real GDP would grow from 39 to 61 per cent by 2000; those estimates have been directly challenged by Rossini and Thomas (1990).
5. Isbell's (1978) account of her experiences in a village near Ayacucho from 1967 to 1975 provides a fascinating description of the process that even she did not understand at the time.
6. There is an extensive and interesting literature on these issues which is generally unfamiliar to economists, coming under the rubric of 'international political economy'. It appears in journals more familiar to political scientists and sociologists, such as the *International Studies Quarterly* or *World Politics*.
7. Jameson (1990) has made this case with regard to the international monetary system. See Bergsten (1990) for a similar but more general treatment.
8. Sen's approach is highly theoretical but has also played a part in the UN Development Program's effort to refocus development on 'human development' (UNDP 1990).
9. GGOs are not part of the ordinary lexicon which includes NGOs and PVOs. GGOs refer to government-sponsored organizations such as the Inter-American Foundation whose resources are specifically dedicated to aiding grassroots organizations, often outside of usual government channels.

REFERENCES

Adams, Dale W. (1988), 'The Conundrum of Successful Credit Projects in Floundering Rural Financial Markets', *Economic Development and Cultural Change*, 355–67.

Agarwal, Bina (1987), 'Who Sows? Who Reaps? Women and Land Rights in India', *Journal of Peasant Studies* ,**15**, 531–81.

Ahluwalia, Montek and Chenery, Hollis (1974), 'The Economic Framework', in Hollis Chenery *et al, Redistribution with Growth,* London and New York: Oxford University Press.

Annis, Sheldon (1988), 'Can Small-Scale Development Be Large-Scale Policy?' in Sheldon Annis and Peter Hakim, *Direct to the Poor: Grassroots Development in Latin America,* Boulder and London: Lynne Rienner Publishers, 209–18.

Annis, Sheldon and Hakim, Peter (1988), *Direct to the Poor: Grassroots Development in Latin America,* Boulder and London: Lynne Rienner Publishers.

Beck, Tony (1989), 'Survival Strategies and Power Amongst the Poorest in a West Bengal Village', *IDS Bulletin* **20**(4), April, 23–33.

Berger, Peter (1974), *Pyramids of Sacrifice,* New York: Basic Books.

Bergsten, C. Fred (1990), 'A New Big Three to Manage the World Economy', *Challenge* **33**(6), November/December, 17–25.

Boeke, J.H. (1953), *Economics and Economic Policy of Dual Societies: as Exemplified by Indonesia,* New York: International Secretariat, Institute of Pacific Relations.

Bromley, Ray (1978), 'The Urban Informal Sector: Critical Perspectives', *World Development* **6**(9/10), September/October.

Brown, Lester (1987), *State of the World,* New York and London: W.W. Norton.

Cernea, Michael (1988), 'Involuntary Resettlement and Development', *Finance and Development* **25,** September, 44–46.

Cline, William (1982), 'Can the East Asian Model of Development be Generalized?', *World Development* **10**(2), 81–90.

Davis, Shelton (1977), *Victims of the Miracle: Development and the Indians of Brazil,* London and New York: Cambridge University Press.

Degregori, Carlos Iván (1987), *Sendero Luminoso,* Lima, Peru: Instituto de Estudios Peruanos.

de Janvry, Alain, Sadoulet, Elisabeth and Wilcox Young, Linda (1988), 'Land and Labour in Latin American Agriculture from the 1950s to the 1980s', *Journal of Peasant Studies* **16**, 396–424.

de Soto, Hernando (1986), *El Otro Sendero: La Revolucion Informal,* Lima: Editorial Barranco.

de Soto, Hernando (1988), 'Constraints on People: The Origins of Underground Economies and Limits to their Growth', paper presented to the Agency for International Development, Washington, DC (processed).

Emmerson, Donald (1977), 'Introducing Technology: The Need to Consider Local Culture', *International Development Review/Focus* **19**(1), June, 17–20.

Feige, E. (1990), 'Defining and Estimating Underground and Informal Economies: The New Institutional Economics Approach', *World Development* **18**(7), July, 989–1002.

Fugelsand, Andreas and Chandler, Dale (1986), *Participation as Process – What We Can Learn from the Grameen Bank. Bangladesh,* Oslo, Norway: North American Air Defense Command.

Goulet, Denis (1981), *Survival with Integrity: Sarvodaya at the Crossroads,* Colombo, Sri Lanka: Marga Institute.

Goulet, Denis (1989), *Incentives for Development: The Key to Equity,* New York: New Horizons Press.

Gran, Guy (1983), *Development by People,* New York: Praeger Publishers.

Griffin, Keith with Ghose, Ajit Kumar (1979), 'Growth and Impoverishment in the Rural Areas of Asia', *World Development*, 7(4/5), 361–84.

Gunder Frank, Andre (1990), 'Revolution in Eastern Europe: Implications for Democratic Social Movements – and Socialists?' *Third World Quarterly* 12(2), April, 36–52.

Hamilton, Clive (1987), 'Can the Rest of Asia Emulate the NICs?' *Third World Quarterly*, 4, 617–32.

Helleiner, Gerald (1989), 'Conventional Foolishness and Overall Ignorance: Current Approaches to Global Transformation and Development', *Canadian Journal of Development Studies*, 107–20.

Hirschman, Albert O. (1958), *The Strategy of Economic Development*, New Haven: Yale University Press.

Hirschman, Albert O. (1982), 'The Rise and Decline of Development Economics', in Mark Gersovitz (ed.), *The Theory and Experience of Economic Development: Essays in Honor of Sir W. Arthur Lewis*, London: George Allen and Unwin.

Hirschman, Albert O. (1984), *Getting Ahead Collectively: Grassroots Experiences in Latin America*, New York and Oxford: Pergamon Press.

IBRD (World Bank), (1984), *Ghana: Policies and Program for Adjustment*, Washington, DC: World Bank.

IBRD, *World Development Report. 1990*, (1990), New York and Oxford: Oxford University Press.

IDB (Interamerican Development Bank), (1989), *Economic and Social Progress in Latin America, 1989*, Washington, DC: IDB.

ILO (International Labor Office), (1972), *Employment, Incomes and Equality: A Strategy for Increasing Productive Employment in Kenya*, Geneva: ILO.

Isbell, Billie Jean (1978), *To Defend Ourselves: Ecology and Ritual in an Andean Village*, Austin, Texas: Institute of Latin American Studies.

Jameson, Kenneth (1990), 'Dollar Bloc Dependency in Latin America: Beyond Bretton Woods', *International Studies Quarterly*, 34(4), December, 519–41.

Kalecki, Michal (1976), 'Observations on Social and Economic Aspects of Intermediate Regimes', in *Essays on Developing Countries*, Atlantic Highlands, NJ: Humanities Press, 30–39.

Keohane, R. (1984), *After Hegemony: Cooperation and Discord in the World Political Economy*, Princeton: Princeton University Press.

Korten, David C. (1990), 'The U.S. Voluntary Sector and Global Realities: Issues for the 1990s', paper presented at University NGO Action Research Network International Conference, October.

Lal, Deepak (1983), *The Poverty of Development Economics*, London: Institute of Economic Affairs.

Lapierre, Dominique (1985), *The City of Joy*, New York: Warner Books.

McCormick, Gordon (1990), *The Shining Path and the Future of Peru*, Santa Monica, Ca: The Rand Corporation.

Malaga, Rosa (1990), 'Peru: Popular Movements Offer the Only Hope', *Latinamerica Press*, 19 July.

Meier, Gerald M. (1989), 'Do Development Economists Matter?', *IDS Bulletin*, 20(3), 17–25.

Meier, Gerald M. (ed.), (1987), *Pioneers in Development: Second Series*, New York and Oxford: Oxford University Press.

Meier, Gerald M. and Seers, Dudley (eds), (1984), *Pioneers in Development*, New York and Oxford: Oxford University Press.

Morawetz, David (1975), *Twenty Five Years of Economic Development. 1950 to 1975*, Baltimore, Johns Hopkins.
Piore, Michael and Sabel, Charles (1984), *The Second Industrial Divide*, New York: Basic Books.
Prudencio, Julio (1986), 'Crisis de Abastecimiento y Estrategias de Resistencia en Bolivia: El Caso de La Paz', manuscript.
Rahman, Anisur (ed.), (1984), *Grass-Roots Participation and Self-Reliance: Experiences in South and South East Asia*, New Delhi: Oxford and IBH Publishers.
Redclift, Michael (1988), 'Sustainability and the Market: Survival Strategies on the Bolivian Frontier', *The Journal of Development Studies*, 93–105.
Rossini, R. and Thomas, J. (1990), 'The Size of the Informal Sector in Peru: A Critical Comment on Hernando de Soto's *El Otro Sendero*', *World Development*, 8(1), January, 125–35.
Sabel, Charles (1986), 'Changing Models of Economic Efficiency and Their Implications for Third World Industrialization', in Alejandro Foxley, Michael McPherson and Guillermo O'Donnell (eds), *Development, Democracy and the Art of Trespassing: Essays in Honor of Albert O. Hirschman*, Notre Dame, Ind: University of Notre Dame Press.
Scott, James C. (1976), *The Moral Economy of the Peasant: Rebellion and Subsistence in Southeast Asia*, New Haven: Yale University Press.
Sell, Ralph R. and Kuniz, Stephen J. (1986), 'The Debt Crisis and the End of an Era in Mortality Decline', *Studies in Comparative International Development*, Winter, 3–30.
Sen, Amartya K. (1983), 'Development: Which Way Now?', *Economic Journal*, **93**, December, 745–62.
Sen, Amartya K. (1989), 'Development as Capability Expansion', in Keith Griffin and John Knight (eds), *Journal of Development Planning*, **19**, 41–58.
Standing, Guy (1989), 'Global Feminization through Flexible Labor', *World Development*, **17**(7), 1077–95.
Truman, Harry (1949), 'Inaugural Address, January 20, 1949', 112–16 in *Public Papers of the Presidents: Harry S. Truman, 1949*, Washington, DC: US Government Printing Office; 1964.
UNDP (United Nations Development Program), (1990), *Human Development Report, 1990*, New York and Oxford: Oxford University Press.
VanSant, J. (1989), 'Opportunities and Risks for Private Voluntary Organizations as Agents of LDC Policy Change', *World Development*, **17**(11), November, 1723–32.
Wasserstrom, Robert (1985), *Grassroots Development in Latin America and the Caribbean*, New York: Praeger Publishers.
Weaver, James and Jameson, Kenneth (1981), *Economic Development: Competing Paradigms*, Washington DC: University Press of America.
Wiarda, Howard (1983), 'Toward a Nonethnocentric Theory of Development: Alternative Conceptions from the Third World', *The Journal of Developing Areas*, **17**, July, 433–52.
Wilber, Charles K. and Jameson, Kenneth P. (1979), 'Paradigms of Economic Development and Beyond' in Kenneth P. Jameson and Charles K. Wilber (eds), *Directions in Economic Development*, Notre Dame: University of Notre Dame Press.
Wilber, Charles K. and Jameson, Kenneth P. (1991), *The Political Economy of Development and Underdevelopment*, 5th ed, New York: McGraw Hill.

Yudelman, Sally (1987), *Hopeful Openings: A Study of Five Women's Development Organizations in Latin America and the Caribbean*, West Hartford, Ct: Kumarian Press.

6. Suggestions for an International Development Strategy for the 1990s

Keith Griffin

The growth of the world economy in the period 1981–88 was disappointingly slow. Per capita income increased about 1.2 per cent a year, a little more than half the rate achieved in the 1970s and about a third of that reached in the 1960s. More distressing, average incomes in the developing countries (excluding China) actually fell by 1.0 per cent a year, whereas they continued to rise in the industrial countries – capitalist and socialist – albeit at a noticeably slower pace than in the previous two decades. Thus the economic distance between the developed and developing countries has widened considerably in recent years. (See Table 6.1 for growth rates of various groups of countries.)

There was marked economic and social retrogression in three regions of the world in particular. Income per head declined 6.8 per cent a year in West Asia, 4.5 per cent a year in Africa and 1.6 per cent a year in Latin America and the Caribbean. Of course within each of these three regions there was a diversity of experience, but among them they highlight the fact that declining living standards tended to be concentrated on primary-producing countries (which suffered a sharp fall in their terms of trade), on a number of countries in sub-Saharan Africa (where misguided domestic policies were aggravated by the debt trap) and more generally on the least developed countries (where severe poverty makes sustained growth difficult even in the best of times).

Elsewhere in the Third World, notably in South and East Asia, average incomes continued to rise although the rate of increase of gross domestic product was well below the 7 per cent target of the International Development Strategy for the 1980s. The newly-industrialized countries of East Asia did especially well. They were able to adjust rapidly to external shocks, to respond to changes in relative international prices, to react quickly (as in South Korea) to the adverse effects of a steep rise in real interest rates and thus were able to sustain economic expansion.

Also impressive was the economic performance of the two giants of Asia – India and China. The development strategy followed by India continued to be rather inward-oriented. Indeed its foreign trade sector relative to total output is less than half as large as China's. India, hence, was insulated from the effects of the collapse in primary commodity prices and, because of its prudent policies towards borrowing on international capital markets, it avoided the international debt crisis. Beginning in the late 1970s, China had introduced a number of major economic reforms, particularly in the rural areas, and at the same time had increased its exposure to world market forces. As a result of this reorientation of policy, the rate of growth of net material product per capita actually accelerated from previously high levels, despite the deceleration in the world economy as a whole. China's net material product per capita grew 8.0 per cent a year during the period 1981–88.

These differences in relative growth performance illustrate a significant fact; namely, the accentuated differentiation that has occurred during this decade within the Third World itself. At one extreme, China and the newly-industrializing countries of East Asia have continued to prosper while, at the other extreme, the least developed countries of sub-Saharan Africa have become further impoverished. Of course each country is different and faces a distinct and possibly unique set of opportunities and obstacles to growth, so

Table 6.1   Rates of growth, 1981–88 (per cent per annum)

	Per capita gross domestic product	Per capita income[a]
World	1.2	1.2
Developed market economies	2.1	2.5
United States	1.8	1.8
Europe	1.9	2.2
Japan	3.4	4.4
USSR and Eastern Europe[b]	2.5	–
Developing countries[c]	−0.4	−1.0
Africa	−3.2	−4.5
Latin America and the Caribbean	−1.1	−1.6
Mediterranean	1.6	1.5
South and East Asia	3.3	2.9
West Asia	−3.9	−6.8
China	8.0	7.8[d]

Notes: [a]Per capita GDP adjusted for changes in the terms of trade and net factor payments.
[b]Net material product.
[c]Excluding China.
[d]1981–87.
Source: Department of International Economic and Social Affairs of the UN Secretariat.

that it is not easy to draw lessons from the experience of a single decade. It does appear, however, that the most successful countries were those which (i) gave high priority to human development, including the creation of a well-trained and educated labour force, (ii) maintained a high rate of investment, and (iii) financed that investment largely through domestic savings without relying on foreign capital to provide the fuel for expansion. High rates of investment in human and physical capital have two advantages. First, they increase the flexibility of an economy and make it easier to adjust to unpleasant and unexpected shocks and to exploit unanticipated opportunities. Second, they increase the economy's growth potential and raise its average productivity. These two factors in combination ensure that trend rates of growth of output are high and departures from trend are modest and short-lived.

It must be said straightaway that while differentiation within the Third World has markedly increased, the problem of slow growth is not confined to the developing countries. Average growth rates have fallen in the industrialized countries too. In the socialist countries of Eastern Europe and the USSR, net material product per head increased only about 2.5 per cent a year during 1981–88 compared to about 4.1 per cent in the 1970s. Growth in the developed market economies was even slower: GDP per capita increased only 2.1 per cent a year during the period 1981–88 as compared to 2.3 per cent a year in the 1970s. The growth rates in Western Europe, previously substantially higher than in the US, were very low in the first half of the 1980s, although growth rates recovered in the second half of the decade as indeed they did throughout the world. Japan was unusual among the advanced capitalist countries in adapting quickly to external disturbances while sustaining a high average rate of growth.

Thus the 1980s were characterized by (i) a slowing down of the rate of growth of the world economy; (ii) increased economic distance between rich countries and poor; (iii) greater differentiation in average standards of living within the Third World; (iv) uneven development, or the presence simultaneously within the Third World of processes of development and underdevelopment; and (v) on average a negative rate of growth of per capita income in the less developed countries excluding China. These patterns of global change were accompanied and partly caused by macroeconomic imbalances in the world economy. Most conspicuous at the end of the decade were (i) the large trade surpluses of Japan and West Germany and the equally large offsetting trade deficit of the US, (ii) the conversion of the US from the leading creditor country to a large borrower of foreign capital, (iii) massive foreign indebtedness of many Third World countries, primarily in Latin America and Africa, combined with (iv) unprecedentedly high real rates of interest charged on foreign loans, such that (v) full repayment of the debt is widely recognized to be impossible. As a consequence of (iii) and (iv) a serious debt crisis emerged in

1982 which persists to this day. Attempts by Third World debtor countries to cope with the crisis and service their debts have resulted (vi) in a perverse flow of finance across the international exchanges and a net transfer of resources from poor debtor countries to rich creditor ones.

THE GLOBAL ECONOMY IN THE 1990s

While the macroeconomic imbalances listed above constitute major obstacles to a resumption of more rapid growth in the world economy and to a less uneven pattern of development, positive changes have also occurred to give grounds for hope for the future. Furthermore, these positive changes can and should be reinforced by policy initiatives at national and international levels to remove barriers to expansion, to increase the flexibility of the economy and its speed of response to changing signals, and to exploit opportunities for constructive change.

The Political Context for International Economic Cooperation

There has been a fundamental change in the political context for international economic cooperation. The two superpowers, the US and the USSR, have reduced the intensity of their ideological conflict and have entered into serious negotiations on disarmament. Already this has diminished the risk of nuclear war. In addition, there has been an outbreak of peace in several regions of the world where violent international conflict has made economic progress impossible. The recent war in the Persian Gulf should not lead us to forget the important instances of the withdrawal of the Soviet Union from Afghanistan, the ending of military support for the Contras by the US government and the end of the civil war in Nicaragua, and arrangements for the independence of Namibia. Progress towards peace in Angola, El Salvador and perhaps even between Israel and the Palestinians may also be possible.

The change in the international political climate creates the possibility for a reduction in the currently massive expenditure on armaments, both in the industrialized countries and in the Third World. Indeed military expenditure has already begun to fall in the Soviet Union, while the Bush administration announced its intention to freeze real expenditure on armaments. If some of the resources absorbed by the armed forces could be released for more constructive purposes during the next ten years, the outlook for social progress in the industrial countries, economic development in the Third World and more rapid expansion of the global economy would be transformed.

Even so, serious political problems would remain in many Third World countries. Civil strife, violence and political instability are often endemic, making broadly-based economic development virtually impossible. Obvious examples include the Sudan, Ethiopia and Mozambique in Africa, the Philippines and Sri Lanka in Asia and Peru in Latin America. Internal peace and national economic development go together, each supporting the other, whereas the absence of one tends to undermine the other.

Adjustment to the World Recession of the Early 1980s

It is an ill-wind that blows no one good. The recession of the early 1980s resulted in widespread bankruptcy and high unemployment. Marginal firms often went out of business. Those firms that survived, however, now enjoy lower costs and increased efficiency: they are leaner and meaner. Moreover, the recession also had profound effects on the labour market. High unemployment weakened the trade union movement and tilted the balance of power in favour of capital. Wage demands under collective bargaining were moderated and real wages sometimes cut. Outside the unionized industries, high unemployment increased competition in the labour market and, once again, the pressure to raise nominal wages was reduced with real wages (and unit labour costs) rising less rapidly than previously. Discipline in the labour market, as seen by management, increased in the 1980s for another reason: the high international mobility of capital by transnational corporations meant that it was possible for management to change (or threaten to change) the location of manufacturing activity to low-wage countries if demands for higher wages in the home country were pushed too hard.

The easing of pressure in the labour market has been accompanied by a fall in the real price of oil and by lower energy costs in general. This is of course a result of the slackening of energy demand in the world market, itself a consequence of the world recession. Moreover, it is not just oil prices that have fallen. The prices of many (but not all) internationally traded raw materials are lower today than they were 10 or 15 years ago, to the great disadvantage of primary commodity exporting countries which have seen their terms of trade deteriorate sharply.

The effect of lower or more slowly rising unit labour costs, lower energy costs and lower prices of raw materials has been to increase profit margins in manufacturing enterprises, especially in those countries (Japan and the East Asian developing countries) which did not allow their exchange rates to become overvalued (as happened in the US, Latin America and Africa). High profit margins have created a potential, on the supply side, for higher investment and faster growth of industry in the 1990s. This potential is sometimes matched, on the demand side, by a backlog of investment needs in the public sector, notably a potential demand for public sector investment in physical infrastructure, urban renewal and public services such as schools and hospitals. Thus recession and slow growth set in motion a number of economic forces which potentially can lead to higher levels of activity and faster growth in future.

Structural Change: Towards a Single International Economy

The conjunctural changes mentioned above are joined by a more powerful set of actual and possible structural developments which together could raise the world economy onto a faster growth trajectory. First, there is the prospect in 1992 of closer economic integration within the European Community. Second, there is the newly-signed free trade agreement between Canada and the US. Third, there is the likely increasing openness of China to the world economy. Lastly, there is a genuine possibility of closer integration of the USSR and the Eastern European socialist countries into the international economy.

These structural changes will lead to an expansion in the size of the world market. Almost certainly, world trade will grow faster than world output; the difference between the two will probably be greater than at any time since the rate of growth of world trade began to decline in 1974. An expanding world market can be a stimulus to overall development, increasing allocative efficiency by permitting greater specialization, by allowing countries – particularly the smaller ones – to exploit the benefits of economies of scale, by creating profit opportunities and thereby encouraging investment, and by facilitating technological transfers as well as product and process innovations.

Such structural changes leading towards a unified world market can of course be perverted. Two dangers must be guarded against. First is that the world will divide into a number of hostile trading blocs which erect high protectionist barriers against imports from non-member countries. One can imagine a trading bloc centred on Western Europe, another on North America and perhaps a third in Asia centred on Japan. Structural change in this case would represent a turning away from liberalism and a unified world market towards protectionism and trade warfare. A second danger is that the structural changes that are likely to occur will in effect marginalize some less developed countries, depriving them of an opportunity to participate fully in the advantages of international trade. This could occur, for example, if preoccupation with the task of integrating the socialist countries into the world trading system led to the neglect of the interests of the Third World or of some of its members. This is not an inevitable consequence of incorporating the socialist countries into the world economy, or even a likely consequence, but it is a point that needs watching.

There is even more reason therefore that the Third World should participate actively in further steps towards trade liberalization and in particular in the negotiations of the so-called Uruguay round. Reduced global trade restrictions on agricultural products, textiles and some service activities are potentially of great benefit to many Third World countries. Greater liberalization naturally implies intensified global competition, but it is almost certainly the case that, on balance, the Third World has more to gain than lose from greater access to world markets.

What seems to be occurring, and what clearly is at stake, is not just the creation of a unified world market, but the emergence of a single international economy where technology can readily be transferred, where capital is highly mobile, where currencies are free to move or where their movement can be stopped only with difficulty, and of course where goods circulate freely and services are sold unhampered across international borders. In such an international economy, major restrictions are likely to remain only on the international mobility of labour, and particularly on the large-scale movement of relatively unskilled labour.

Adjustments will be required of all countries, but most profoundly of the socialist countries which will have to adapt their policies and systems of economic management so as to be compatible with capitalist practices. The exchange rate, for example, will have to be brought in line with relative international costs and prices; monetary policy and interest rates will have to be adjusted so that the cost of finance capital bears some relationship to the return on investment in plant and equipment. Capital flows into and out of socialist countries may eventually become significant, although (with the exception of East Germany) this is unlikely to occur during the next ten years, given the high foreign indebtedness that some of them already carry. It is enough to recognize for now that major structural change is likely to occur during the next decade as a result of the incorporation of the socialist countries into the international economy, that this will necessitate accommodation by other countries and that, once the transitional problems have been overcome, all countries can potentially benefit.

Projected Growth Rates to the Year 2000

The conjunctural and structural changes that have been identified will help to ensure that average growth rates in the 1990s are higher than in the 1980s. Since they could hardly be much lower, this in itself is not a great achievement. Assuming unchanged government policies, various projections of UN bodies indicate that world gross domestic product would rise between 3.1 and 3.3 per cent a year during the period 1991–2000, with a corresponding increase in per capita GDP of between 1.5 and 1.7 per cent a year.

Constancy or a slight acceleration in per capita growth is projected for the developed market economies, the range being between 2.0 per cent a year (projected by UNCTAD) and 2.4 (the World Bank). A sharper acceleration is projected for the USSR and Eastern Europe, the range being between 3.2 per cent a year (projected by the Department of International Economic and Social Affairs and by UNCTAD) and 3.3 per cent (the Economic Commission for Europe).

Projections indicate that China will continue to grow rapidly, with DIESA predicting a 5.5 per cent annual rate of growth per capita. This evidently is more than satisfactory; however, after the events at Tienanmen Square in June 1989, such projections may be rather optimistic. The projected growth rates for the developing countries excluding China are clearly unsatisfactory. UNCTAD anticipates a growth of income per head in the Third World of only 1.3 per cent a year, largely due to pessimism about the situation in Africa. DIESA is somewhat more hopeful, projecting a growth of per capita output for the Third World as a whole of 2.0 per cent a year. Within the Third World, however, DIESA envisages zero growth per head in sub-Saharan Africa and only modest growth in Latin America, West Asia and the Mediterranean. Growth is projected to be relatively high in South and East Asia and in North Africa, 2.4 per cent per capita per year. (The projections are summarized in Table 6.2.)

Table 6.2   Projected rates of growth of per capita GDP, 1991–2000 (per cent per annum)

	DIESA	ECE	UNCTAD	IBRD
World	1.8	1.6	1.5	1.7
Developed market economies	2.0	2.2	2.0	2.4
USSR and Eastern Europe	3.2	3.3	3.2	–
Developing countries	2.0[a]	1.5[b]	1.3[a]	2.8[b]
North Africa	2.4	–	–	–
Sub-Saharan Africa	0.0	–	–	0.3
Latin America	1.3	–	1.6	2.2
West Asia	1.4	–	1.5	–
South and East Asia	2.4	–	–	–
Mediterranean	1.4	–	–	–
China	5.5	–	5.1	–

Notes: [a]Excluding China.
            [b]Including China.

Source: ACC Task Force on Long-Term Development Objectives, "Monitoring Development Progress During the Decade of the 1990s: Economic and Social Indicators in a New Strategy for Development', Preliminary Draft, February 1989, Table 2, p.10; United Nations, DIESA, *Development and International Economic Co-operation: Long-Term Trends in Social and Economic Development,* A/43/554, 20 September 1988, Table 10, p. 38.

Only in China is total output projected to rise as much as 5.0 per cent a year, and only in China, the USSR and Eastern Europe is output per head calculated to rise as much as 2.5 per cent a year. The achievements of the 1960s and 1970s indicate that much better progress is possible and that the retrogressions in the 1980s in Africa, Latin America and West Asia must be reversed since currently projected growth rates cannot be acceptable to informed world opinion.

Moreover the projected growth rates make no provision for any shocks that might beset the world economy, as happened in the 1970s with the two oil price rises and in the 1980s with the debt crisis. Yet it is not difficult to imagine a number of unpleasant possibilities: negotiations could break down and the political situation in South Africa explode, engulfing the whole of southern Africa in violent conflict; the debt problem could remain unresolved and plunge Latin America and Africa into another period of negative growth; or the economic reforms in the socialist countries could fail and seriously disrupt the pace of production. These considerations suggest that in the International Development Strategy for the 1990s the aim should be for higher rates of growth than those currently projected.

ACCELERATING GROWTH IN THE 1990s

Growth, of course, is not an end in itself; it is a means to improve the well-being of people throughout the world. If the growth of income per head is negative or negligible it is almost impossible to reduce poverty substantially, particularly in countries where the incidence of poverty is high. But even when the rate of growth of per capita income is positive, poverty – or unemployment or hunger – will not automatically decline. Much depends on the pattern of growth. If, for example, growth is accompanied by greater inequality in the distribution of income, the reduction in poverty could be rather modest. Similarly, the effects of growth on unemployment depend not so much on the average rate of expansion as on the employment intensity of the sectors of the economy that expand most rapidly. Even the elimination of famine in countries such as the Sudan and Ethiopia depends less on economic growth than on bringing civil war to an end.

Population trends will evidently affect the possibility of accelerating growth in per capita income in the 1990s. No direct relationship exists between a slower rate of growth of population and faster growth of average incomes, but generally the slower the former, the more rapid the latter.

Population growth rates began to decline around 1965 and fell sharply until 1980. No significant change has occurred since, but recent projections indicate that population growth rates should begin to fall again, albeit at a modest rate, after 1995. Demographic expansion occurred at a rate of 2.06 per cent a year for the world as a whole during 1965–70, according to UN estimates, but should be only 1.62 per cent a year during 1995–2000. This fall in population growth rates is expected to occur in all groups of countries, be they rich or poor, capitalist or socialist, but not in all regions. Thus in the capitalist developing countries the population growth rate is expected to fall from 2.5 per cent a year in 1960–70 to 2.1 per cent in 1990–2000, while in China and the other Asian planned economies the decline is expected to be from 2.36 per cent in 1960–70 to 1.18 per cent in 1990–2000.

Within the Third World, population growth rates are expected to remain high, at 2.92 per cent a year in West Asia, and to continue to accelerate to 3.29 per cent a year in sub-Saharan Africa. Elsewhere they should fall, sometimes sharply. It is perhaps too early to claim that the population problem has been solved, but attention in future is likely to be less concerned with the overall rate of increase and directed instead to the rate of increase in urban areas, which continues to be high despite the diminished overall rate of population growth. In 1980–85, for instance, the urban population grew 4.0 per cent a year in the low-income economies and 3.5 per cent a year in the middle-income ones, as compared to total population growth rates in the two groups of countries of 1.9 and 2.3 per cent respectively.

Rapid demographic expansion is thus not likely, in general, to be as great an obstacle to accelerating economic growth in the 1990s as perhaps it was in earlier decades. The main international and domestic barriers are likely to lie elsewhere, and it is to these that we now turn.

The Responsibilities of the Industrialized Countries for Global Macroeconomic Management

The major industrialized countries of Western Europe and North America have for a number of years given priority to restraining inflation. While price increases have indeed been less rapid than in the late 1970s, the restrictive monetary and expenditure policies adopted to combat inflation have resulted in universally high (open and disguised) unemployment, low investment, sluggish growth and a generally low level of aggregate demand. One of the most important conditions for accelerating world growth in the 1990s is wider recognition in the industrialized countries that while resistance to inflation is one objective of the international community, it is not the only objective nor, under current conditions, the most important one.

The solution of many economic problems, domestic as well as international, would be greatly facilitated if expansion were given a higher priority by the OECD countries in general, following the example of Japan. This expansion would almost certainly exert some upward pressure on wages and other costs and hence on final prices, but a modest increase in the rate of inflation would be an acceptable price for improved global economic performance. At the very least, within a given pressure of aggregate demand, there is a strong case for a change in the composition of demand away from military spending and personal consumption in favour of investment.

Next, a reassessment of monetary policy in the industrialized countries is in order, starting with the US. Nominal world interest rates (for example as measured by LIBOR) have fluctuated sharply over short periods and reached unprecedented heights in the early 1980s. (The LIBOR climbed to 16.9 per cent a year in 1981.) At the same time the export prices of developing countries, beginning in 1982, fell sharply. As a result, the 'real' rate of interest paid by developing countries on their foreign debt rose to nearly 20 per cent in 1983 and has remained high. Interest rates of this magnitude are clearly incompatible with repayment of debt by debtor countries since they reflect neither the real rate of return on assets that might have been acquired with the loans, nor possible rates of growth of foreign exchange earnings necessary to service dollar-denominated liabilities. Continuation of tight monetary policies in the creditor countries will prolong the debt crisis and continue to act as a barrier to accelerated growth in the 1990s.

Third, the burden of solving the debt crisis should be more equitably shared. Most of the costs of adjustment have so far been borne by the debtor countries and particularly by the lower-income groups in the debtor countries. Neither the lending institutions nor the governments of the creditor countries has assumed any responsibility for the financial imbalances caused by excessive lending at high real rates of interest at a time of slower growth in the volume of world trade. The international banks, moreover, are now well able to bear part of the costs of adjustment. They have established substantial reserves against non-payment of debt; they have written down the book value of their loans; and in a few cases they have sold part of their loan portfolio at a heavy discount on the secondary market. The balance sheets of the banks are much healthier today than they were in 1982 when the debt crisis erupted. Indeed, the banks should play a much larger role in solving the international debt problem which, after all, they helped to create.

The governments of the industrialized countries also have a role to play in solving the problem. Tight monetary policies and contractionary expenditure policies pushed up interest rates, slowed the growth of the world economy and depressed commodity prices, all of which seriously aggravated the debt problem and made it impossible for many debtor countries even to maintain previously achieved levels of income, let alone sustain the momentum of growth. To make matters worse, the debtor countries have been compelled to run trade surpluses in a desperate attempt to avoid default on their debts, resulting in a net transfer of resources from increasingly impoverished debtor countries to increasingly prosperous rich ones. In fact, the net transfer to developing countries as a whole became negative in 1984 (when it was minus $10.2 billion) and has risen steadily (to minus $43 billion in 1988). Over the entire five-year period the negative net transfer from the Third World was $142.9 billion which exceeded the amount of official development assistance received by its members.

No international development strategy for the 1990s can succeed unless the debt problem is resolved. Some combination of debt forgiveness, lower real interest rates and faster growth of international trade will be necessary to avoid outright default. What is perhaps not yet widely appreciated is that a resolution of the debt problem is in the interests of both creditor and debtor countries. Debt forgiveness would not be an act of charity; it would be a matter of enlightened self-interest. That is, there are mutual gains to be had from debt reduction in the form of expanded exports from creditor to debtor countries, faster overall growth of world trade and a resumption of growth in sub-Saharan Africa and Latin America. The industrialized countries find themselves in the happy situation in which their duty to the international community coincides with their national interest.

Fourth, the industrialized countries also have a responsibility to reduce tariff and non-tariff barriers to trade, and particularly to ensure Third World access to markets in developed countries. Indeed GATT rules now cover only 7 per cent of world trade leaving much potential for further liberalization. The Uruguay round has already been mentioned. Discriminatory protectionist restrictions against exports from developing countries merit special attention in future negotiations. The unfavourable treatment of textile exports from developing countries illustrates a more general tendency. The current arrangements had their origin in 1962 when exports of cotton textiles were restricted, supposedly only temporarily, for a period of five years. In the event, the arrangements (i) have been repeatedly renewed, (ii) have been expanded steadily to include additional textiles, and (iii) have become progressively more restrictive. One of the aims of international trade policy in the 1990s should be to reverse these tendencies. There may actually be a case for discriminating in favour of trade from the least developed countries; certainly there is no case for discriminating against them.

Lastly, there is the issue of macroeconomic adjustment among the developed countries. The key here is the elimination of the massive American trade deficit and the absorption by the US of a significant portion of the rest of the world's savings. One possibility would be to aim for the simultaneous reduction in the trade deficit of the US and the trade surpluses of Japan and West Germany, which together are about as large as the US deficit. An alternative would be to reduce the US deficit while allowing Japan and West Germany to continue to run large trade surpluses. The Japanese and West

German savings currently used to finance the US deficit would then become available to finance investment and growth in the Third World. The danger is that neither option may be adopted, hence postponing indefinitely any global macroeconomic adjustment. Moreover, even if policies intended to bring about adjustment are adopted by some countries, there is no guarantee that all other important countries will pursue policies equally compatible or consistent with global adjustment. The international economy lacks effective coordinating machinery; in particular, there is no mechanism for harmonizing fiscal policies within, say, the Group of Seven (G7). This is something that may deserve careful consideration.

Stimulating Growth in the Third World: Domestic and International Policies

The need for faster growth is undeniable, especially in the Third World and in those parts of it where per capita incomes fell during the 1980s. However, no purpose is probably served in specifying precise targets for rates of growth for the International Development Strategy for the 1990s, particularly since the international community does not possess the policy instruments necessary to translate targets into attainments. Yet a desirable minimum rate of growth in the Third World during the next decade could be agreed at about 5.0 per cent a year. This implies a rate of growth of per capita income of 2.5 to 3.0 per cent a year. Such a growth rate, while modest, is faster than the rates currently projected for the Third World as a whole, and under present circumstances represents a real challenge to national policy-makers. Moreover, even if the desirable minimum rate of growth were achieved, per capita incomes in Africa and West Asia would still be lower at the turn of the century than at the end of the 1970s. This is a measure of how much ground has been lost in recent years.

A central policy objective during this decade must be to raise the rate of accumulation of capital. In a great many countries gross domestic investment actually declined during the 1980s – a pattern that clearly must be reversed if even minimum growth objectives are to be attained. As can be seen in Table 6.3, investment increased at an extraordinarily rapid rate in China and at a modest rate in India. In the other low-income economies as a group, however, investment increased only 0.4 per cent per annum, which implies a heavily negative rate of growth in per capita terms. Middle-income economies experienced a negative growth of investment, with lower middle-income economies faring worse than upper middle-income ones.

The most serious situation as regards investment occurred in two overlapping groups of countries: sub-Saharan Africa and the highly indebted countries. In sub-Saharan Africa gross investment declined at an annual rate of

Table 6.3   Rates of growth of gross domestic investment, 1980–86 (per cent per annum)

Low-income economies	13.2
China	19.3
India	4.6
Other low-income	0.4
Middle-income economies	−2.3
Lower middle-income	−3.4
Upper middle-income	−1.9
Other groupings	
Highly indebted countries	−6.3
Sub-Saharan Africa	−9.3

Source: World Bank, *World Development Report 1988*, Oxford University Press, 1988, Table 4, p. 228.

9.3 per cent a year, and in the highly indebted countries by 6.3 per cent a year. The stock of capital per head of population obviously declined sharply in many Third World countries which should now adopt a public policy objective of restoring those ratios to previously attained levels.

Unfortunately it is not enough merely to raise the rate of growth of investment. Governments must also ensure that investment is allocated efficiently so that every addition to the stock of capital makes the largest possible contribution to increased output. However, there has been a tendency throughout the Third World for the efficiency of investment to decline, or, conversely, for the incremental capital-output ratio (ICOR) to rise. DIESA has estimated ICORs for 1971–80 and 1981–85 for the developing countries as a whole, for China and for five separate groups of developing countries.[1] Apart from China, where the ICOR fell quite substantially, the efficiency of investment appears to have deteriorated virtually everywhere, in the developing countries as a whole and in each of the five separate groups. In the least developed countries, for instance, the ICOR is reported to have nearly doubled, from 4.1 in 1971–80 to 8.0 in 1981–85.

In the present decade it will be important for governments to take what steps they can to increase the efficiency of investment at least to regain the levels experienced in the 1970s. In addition to a restructuring of output, this may require reform of investment procedures within central government ministries; improved criteria for investment decisions in public sector enterprises; and price reforms designed to channel private investment in more socially optimal directions. State-owned enterprises in particular have tended to serve limited interests, have been inefficient and often operated at a loss, thereby constituting a drain on resources available for development. Whether such enterprises are retained in the public sector or privatized, they should be forced to become more competitive by increasing their exposure to market forces.

The savings effort in developing countries remained surprisingly large on the whole, the average savings rate being 23.6 per cent of GDP in 1987 or about the same as it was in 1973 before the first sharp increase in oil prices. In sub-Saharan Africa, however, the savings rate was less than half the average in the rest of the Third World (10.9 per cent in 1987) and much below the rate of savings achieved in 1973 (17.5 per cent). In this region a major effort will be required in the coming decade to raise the savings rate to a level compatible with the minimum desired rate of growth. Failure to do so will almost certainly result in further impoverishment.

Public expenditure in developing countries increased its share of GNP by nearly 41 per cent between 1972 and 1986, central government expenditures rising from 18.7 per cent of GNP in 1972 to 26.3 per cent in 1986. Much of this was due to rising interest payments on foreign debt. When examining the composition of central government expenditure, two things stand out. First, the share of expenditure devoted to human development (notably education and health) declined, especially on education; and, second, the proportion of expenditure devoted to the military also fell (see Table 6.4). These were of course falling shares of a total which was itself an increasing proportion of GNP. Thus when these expenditure categories are expressed as proportions not of total central government expenditure but of GNP, it transpires that public expenditure b⸱th on the military and on education and health rose. It would be highly desirable if developing countries in the 1990s

Table 6.4   *Central government expenditure in the developing countries,*
           1972 and 1986

	% of GNP		% of central government expenditure	
	1972	1986	1972	1986
Total central government	18.7	26.3	100	100
expenditures, of which,				
Military expenditure	2.7	3.3	14.3	12.5
Education	2.2	2.7	12.5	10.3
Health	0.9	1.2	4.7	4.5

Note: In some large developing countries central government expenditure excludes
         significant expenditure by lower levels of government on such things as education.
Source: World Bank, *World Development Report 1988*, Oxford University Press, 1988,
         Table 23, p. 267.

could take advantage of the improved international political climate and curtail military expenditure, thereby releasing additional resources for human development (which as we shall see below is essential) and for physical investment. The central government current deficit, which can be interpreted as negative savings, rose very sharply from 3.5 per cent of GNP in 1972 to 6.2 per cent in 1986. This is a further indication of the need to reform public finances through improved tax and expenditure policies in order to make a larger contribution to accelerating growth.

Indeed in many countries, above all in those affected by serious debt-servicing problems, the fiscal deficit of central government is the major contraint on development. The ease with which several countries have generated trade surpluses indicates that the balance of payments constraint is not always as severe as was once thought, and widespread evidence of massive capital flight indicates that in those countries, at least, a savings constraint is not binding. Fiscal reforms (designed to raise more revenue) and debt relief (which would release public sector funds for development purposes) are often the main priorities.

Other internal policy reforms are also likely to be necessary in many countries. These include measures to improve the efficiency of domestic capital markets and alleviate financial repression; a realignment of the exchange rate to ensure that incentives are not biased against production for sale in export markets; and controls to prevent capital flight, supplementing interest rate and exchange rate policies. The deficits of public sector enterprise are quite large in some countries and these, too, represent negative savings and hence a restraint on growth. Where deficits are quantitatively important, governments should reconsider the pricing policies of public-sector enterprises as well as the desirability of transferring such enterprises to the private sector. The objective should be to accelerate savings and capital formation in support of faster growth, while policies towards public-sector enterprises should be made consistent with this overall priority.

In an ideal world, enhanced domestic effort and improved domestic policies in the developing countries would be supported by international efforts to accelerate growth. Perhaps foremost among such efforts would be a net resource transfer from rich countries to poor. Since we do not live in an ideal world, it would be unwise to formulate an international development strategy for the 1990s based on an untenable assumption that past patterns of resource transfer could suddenly and miraculously be transformed.

First, as was indicated above, the net transfer of resources is often from poor countries to rich, not the other way round. It would be an achievement to stop this let alone suggest that the net flow should substantially favour the developing countries. If one considers the main sources of international capital one by one, the picture is no less bleak.

Thus, second, direct private foreign investment in the Third World is more likely to be an effect of accelerated growth than the stimulus that lifts a country out of stagnation or retrogression. In any case, direct foreign investment at its peak in 1975 was equivalent to only 0.9 per cent of the GDP of developing countries, and by 1985 had fallen to 0.2 per cent. Third, portfolio investment, primarily by large international commercial banks, is even less important. The peak was reached in 1978 when portfolio investment was 1.2 per cent of the GDP of developing countries, but by 1985 it had become minus 0.1 per cent. It is unlikely that bank lending will resume on a significant scale until long after the debt crisis has been resolved. Again, portfolio investment is more likely to be a consequence of growth than a cause of it.

That leaves us, fourth, with official development assistance. Foreign aid to the Third World reached its peak in 1961 and 1962 when it amounted to 1.9 per cent of the GDP of developing countries. Thereafter it declined steadily and by 1985 amounted to only 0.8 per cent of Third World GDP.

It has long been a target of the international community that the wealthy donor countries should contribute 0.7 per cent of their GNP as foreign aid to assist developing countries. This target has never been attained and we are further from achieving it today than ever before. Indeed between 1980 and 1989 the net transfer of foreign aid to developing countries declined by nearly two-thirds, from just over $29 to about $10 billion. Perhaps it would be realistic to admit failure and abandon the target rather than continue to raise false hopes that foreign aid will play a prominent part in the International Development Strategy of the 1990s. Foreign aid has lost momentum and it would be best to accept that this is so.

The story of the US foreign assistance programme dramatizes the point.[2] In the late 1940s the US aid programme accounted for 2–3 per cent of that country's GNP. A decade later it was down to 1 per cent and today it is 0.3 per cent of the US gross national product. Military aid represents 35.8 per cent of the total; if this is excluded, US economic assistance accounts for only 0.2 per cent of GNP – the lowest aid ratio of any member-country of the Development Assistance Committee of the OECD.

Expressed in terms of dollars rather than as a percentage of GNP, the decline in US aid is even more dramatic. In 1946–52, measured in 1989 prices, the real value of the US foreign assistance programme was $32 billion. This fell to $22 billion in 1953–74, to $17 billion in 1975–85 and to $15 billion since 1986. That is, in real terms the value of US aid today is less than half what it was 40 years ago. Moreover 47 per cent of the aid goes to just two countries, Israel and Egypt. Finally, Japan, with a population only half the size of the US and a per capita income only 73 per cent as large, has since 1989 replaced the US as the largest aid donor. At least as regards US aid, an era has ended.

HUMAN DEVELOPMENT

In formulating an international strategy for the 1990s it would be prudent to assume that the Third World will have to rely largely on its own resources to finance development. Foreign capital is likely to be meagre; domestic savings also are unlikely to be abundant. For these reasons alone it will be essential to make full use of the human resources available within the Third World itself. People, in the 1990s, should be placed firmly in the centre of development.

The most compelling reason for doing so is that the process of economic development is coming increasingly to be understood as a process of expanding the capabilities of people. The ultimate focus of economic development has of course always been human development, but at times this has become obscured by too narrow a concentration on expanding the supplies of commodities. Economic growth should be seen as merely one means among several to the end of enhancing people's capabilities. Commodities and capabilities are of course linked, for example through the distribution of income which affects the degree to which the basic needs of the entire population are satisfied and through the system of entitlements that determines to what extent specific needs in society are met. But commodities and capabilities are distinct categories and should be kept separate. In the final analysis it is capabilities that matter and this is underlined by putting people first. An emphasis on human development has the virtue of forcing policymakers to ask themselves the question, growth for what?

Human Development as a Means

Human development also has instrumental value in accelerating economic growth.[3] Indeed expenditures on improving human capabilities have the potential to yield a return to society at least as high as the return on physical investment. Estimates of the rate of return on expenditure on education have made this very clear, even after allowing for possible upward biases in the rates of return.[4] Countries that neglect human development not only retard the expansion of human capabilities in the broadest sense; they also undermine the country's long-run potential rate of economic growth.

Until the beginning of the last decade public expenditure on education rose rapidly throughout the Third World. Starting around 1980, however, real per capita expenditure on education began to fall in some countries and in others the rate of increase began to diminish. As a result, for the 94 countries represented in Table 6.5, real public expenditure per capita on education increased only 1.95 per cent between 1980 and 1985. More worrying, in regions accounting for 74 of the 94 countries in the Table, per capita

*Table 6.5   Real public expenditure per capita on education, 1980 and 1985
(US dollars; 1980 prices)*

	Number of countries	1980	1985
Developing countries, of which:	94	37.94	38.68
North Africa	5	82.71	87.31
Sub-Saharan Africa	39	21.50	20.93
South Asia	5	6.55	8.95
East Asian NICs	3	72.63	126.07
Other East Asian	7	18.26	22.44
West Asia	6	218.34	192.12
Mediterranean	4	93.95	74.66
Western Hemisphere	25	84.08	77.88

Source: UN Department of International Economic and Social Affairs, *Development and
International Cooperation: Long Term Trends in Social and Economic
Development*, A/43/554, 20 September 1988, Table 35, p.107.

expenditure on education actually declined. This occurred in four regions:
sub-Saharan Africa, the Western Hemisphere, West Asia and the Mediterranean. These regions include many countries in which average incomes fell
and hence it is hardly surprising that expenditure on education also fell, but
the decline in this component of human capital formation is cause for concern.

If one disaggregates total educational expenditure among first-level (primary), second-level (secondary) and third-level education and examines
expenditure per pupil further, interesting points emerge (see Table 6.6). The
first point to note is that in the developing countries as a whole, real expenditure per pupil declined between 1980 and 1985 in each of the three
levels of education. Second, this same pattern is found in the four regions
previously identified as ones where total expenditure on education per capita
declined (sub-Saharan Africa, the Western Hemisphere, West Asia and the
Mediterranean). Third, real expenditure per student in secondary education
also fell in North Africa where the reduction was severe – 30.5 per cent. It is
quite possible therefore that the quality of secondary education deteriorated
in North Africa. Finally, in both the East Asian newly-industrialized countries and in the Other East Asian countries, real public expenditure per
student on third-level education declined. In only one group of countries –
South Asia – did expenditure per pupil increase in all three levels of education.
In every other group there was a decline in at least part of the educational
system. It is a sad record to report.

Table 6.6   *Real public expenditure on education per student, 1980 and 1985 (US dollars; 1980 prices)*

	First level		Second level		Third level	
	1980	1985	1980	1985	1980	1985
Developing countries, of which:	95	92	168	154	771	641
North Africa	166	178	610	424	982	998
Sub-Saharan Africa	63	62	210	198	2915	1940
South Asia	20	31	40	63	128	220
East Asian NICs	200	360	211	325	514	473
Other East Asia	68	94	103	125	197	170
West Asia	369	200	737	456	2652	1861
Mediterranean	86	81	142	121	1700	1125
Western Hemisphere	187	171	229	176	1439	1132

Source: UN Department of International Economic and Social Affairs, *Development and International Co-operation: Long Term Trends in Social and Economic Development*, A/43/554, 20 September 1988, Table 36, p. 109.

Table 6.7   *Real public expenditure per capita on health, 1980 and 1985 (US dollars; 1980 prices)*

	Number of countries	1980	1985
Developing countries, of which:	26	7.39	7.63
North Africa	2	10.55	13.03
Sub-Saharan Africa	8	8.09	7.76
South and East Asia	9	2.96	3.93
West Asia	2	118.10	151.39
Mediterranean	2	175.41	135.34
Western Hemisphere	3	39.39	37.21

Source: UN Department of International Economic and Social Affairs, *Development and International Co-operation: Long Term Trends in Social and Economic Development*, A/43/554, 20 September 1988, Table 43, p. 127.

The record in health care is not much better, as can be seen in Table 6.7. In the developing countries as a whole per capita government expenditure on health increased 3.2 per cent in real terms between 1980 and 1985. This modest rise in average expenditure obscures the fact that in three of the six regions represented, per capita expenditure on health actually fell. The decline varied from 4.1 per cent in sub-Saharan Africa to 5.5 per cent in the Western Hemisphere and 22.8 per cent in the two Mediterranean countries of Yugoslavia and Malta.

Considering the evidence on both educational and health expenditure, it seems clear that in the first half of the 1980s many Third World countries experienced a deterioration of the human condition and of their potential for long-run growth. One of the tasks of the International Development Strategy of the 1990s should be to reverse that deterioration wherever it has occurred and, in the other countries, to push for further improvements.

Strategic Activities

Human development encompasses a wide range of activities, but here, as in other areas, selectivity is essential. Certain activities can be regarded as strategic and hence deserving of priority. Obvious candidates are (i) education and training, (ii) health and nutrition, and (iii) housing. If these three areas receive the attention they deserve, human development as a whole will likely occur at a rapid pace.

The recommended approach during the next ten years is to emphasize those aspects of expenditure on human development which are akin to capital formation, and to give lower priority to the purely social welfare aspects of expenditure programmes. Such an approach will have several advantages. First, the development of human resources in almost any form will inevitably contribute directly to the well-being of the poor. Second, an emphasis on human capital formation will help to create a more equal distribution of income.[5] Third, it will create an environment in which equality of opportunity is not likely to lead to great inequality of outcome. Fourth, by providing comprehensive health, nutrition and educational services, complementarities between the various services can be exploited. For example, better health for the poor (as a result of primary health care services) increases the efficiency with which the body transforms calories into improved nutrition; and improved nutrition, in turn, leads to increased attendance at school and improves the ability of children to learn. Similarly, there are important linkages between women's health, female life expectancy, the education of young women, the birth rate and population growth. There are linkages between literacy and health; between education, literacy and labour productivity, etc. Indeed, because of the complementarities among different types of human development programmes, there may be increasing returns to expenditure on human development over quite a large range.

Finally, there are complementarities between physical and human capital which a strategy of the type being suggested can exploit. Investment in modern industry requires skilled labour; agricultural mechanization requires people who can, for example, operate and repair irrigation equipment; modern services (banking, tourism, public administration) require a literate and numerate labour force. Thus an emphasis on human capital formation can in principle yield high returns in the form of an increase in the productivity of investment in physical assets.

Half our People, All our Future

The crucial role of women in development has come to be acknowledged. Women in the Third World perform the fundamental tasks of feeding and nurturing the population. They are responsible (particularly in Africa) for growing and marketing most of the food crops. They do most of the food preparation, obtain the water and fuel for the household, are responsible for health, nutrition and hygiene, and provide the early education of the young. Increasingly, too, women are engaged in wage employment or self-employment in the modern sector of the economy. It is not surprising that women are so important since they are, after all, half our people.

Yet in many countries women have been neglected by development programmes and discriminated against by public policy. Both literacy rates and female enrolment rates in all three levels of education are lower for women than men. Females spend less time in education than males, probably because, from the age of five upwards, girls' time is consumed by work in the home and in the fields. The nutrition and health of women often are neglected in favour of men. In India, Bangladesh and Pakistan there is evidence of discriminatory feeding and health practices favouring male children right from birth.[6] Despite the fact that women enjoy a biological advantage in longevity over men, life expectancy for women in many developing countries is lower than for men in age groups below 50 years. This is due largely to two facts. First, there is generally a higher mortality rate for female than for male children above five years of age and, second, there is a higher mortality rate for women of child-bearing age (15 to 44 years) than for men of the corresponding group.[7] In addition, in India and Pakistan, contrary to the usual pattern, the mortality rate among infant girls zero to five years old is higher than for boys in the same age group. These patterns of mortality are indicative of discrimination against girls from the time of birth onwards.

In the 1990s the task is to translate greater understanding of the problems of women into altered priorities to correct such problems. It is essential that women receive equal access to education and training programmes, to health and nutrition services and, in the sphere of production, to credit, extension services, technology and income-generating activities. Beyond this, specific investments favouring women are needed, such as in safe motherhood and in relevant labour-saving devices (more fuel-efficient methods of cooking, less labour-intensive ways of preparing food and more accessible sources of water, fuel and fodder). Empowering women for development should have high returns in terms of increased output, greater equity and social progress.

If women are half our people, the young are all our future. Any society that neglects its youth does so at its peril. Winston Churchill expressed this well when he said, 'There is no finer investment than putting milk into babies'. If that were true of wartime Britain, it is no less true of the contemporary Third World.

We have already referred to the decline in real public expenditure on education per pupil in many Third World countries. To that should be added the decline in primary school enrolment ratios in a number of African and Caribbean countries, and a widespread decline in the quality of education. There is a danger that unless these tendencies are quickly reversed, this generation of young people – and the next – will be even less well equipped for the future than the last.

UNICEF reports that about 45 per cent of children under five in the developing countries excluding China are living in absolute poverty.[8] This is roughly 155 million young people, 74 per cent of whom live in rural areas. About 40 per cent of children under five years of age suffer from protein-energy malnutrition. About 20 per cent of infants in the Third World are born with low birth weight. Nearly half the children have no access to clean drinking water and two-thirds do not have access to adequate sanitation. About 20 per cent of children of primary school age do not attend school and of those who attend, one-third drop out before completing four grades.[9] Here is an agenda for action that deserves high priority, for the future of our children is no less the future of ourselves.

Participation and Human Development

People in the Third World, women and men, the young and old, but above all the poor, often feel and indeed are relegated to the status of subjects. Recognition of this in recent years is what lies behind the call for greater popular participation in development. Broadly-based development of the type recommended is most likely to succeed when the various groups in poverty are well organized. Participation, or the opportunity to participate if one wishes, is of course an end in itself, but participation also has a number of instrumental values which makes it an important feature of human development. First, participation in representative community-based organizations can help to identify local priorities, to determine which needs are essential or basic and which of secondary importance, and to define the content of development programmes and projects so that they reflect accurately local needs, aspirations and demands. Next, having identified priorities and designed the programmes which incorporate them, participation in functional organizations (service cooperatives, land reform committees, irrigation societies, women's groups) can be used to mobilize support for national and local policies and programmes and local projects. Last, participation can be used to reduce the cost of public services and investment projects by shifting responsibility from central and local government (where costs tend to be relatively high) to the grassroots organizations (where costs can be low). In some cases, for example, it may be possible to organize the beneficiaries of an investment project and persuade them to contribute their labour voluntarily to help defray construction costs. In other cases some of the public services (clinics, nursery schools) can be organized, staffed and run by local groups rather than by relatively highly-paid civil servants brought in from outside. Thus in an appropriate context participation can flourish and in so doing contribute much to development.

Desirable Goals for the Year 2000

Each country will of course set its own national goals for human development, taking into account its particular social, economic and financial circumstances. However there are minimum desirable goals that may commend themselves to the international community as a whole. One such goal is the attainment of universal primary education but, short of this, special efforts should be made to increase primary education for girls. A second goal is a reduction of the infant mortality rate to no more than 50 per 1000 or, in countries where this has already been achieved, a reduction of the infant mortality rate by 50 per cent. Third, it is now possible virtually to eliminate severe malnutrition in all countries, and it is suggested that this should be a goal for the 1990s. The measures necessary to reach this goal will vary from one country to another – including increased agricultural production, food entitlement programmes and improvements in primary health care systems – but the knowledge and resources necessary to banish severe hunger from the globe exist and the time surely has come to make this a high priority. Lastly, a basic need of all people is access to safe drinking water and sanitation, and it is suggested that universal access to such services should be a goal for the year 2000.

It was indicated earlier that population growth rates are projected to decline in most regions of the world over the next ten years. If the recommended policies are adopted to accelerate the rate of economic growth, the actual pace of demographic expansion should decline below the projected rates. If, in addition, high priority is given to human development, as we urge, a further reduction in the rate of growth of the population can be anticipated. Even so, in some countries, particularly in Africa, population growth rates may remain extraordinarily high, and governments in these countries may wish to consider specific measures to reduce the rate of growth of the population.

THE REDUCTION OF SEVERE POVERTY AND DEPRIVATION

While it is important to increase the aggregate rate of economic growth, reduce the pace of demographic expansion and give much higher priority in coming years to human development, these measures, separately or together, will not suffice to eliminate severe poverty and deprivation. It is now widely understood that one cannot rely on the benefits of increased production to trickle down automatically to all sectors of society, particularly to those most in need. Growth is not enough. Even in the US, which has enjoyed more or less sustained growth for over 200 years, it is estimated that 20 million people do not have enough to eat.

The poorest people in any society are the hardest to reach. They live in remote and inaccessible areas, are scattered and isolated, or else crowded into urban slums. They are the least skilled; they have the fewest productive resources and little access to high productivity employment. Growth tends to pass them by, and public services fail to touch their lives unless specific measures are taken to see that they do. It is important in formulating national strategies for the present decade of development that policy-makers repeatedly ask themselves the question, growth for whom?

Considering the Third World as a whole, roughly 90 per cent of the absolute poor[10] live in rural areas. Within these areas the percentage of the population in poverty rises from 32 per cent in the Near East, to 49.8 per cent in Asia, to 53.4 per cent in Latin America, to 65.2 per cent in Africa.[11] Given this high incidence of poverty in rural areas and the location of most of the poor in the countryside, reductions in poverty depend (i) on achieving sustained growth of agricultural income per head of the rural population, combined with (ii) guaranteed access of all sections of the rural working population to productive resources (land, water, pasture, forests). Unfortunately neither condition was satisfied in the 1980s. Agricultural GDP per head of the agricultural population actually fell in Africa, Latin America and the Near East, and rose only in Asia. Land concentration remained high almost everywhere and appears to have increased in such countries as Pakistan, the Philippines, Sri Lanka, Brazil, Panama and Uruguay.[12] Moreover, the size of the landless population increased by 11 million between 1980 and 1985 or by 5.3 per cent.[13] The conclusion is inescapable that 'with notable exceptions, the basic needs of the rural poor are being less well met today than they were at the beginning of the decade'.[14]

Taking both rural and urban poverty into account, the ILO estimates that the number of people in the Third World living in extreme poverty increased from 819 million in 1980 to 881 million in 1985. This is a rise of 62 million or 7.6 per cent in just five years. Moreover, on the basis of present growth projections, and assuming that distribution of income remains unchanged, the ILO projects a further rise in the number living in poverty to 913 million by 1995 (see Table 6.8). It must be one of the objectives of the International Development Strategy for the 1990s to ensure that the projections of the ILO do not in fact materialize.

Table 6.8   *Number of persons in extreme poverty (millions)*

	1980	1985	1995 projection
Africa	210	278	405
Asia	562	538	450
Western Hemisphere	47	65	58
TOTAL	819	881	913

Source: ILO, High-Level Meeting on Employment and Structural Adjustment, *Background Document*, Geneva, 23–25 November 1987, p. 17, cited in Jean Mouly, 'Reviving the World's Economic Growth: Chances and Risks', mimeo., February 1989, p. 4.

Turning from global estimates to regional figures, it can be seen at a glance that rising poverty is most serious in Africa. Between 1980 and 1985 extreme poverty in Africa increased by 68 million and, if nothing is done to reverse the trend, poverty is expected to rise by a further 127 million by 1995. In Latin America, extreme poverty rose by 18 million in the first half of the 1980s. This is much less than in Africa but, because of the smaller base, the proportional increase was larger: 38.3 per cent in Latin America compared to 32.4 per cent in Africa. Under present conditions, poverty in Latin America should decline between 1985 and 1995 but (according to the ILO's projections) the number of poor people in 1995 will still be higher than in 1980.

The unfavourable developments in Africa and Latin America were partly offset by favourable trends in Asia. The number of poor people in Asia is estimated to have declined by 24 million during 1980–85 and the ILO projects a further decline of 88 million by 1995. This is encouraging. ESCAP, however, takes a different view, regarding progress towards the elimination of poverty as being 'disappointing throughout the region'.[15] This judgement appears to be based on a relative rather than an absolute view of poverty, in particular on the high degree of inequality, the apparent stability of the overall distribution of income and, in one or two cases (Sri Lanka, Bangladesh), on the fall in the share of household income received by the poorest quintile. At the very least this assessment of the situation in Asia shows that there are no grounds for complacency, particularly when one considers that under the ILO's projections there will still be more poor people in Asia than in any other region, and almost as many as in Africa and Latin America combined.

Thus the necessity to tackle poverty directly remains in all regions. The required direct measures are likely to include a combination of the following: (i) welfare services and entitlement programmes which place a safety net under the poor; (ii) policies directed towards satisfying the basic needs of the poor, partly by giving priority to the production of goods consumed by low-income groups (wage goods) and partly by redirecting public expenditure programmes on essential infrastructure (transport, power) and services (education, primary health care) to benefit the poor; (iii) public works programmes aimed at providing employment for the poor; (iv) redistribution of income and productive assets in favour of the poor, notably land reform, and (v) investment and credit programmes aimed at the poor.

This may require a fundamental change in attitude by policy-makers, a change from regarding poverty alleviation as essentially an act of charity and a drain on the exchequer that should be minimized, to recognition that poverty alleviation should be seen as an investment in the poor, and moreover an investment that can produce a high rate of return. Such an approach would be likely in most countries to imply greater emphasis on peasant agriculture and small-scale rural entrepreneurship, greater freedom for the urban informal sector and reduced emphasis on large-scale, capital-intensive, often state-owned manufacturing enterprises. Within the international community this is the approach that was adopted from the very beginning by the International Fund for Agriculture Development (IFAD) and IFAD's success has demonstrated the validity of the approach. It is now time for national governments throughout the Third World to apply on a large scale the lessons learned from IFAD's experience.

Desirable Anti-Poverty Goals for the Year 2000

The minimum objective for the new International Development Strategy should be to reduce the absolute number of people living in poverty by the year 2000. The present tendency for the numbers in absolute poverty to increase is not acceptable; the trend must be reversed. Each country should set its own standard, its own definition of poverty, and then direct its energies to ensure that by its own standard development is accompanied by a reduction in the number of people living in conditions of severe poverty and deprivation. This is a readily attainable goal and so central to what development is all about that its enunciation as international policy could serve as a rallying point for renewed national commitment and enhanced international cooperation.

If the reduction of severe poverty and deprivation is to be a central objective of the next decade of development, it will be necessary for each country to create a monitoring and reporting system that enables it to trace changes in the living conditions of the poor with a reasonable degree of accuracy. Existing data on poverty are sparse and often years out of date. Alternative economic and social indicators, where they exist, are often not accurate. Further work will be necessary to fill important gaps in the data, to improve reliability and to develop 'simpler, lower cost, non-conventional methods of information collection and analysis'.[16] Lack of complete information should not be used as an excuse to delay the design and implementation of policies to reduce absolute poverty, but nor should the need to monitor progress be neglected.

ENVIRONMENT AND DEVELOPMENT

If development is to have meaning it must be long term; it must be sustainable. More and more frequently, however, doubts are being expressed that present patterns of development, in rich countries and poor, cannot be sustained indefinitely and perhaps not for much longer. Many people have come to believe that the world cannot continue as it is. So much damage and stress are being inflicted on the environment that its capacity to sustain productive activities and eventually life itself is being undermined. Views such as these are widely held throughout the world, but it would be a mistake to assume that perceptions of environmental problems are identical in the industrialized and developing countries. They are not.

Many environmental problems in the industrialized countries are regarded as consequences of affluence. The use of large numbers of private automobiles, many for recreational purposes, result in air pollution; the intensive agriculture required to supply an over-fed and over-weight population results in soil and water contamination by high levels of nitrates; the high consumption per head of manufactured products is associated with huge quantities of industrial waste, some of which ends up polluting the soil, rivers and coastal waters. Environmental damage in affluent societies is a consequence of excessive development and unrestrained demands for ever-larger quantities of goods and services. It is thus a consequence of materialism and acquisitiveness.

Environmental problems in the developing countries are seen as consequences of poverty, not of affluence. A rapidly growing population puts pressure on a country's natural resources. The ever-increasing demand for food and firewood, for example, results in the destruction of the forests, degradation of the soil and depletion of water supplies. Thus the basis for future growth is eroded. Issues of economic development consequently cannot be separated from environmental issues.[17] Poverty and the environment are closely linked, not least because it is the poorest members of society that typically suffer most from environmental deterioration.

Despite these differences in perception there is broad agreement that attempts by men and women to improve their economic well-being have resulted occasionally in huge disasters (the explosion of a chemical plant at Bhopal, the nuclear explosion at Chernobyl) and more frequently in gradual destruction of the resources on which material betterment depends (desertification in the Sahel, flooding in the Indo-Gangetic plain). There is also broad agreement that the situation in the Third World is sufficiently different from that in the industrialized countries that it would be a mistake to adopt identical technical standards for, say, air and water pollution throughout the globe. Environmental problems may be present in all countries, but the appropriate response will differ from one country to another. Environmental standards are needed, but in many cases these should be specific to each country.

The Possible Threat to the Global Economic System

Some issues, however, transcend individual countries and threaten the entire globe. Foremost among these is the possible warming of the planet from the emission of carbon dioxide into the atmosphere, the so-called greenhouse effect. The main source of the greenhouse effect is the emission of carbon dioxide from burning large quantities of fossil fuels, above all in the advanced, affluent industrialized countries. Precise and continuous measurements of atmospheric carbon dioxide show a clear increase from 315 ppmv (parts per million, by volume) in 1958 to 343 ppmv in 1984. If the present rate of increase of carbon dioxide emission continues for 40 years (namely, 1–2 per cent per year), with a slower increase thereafter, the carbon dioxide concentration towards the end of the next century will be about 600 ppmv, or more than twice the level of 280 ppmv in 1750 (based on analysis of glacier ice cores).[18] Carbon dioxide absorbs heat that might otherwise escape from the atmosphere and redirects it back towards the earth's surface.

The consequence of this for average global temperatures is still uncertain, but computer-based simulation models predict that average temperatures will rise by 1°C by the year 2010 and possibly by 4.5°C by 2050. The temperatures in the Arctic would rise more and increase more rapidly than temperatures elsewhere. These temperature changes would in turn lead to alterations in rainfall patterns, in particular to a deterioration in growing conditions in the major temperate cereal-producing areas of the world.

Higher average temperatures would also result in a rise in the sea level, largely as a result of an expansion of the oceans as the water warms. A 1°C rise in temperature could raise the sea level by 30 cm by 2010 and a 4.5° rise could raise it by as much as 150 cm by 2050. 'Since more than half of the human population lives within 40 km of a coastline, a relatively modest 30 cm rise in sea level could have profound implications for many countries, particularly in Asia.'[19]

A second threat to the entire globe comes from the depletion of the ozone layer in the upper atmosphere. This is due to the emission of chlorofluorocarbons or CFCs into the air, again largely in the developed countries. The depletion of ozone in the stratosphere increases the exposure of the earth to the sun's radiation and could result in serious health problems for the human population. Fortunately the potential seriousness of the situation has been recognized and agreement has been reached by the industrial countries to curtail sharply the use of CFCs. Several important developing countries, including China and India, have expressed a willingness to restrain the growth of CFC technology on condition that the wealthy nations create a special fund to assist developing countries to convert to ozone-safe technologies.

The image of spaceship earth is widely used to underline the increasing fragility of our shared environment. But we have not yet come to recognize fully that the common global heritage – space, the sea, Antarctica – is threatened by pollution and undiscriminating exploitation and deserves protection for the benefit of mankind as a whole. The pollution of the sea is occurring at an alarming rate, that of Antarctica and space has just begun, but the international community has yet to take action. The time for it to do so has arrived.

Affluence, Pollution and International Conflict: Fouling the Rich Man's Nest

Not all environmental issues are global in scope or require universal agreement to be resolved. Indeed the number of such issues, although growing, is relatively small. More common are environmental problems that affect a number of countries in close proximity; they are international in character but not global. The industrialized countries provide many examples of such environmental problems, though the issues raised are not unique to them.

One example is the nuclear power industry. After Chernobyl everyone is aware of the possible consequences to the surrounding community of an explosion in a nuclear power plant. Everyone is also aware that the consequences are not limited to the immediate vicinity; they spread widely and quickly to other communities and countries downwind of the plant. Radiation threatens not just the local citizens, but animals and livestock, agriculture and the human population in many nations, including those which do not even share a border with the affected country. Quite apart from the rare horrific accident, the nuclear power industry suffers from a chronic, daily problem of how to dispose of dangerous radioactive waste. Since this waste remains radioactive and hence dangerous forever, methods must be found to guarantee safe disposal until the end of time. No such method has yet been found; hence every country exploiting nuclear reactors poses a potential and permanent environmental threat to the safety and well-being of itself and its neighbours.

Even conventional industry, we now know, can damage the environment of communities and countries hundreds of miles away from the origin of pollution. A prime example is the emission of sulphur into the air by conventional coal-fired power stations and manufacturing enterprises. The sulphur returns to earth later as acid rain, a very dilute solution of sulphuric acid, which damages forests and fresh-water fishing and even corrodes stone buildings in areas downwind of the source. Yet another typical example is the pollution of international rivers by chemical industries built along the banks disposing of their waste products by dumping. The river may seem to one country an inexpensive way of getting rid of unwanted substances, yet to others downstream the same river may be a source of drinking water. In effect, the upstream country is shifting part of the costs of industrialization onto its defenceless neighbours.

Poverty and Environmental Degradation

Many of the environmental problems found in developing countries are different from those characteristic of the industrialized world. Shrinking forests, eroding soils, more frequent flooding of river basins and plains, overgrazed pastures and expanding deserts – these are the special problems one encounters in the Third World. In these cases a close link exists between the persistence of poverty and restricted economic opportunities for the poorest people in society and the processes that result in the deterioration of the physical environment. Deforestation, desertification and degradation of existing cultivated land are inevitable as long as (i) inequality in the distribution of productive resources is great, and (ii) the pressure of the poor upon the physical environment is high. If there are many people, if most of them are poor and if the poor are denied access to produced means of production, it is obvious that they will have no alternative but to earn a living as best they can by extracting the maximum possible output from the natural resources available. This will occur even if short-term maximization of output reduces long-term potential; that is, even if development is unsustainable.

Some problems could be ameliorated if the poor were organized to protect common resources. This would help to avoid over-exploitation and 'the tragedy of the commons' by, in effect, internalizing some negative externalities. If nothing else were done, however, a serious problem would still remain because of the high time rate of discount of the poor and the associated high optimal rate of extraction, as seen from the perspective of the poor. The only real or permanent solution is to alter the strategy of development, redistributing resources in favour of the poor, giving high priority to human development and adopting policies that ensure that the benefits of growth accrue directly to those most in need.

Failing a reorientation of the development strategy, the question arises whether growth in the Third World can be sustained in the face of a deteriorating environment. The answer is that aggregate rates of growth probably can be sustained. Environmental deterioration has not in general reached such a point that it will bring growth to a halt, or even reduce the rate of growth markedly, but it definitely is costly and represents a misallocation of scarce resources. In some countries, for instance those which run the risk of exhausting usable supplies of water, environmental constraints may affect the rate of growth, but it is not likely to occur in many. The more immediate danger is that if environmental deterioration continues, it may be impossible to sustain the income of the poor. Development on average may proceed while the poorest sections of the community enter into a process of underdevelopment, with falling incomes, consequently greater pressure upon those parts of the physical environment to which they have access, and consequently lower incomes still in subsequent periods. A vicious spiral of environmental degradation and falling incomes for the poor certainly is possible.

Priorities for the Year 2000

Environmental damage is not something that will be corrected automatically by the operation of market forces. Intervention by public actors is essential. Sometimes intervention by a single government will suffice, notably when a specific problem is limited to a single country. This could take the form of taxes or charges, prohibitions on the use of certain materials or the implementation of environmental standards. At other times collective action by a group of countries will be necessary, as when pollution originating in one country affects people living in another. On still other occasions, global action may be necessary, as in the case of global climatic change.

Because of the diversity of environmental problems it is not possible to quantify targets for the International Development Strategy for the 1990s. However, priorities for the international community can be listed and used as a basis for action. In our judgement the priorities should be as follows:

1. restraining land degradation, deforestation and the process of desertification;
2. reducing water pollution and overcoming the shortage of freshwater resources;
3. reducing the rate of deterioration of coastal areas and oceans;
4. controlling atmospheric pollution; and
5. regulating the production, international trade and disposal of hazardous waste and toxic chemicals.

Each country no doubt will have its own environmental problems, its own priorities for dealing with them, its own technical standards and policy measures. But these five problems should perhaps be at the top of the international agenda in the 1990s and merit priority in the search for collective solutions.

CONCLUSIONS

Any development strategy, be it national or international, must have priorities and hence be selective. There can be no escape from the necessity to choose. In formulating an International Development Strategy for the 1990s it has been suggested that the priorities be few in number and that international action be organized around four themes:

1. accelerated economic growth;
2. greater concern for human development;
3. an absolute reduction in the number of people suffering from severe poverty and deprivation; and
4. restraining the deterioration in the natural environment.

These themes should be seen not as separate issues to be addressed one by one but as four strands of a coherent approach to development policy in this decade. Faster growth is absolutely essential, especially in those countries which experienced a fall in average incomes in the 1980s. Growth is not the end of development, but it is the foundation on which other policies to improve the well-being of mankind rest. One must ask, growth for what? And the answer we give is that growth should aim at enlarging the capabilities of people. This implies greater concern with human development as an ultimate objective. Moreover, because of the recent neglect of education, health, nutrition, etc, the return on expenditure on human development programmes can be expected to be at least as high as that on ordinary investment. Human development is thus not only an end in itself; it is also an efficient way of achieving growth. To repeat, the return on human capital is likely to be as high as the return on capital embodied in plant and equipment.

But one must also ask, growth for whom? Our answer is that growth, human development expenditure and indeed all social and economic policy should be designed to ensure that the number of people in poverty declines absolutely. This will not happen automatically either as a result of faster growth or of a greater emphasis on human development programmes, although both will help. The reduction of poverty and deprivation also will require positive action; because of the tendency for severe poverty to increase during the 1980s, such action should be a top priority for the 1990s.

Environmental degradation in the Third World is frequently a symptom or consequence of poverty. Those who possess neither human capital nor produced means of production often have no alternative but to exploit to the full the natural resources (land, forests, fisheries) to which they have access. Poverty is thus a major cause of the deterioration of the natural environment. At the same time, the deterioration of the environment accentuates poverty with the two processes interacting, there is always a danger that the results will be cumulative, producing an accelerating downward spiral of underdevelopment of those who are already impoverished. The sustainability of development for poor people in poor countries often depends on measures to improve the physical environment.

In these ways the four strands of the suggested International Development Strategy interact with and reinforce each other. Each strand is worthy of attention in its own right, but when taken together the whole is greater than the sum of the parts.

Implications for the United Nations System

If the International Development Strategy is to be meaningful it must have the full support of the United Nations family. Indeed the first test of the new strategy will be whether it encourages the UN system to adapt its internal structures so that it can contribute to the implementation of agreed international objectives. The entire organization – the financial institutions (IMF, IBRD, IFAD, the regional banks), the specialized agencies (UNESCO, WHO, ILO, FAO, UNICEF, etc), the regional commissions and UNDP – should commit itself to harmonizing its separate activities in support of the objectives of the strategy. If the UN cannot act in a planned, coherent manner, it is utterly unrealistic to suppose that other members of the international community (countries, NGOs and other international agencies) can do so. If the UN system as a whole believes in the new strategy, then it must take vigorous steps to do whatever possible to implement it.

Beyond implementation, there is a need to monitor change. Each country will presumably have its own monitoring system, but the UN will have a role to play in collecting information from member-countries all over the globe and presenting it in such a way that the findings are comparable and can readily be understood. In some cases, additional work will be necessary to improve existing economic and social indicators and to devise new ones. This can best be done within a UN research framework rather than by encouraging each country to go its own way.

Monitoring progress is important – governments, international agencies and independent observers must know what is going on – but there is no need to set up an elaborate and expensive monitoring and reporting system. What is most important during the next ten years is to implement the agreed international strategy so that there will be progress to report.

Managing the Global Economy

The process of creating a single, global economy is likely to continue during the next ten years and, with increased globalization, will come greater interdependence of all aspects of economic life. National economies will gradually lose their separate identities and become closely linked into an international economic system. The world will be one, economically, for the first time in its history.

The transformation of the world economy through globalization and close interdependence will not necessarily occur smoothly. Adjustments will be required which will sometimes be painful. On the other hand, the transformation of the world economy will create numerous opportunities for mutually beneficial change and development. The task is to minimize the pain of adjustment while taking full advantage of the potential benefits that are created. This is easier said than done.

Politically we are witnessing the disappearance of a hegemonic power (the US), the decline of its international leadership in economic affairs and the slow emergence of a multi-polar world. Thus precisely at the time when we approach the formation of a single world economy, the possibility of a single nation taking the lead and guiding the collectivity of nation-states through the transition appears to be waning. Moreover, the declining leadership of the once hegemonic power has been accompanied by a weakening of the authority of the major international economic institutions – GATT, the IMF and the World Bank. The two phenomena are of course closely connected since the authority of the international economic institutions depended upon the support of the hegemonic power and its allies.

Be that as it may, the world now finds itself facing a pressing need to strengthen and reform existing global institutions for the benefit of the international system as a whole. Three points in particular deserve attention by statesmen in the near future. First, there is a need to design improved coordinating machinery for international economic cooperation between developed and developing countries. Neither the UN secretariat, UNCTAD nor the World Bank was intended to play such a role or is capable of doing so. Yet without machinery for policy coordination it is difficult to see how an international development strategy can be implemented. Second, there is a need substantially to increase the resources of the multilateral financial agencies so that they can begin to assume a role not too dissimilar from that played by their national counterparts. The lending capacities of the World Bank, the regional development banks, IFAD and the IMF (preferably by the issue of SDRs) should be raised so that they can contribute in a significant way to the implementation of the International Development Strategy. Third, in a highly interdependent world, a mechanism should be invented to allow the introduction of international accountability for national economic policies since these have international as well as national consequences. In effect national actions produce widespread externalities, both positive and negative, and the time has arrived to recognize this explicitly by creating appropriate international institutions.

The International Development Strategy as a World Social Contract

We are presented with a rare opportunity during these ten years to create a much better world for all people. We have a chance to reduce military expenditure and reallocate resources devoted to armaments to activities which increase material and social well-being. We have the possibility of moving away from ideological confrontation and of integrating the socialist countries into a single global economy. We have a chance to negotiate debt relief in the Third World, provide greater access to markets and diminish protectionism. We also have an opportunity to make resources available for human development and to invest in the poor.

The suggested International Development Strategy can thus be seen as a world social contract. The developed countries, capitalist and socialist, would give priority to maintaining and if possible accelerating growth. Reduced military expenditure would help to make this possible. The developing countries would benefit from faster growth in the rest of the world and expanding international commerce; where possible, particularly in Africa and Latin America, they would take steps of their own to stimulate expansion.

Further, the industrial countries would do what is necessary to reduce the debt overhang, to eliminate discriminatory trade practices against exports from Third World countries and generally to reduce protectionist barriers all round. This would facilitate growth in the developing countries. As its part of the bargain, the Third World would give high priority to human development and to reducing the number of people in poverty. Globally, there would be an international effort to halt the deterioration of the natural environment. Finally, the UN system would put its moral authority, its expertise and its resources behind the world social contract.

Such a scheme, we suggest, has many attractions. There is something in it for every country. No country would lose; every country would gain – from faster growth, a better environment, diminished political discord. The poor of the Third World would benefit most of all. They deserve to; they have suffered much and in recent years many have seen their gains erode. No person of goodwill could grumble about putting the poor first. Indeed for many it is this that gives the contract a noble purpose. We do not pretend that the international development strategy we recommend will be easy to implement, but it is worth the effort; if successful, it will herald a new era in international economic cooperation and represent a major step forward in translating into practice the ideals of a truly global community.

NOTES

1. United Nations, Department of International Economic and Social Affairs (1988), *Development and International Economic Co-operation: Long Term Trends in Social and Economic Development*, A/43/554, 20 September, Table 3, p. 22. The five groups of countries are the developing petroleum-exporting countries, major exporters of manufactures, highly indebted developing countries, least developed countries and primary commodity and services exporters.
2. The data were obtained from the 1989 *Report of the Task Force on Foreign Assistance* to the Committee on Foreign Affairs, US House of Representatives, 101st Congress, 1st Session, February.
3. See the report of the United Nations, Committee for Development Planning (1988), *Human Resources Development: A Neglected Dimension of Development Strategy*, New York.
4. See, for example, World Bank (1986), *Financing Education in Developing Countries. An Exploration of Policy Options*, Washington, DC. Most estimates are of average rates of return. A careful study of the return on marginal expenditure in Kenya, however, concludes that the social marginal rate of return is 12 per cent in primary education and 13 per cent in secondary education. J.B. Knight, R.H. Sabot and D.C. Hovey, 'Is the Rate of Return on Primary Schooling Really 26 percent?', *American Economic Review*, forthcoming.
5. It has been shown, for example, that expanded educational expenditure in both East Africa and Colombia reduces urban income inequalities. See J.B. Knight and R.H. Sabot (1983), 'Educational Expansion and the Kuznets Effect', *American Economic Review*, December; also Rakesh Mohan and Richard Sabot (1988), 'Educational Expansion and the Inequality of Pay: Colombia 1973–78', *Oxford Bulletin of Economics and Statistics*, May.

6. World Health Organization, Division of Family Health (1980), *Health and the Status of Women*, Geneva; L.C. Chen, E. Huq and S.D. D'Souza (1981), 'Sex Bias in the Family Allocation of Food and Health Care in Rural Bangladesh', *Population and Development Review*, 7(1).
7. WHO, *op cit*; S. Hamilton, B. Popkin and D. Spicer (1984), *Women and Nutrition in Third World Countries*, New York: Praeger; H. Ware (1981), *Women, Demography and Development*, Canberra: Australian National University.
8. UNICEF (1989), *Strategies for Children and Development in the 1990s*, New York, February, p. 10.
9. *Ibid.*, See UNICEF (1989), p. 11.
10. By absolute poor is meant those who fall below the (essentially nutritionally-determined) official Indian poverty line.
11. FAO (1981), *Sound Progress Report on WCARRD Programme of Action Including the Role of Women in Rural Development*, Rome, C87/19, August, Table 1, p. 102.
12. FAO (1987), Table 3, pp. 42–3.
13. FAO (1987), Table 4, p. 45.
14. United Nations, ECOSOC (1988), *Food and Agriculture, Review and Analysis of Agrarian Reform and Rural Development, Note by the Secretary General*, 21 April, p. 29.
15. ESCAP (1989), *Towards a New International Development Strategy: Economic, Social and Environmental Concerns in the Asian and Pacific Region in the 1990s*, E/ESCAP/645, Bangkok, 16 February, p. 8.
16. Ghai, Dharam, Hopkins, Michael and McGranahan, Donald (1988), 'Some Reflections on Human and Social Indicators for Development', UNRISD Discussion Paper No 6, Geneva, October, p. 28.
17. This argument is made at length in the Brundtland Report, *Our Common Future*.
18. UNEP (1987), *The State of the World Environment 1987*, Nairobi, April, p. 10.
19. FAO (1989), *Position Paper on Climate Change and Its Implications for Agriculture, Forestry and Fisheries*, Rome, February, p. 3.

REFERENCES

Chen, L.C., Huq E. and D'Souza, S.D. (1981), 'Sex Bias in the Family Allocation of Food and Health Care in Rural Bangladesh', *Population and Development Review*, 7(1).

ESCAP (1989), *Towards a New International Development Strategy: Economic Social and Environmental Concerns in the Asian and Pacific Region in the 1990s*, E/ESCAP/645, Bangkok, 16 February.

FAO (1987), *Sound Progress Report on WCARRD Programme of Action including the Role of Women in Rural Development*, C87/19, Rome, August .

FAO (1989), *Position Paper on Climate Change and Its Implications for Agriculture, Forestry and Fisheries,* Rome, February.

Ghai, D., Hopkins, M. and McGranahan, D. (1988), 'Some Reflections on Human and Social Indicators for Development', UNRISD Discussion Paper No 6, Geneva, October.

Hamilton, S., Popkin, B. and Spicer, D. (1984), *Women and Nutrition in Third World Countries,* New York: Praeger.

Knight, J.B. and Sabot, R.H. (1983), 'Educational Expansion and the Kuznets Effect', *American Economic Review,* December.

Knight, J.B., Sabot, R.H. and Hovey, D.C. 'Is the Rate of Return on Primary Schooling Really 26 per cent?', *American Economic Review* (forthcoming).

Mohan, R. and Sabot, R.H. (1988), 'Educational Expansion and the Inequality of Pay: Colombia 1973–78', *Oxford Bulletin of Economics and Statistics*, May.

UNEP (1987), *The State of the World Environment 1987*, Nairobi, April.

UNICEF (1989), *Strategies for Children and Development in the 1990s*, New York, February.

United Nations, Committee for Development Planning (1988), *Human Resources Development: A Neglected Dimension of Development Strategy*, New York.

United Nations, Department of International Economics and Social Affairs (1988), *Development and International Economic Co-operation: Long-Term Trends*, A/43/554, New York, 20 September.

United Nations, ECOSOC (1988), *Food and Agriculture. Review and Analysis of Agrarian Reform and Rural Development. Note by the Secretary-General*, 21 April.

United States House of Representatives, Committee on Foreign Affairs (1989), *Report of the Task Force on Foreign Assistance*, 101st Congress, 1st Session, February.

Ware, H. (1981), *Women, Demography and Development*, Canberra: Australian National University.

World Bank (1986), *Financing Education in Developing Countries. An Exploration of Policy Options*, Washington DC.

World Health Organization, Division of Family Health (1980), *Health and the Status of Women*, Geneva.

Index